Legalines

MW01109992

Editorial Advisors:
Gloria A. Aluise
   Attorney at Law
David H. Barber
   Attorney at Law
Jonathan Neville
   Attorney at Law
Robert A. Wyler
   Attorney at Law

Authors:
Gloria A. Aluise
   Attorney at Law
David H. Barber
   Attorney at Law
Daniel O. Bernstine
   Professor of Law
D. Steven Brewster
   C.P.A.
Roy L. Brooks
   Professor of Law
Frank L. Bruno
   Attorney at Law
Scott M. Burbank
   C.P.A.
Jonathan C. Carlson
   Professor of Law
Charles N. Carnes
   Professor of Law
Paul S. Dempsey
   Professor of Law
Ronald W. Eades
   Professor of Law
Jerome A. Hoffman
   Professor of Law
Mark R. Lee
   Professor of Law
Jonathan Neville
   Attorney at Law
Laurence C. Nolan
   Professor of Law
Arpiar Saunders
   Professor of Law
Robert A. Wyler
   Attorney at Law

DOMESTIC RELATIONS

Adaptable to Third Edition of Wadlington Casebook

By Gloria A. Aluise
Attorney at Law

HARCOURT BRACE LEGAL AND PROFESSIONAL PUBLICATIONS, INC.

EDITORIAL OFFICES: 176 W. Adams, Suite 2100, Chicago, IL 60603

Legalines

REGIONAL OFFICES: New York, Chicago, Los Angeles, Washington, D.C.
Distributed by: **Harcourt Brace & Company** 6277 Sea Harbor Drive, Orlando, FL 32887 (800)787-8717

EDITOR
Stephanie A. Kartofels, J.D.
Attorney at Law

PRODUCTION COORDINATOR
Sanetta Hister

FIRST PRINTING—1997

Legalines™

Features Detailed Briefs of Every Major Case, Plus Summaries of the Black Letter Law.

Titles Available

Administrative Law . . . . .Keyed to Breyer
Administrative Law . . . . .Keyed to Gellhorn
Administrative Law . . . . .Keyed to Schwartz
Antitrust .Keyed to Areeda
Antitrust .Keyed to Handler
Civil Procedure . . . . .Keyed to Cound
Civil Procedure . . . . .Keyed to Field
Civil Procedure . . . . .Keyed to Hazard
Civil Procedure . . . . .Keyed to Rosenberg
Civil Procedure . . . . .Keyed to Yeazell
Commercial Law . . . . .Keyed to Farnsworth
Conflict of Laws . . . . .Keyed to Cramton
Conflict of Laws . . . . .Keyed to Reese
Constitutional Law . . . . .Keyed to Brest
Constitutional Law . . . . .Keyed to Cohen
Constitutional Law . . . . .Keyed to Gunther
Constitutional Law . . . . .Keyed to Lockhart
Constitutional Law . . . . .Keyed to Rotunda
Constitutional Law . . . . .Keyed to Stone
Contracts . . . . .Keyed to Calamari
Contracts . . . . .Keyed to Dawson
Contracts . . . . .Keyed to Farnsworth
Contracts . . . . .Keyed to Fuller
Contracts . . . . .Keyed to Kessler
Contracts . . . . .Keyed to Knapp/Crystal
Contracts . . . . .Keyed to Murphy
Corporations . . . . .Keyed to Cary
Corporations . . . . .Keyed to Choper
Corporations . . . . .Keyed to Hamilton
Corporations . . . . .Keyed to Vagts
Criminal Law . . . . .Keyed to Boyce
Criminal Law . . . . .Keyed to Dix
Criminal Law . . . . .Keyed to Johnson
Criminal Law . . . . .Keyed to Kadish
Criminal Law . . . . .Keyed to LaFave
Criminal Procedure . . . . .Keyed to Kamisar
Decedents' Estates & Trusts . . . . . .Keyed to Ritchie

Domestic Relations . . . . .Keyed to Clark
Domestic Relations . . . . .Keyed to Wadlington
Enterprise Organizations . . . . .Keyed to Conard
Estate & Gift Tax . . . . .Keyed to Surrey
Evidence .Keyed to Sutton
Evidence .Keyed to Waltz
Evidence .Keyed to Weinstein
Family Law . . . . .Keyed to Areen
Federal Courts . . . . .Keyed to McCormick
Income Tax . . . . .Keyed to Andrews
Income Tax . . . . .Keyed to Freeland
Income Tax . . . . .Keyed to Klein
Labor Law . . . . .Keyed to Cox
Labor Law . . . . .Keyed to Merrifield
Partnership & Corporate Tax . . . . . .Keyed to Surrey
Property .Keyed to Browder
Property .Keyed to Casner
Property .Keyed to Cribbet
Property .Keyed to Dukeminier
Real Property . . . . .Keyed to Rabin
Remedies . . . . .Keyed to Re
Remedies . . . . .Keyed to York
Sales & Secured Transactions . . . . .Keyed to Speidel
Securities Regulation . . . . .Keyed to Jennings
Torts . . . . .Keyed to Dobbs
Torts . . . . .Keyed to Epstein
Torts . . . . .Keyed to Franklin
Torts . . . . .Keyed to Henderson
Torts . . . . .Keyed to Keeton
Torts . . . . .Keyed to Prosser
Wills, Trusts & Estates . . . . .Keyed to Dukeminier

Other Titles Available:
Accounting For Lawyers
Criminal Law Questions & Answers
Excelling on Exams/How to Study
Torts Questions & Answers

All Titles Available at Your Law School Bookstore, or Call to Order: 1-800-787-8717

Harcourt Brace Legal and Professional Publications, Inc.
176 West Adams, Suite 2100
Chicago, IL 60603

SHORT SUMMARY OF CONTENTS

TABLE OF CONTENTS AND SHORT REVIEW OUTLINE

I. CHANGING CONCEPTS ABOUT THE NATURE OF MARRIAGE

A. CHANGING PERSPECTIVES

1. **Constancy Amidst Change.** Two things that have characterized American family law historically and contemporaneously are the variety of laws (from state to state) and the ongoing changes in them. Yet many scholars note that family relations and families are among the most "primitive," *i.e.,* the most relatively unchanged social relations and institutions in human history.

   a. **Commitment to a permanent relationship and reciprocal support obligations are the essence of a "family"--City of Ladue v. Horn,** 720 S.W.2d 745 (Mo. Ct. App. 1986).

   City of Ladue v. Horn

   1) **Facts.** A City of Ladue (P) zoning ordinance restricted certain zones to "one-family residential" housing. It defined a family as one or more persons related by blood, marriage, or adoption. Ms. Horn and Mr. Jones (Ds) were unmarried cohabitants who purchased a home in such a zone and resided there with their respective children. P sued to enjoin Ds from violating the zoning ordinance and Ds counterclaimed seeking a declaration that the ordinance violated federal and state constitutional standards. The trial court entered a permanent injunction for P and dismissed Ds' counterclaim. Ds appeal.

   2) **Issue.** Does the zoning ordinance definition of family violate the constitutional rights of association, privacy, or equal protection, or state constitutional rights?

   3) **Held.** No. The injunction is affirmed.

      a) Ds' relationship is not the functional equivalent of a family. A commitment to a permanent relationship and a perceived reciprocal obligation to support and care for each other is the functional essence of a family.

      b) Following *Village of Belle Terre v. Boraas*, 416 U.S. 1 (1974), the zoning ordinance is examined under the rational relation standard because it deals with economic and social legislation, not any fundamental interest or suspect classification. The zoning ordinance is reasonable and not arbitrary.

      c) State cases holding that nontraditional families came within the scope of other ordinances merely interpreted those ordinances.

   4) **Comment.** The definition of family is important for zoning, rent control, unemployment insurance, and numerous other local regulations. Some recent cases have construed the term "family" in some such regulations to include homosexual and non-marital relations, relying on the policy behind the regulation or the equities of the particular case.

2. **The Dualistic Nature of Marriage.** The foremost controversy regarding marriage historically has concerned whether marriage is a fixed institution whose characteristics are set by God or by the state, or whether it is a relationship with attributes that are determined by the parties.

   a. **Status or contract.** Marriage is a relationship created by contract. But, traditionally the basic legal incidents of marriage have been governed by law. Thus, marriage is a hybrid legally—both a "status" and a "contract." The tension between these two competing ways of looking at marriage is as old as the law of marriage and as modern as the controversy concerning the validity of common law marriage or nonmarital cohabitation.

   b. **Public interest.** In the nineteenth century, the U.S. Supreme Court once described marriage as "something more than a mere contract. . . . It is an institution, the maintenance of which in its purity the public is deeply interested . . . . " [Maynard v. Hill, 125 U.S. 1980 (1888)]

Fisher v. Fisher

   c. **Consent is the heart of marriage--Fisher v. Fisher,** 165 N.E. 460 (N.Y. 1929).

      1) **Facts.** Wife (P) sought separation from husband (D). The parties were married by the captain of a ship on which they were traveling. The ceremony was followed by cohabitation. D had been married previously; his former wife had divorced him for adultery. According to the terms of the divorce decree and the laws of the state of New York, D was forbidden to remarry during the first wife's lifetime. The ship, which was registered in the port of New York, was wholly owned by the United States of America represented by the United States Shipping Board. The Shipping Board had its domicile in the District of Columbia. The trial court declared the marriage valid. P appeals.

      2) **Issue.** Did the laws of the state of New York follow the steamship in its journey upon the high seas?

      3) **Held.** No. The judgment is affirmed.

         a) Marriage is a civil contract; consent is the essence of the contract; in the absence of any positive law prohibiting marriage by consent only, the marriage will be deemed valid.

         b) Although Wharton, Conflict of Laws section 356, states that a ship at sea is presumed to belong to the state in which it is registered, Wharton misconceived the decision on which he based this statement. A ship on the open sea is regarded by the law of nations as part of the territory whose flag the ship carries.

         c) Congress recognizes shipboard marriages notwithstanding the absence of municipal marriage laws. In this view, the marriage between the parties to this action, by force of a federal statute, was a solid marriage.

d)   If the federal statute cannot be so interpreted, then the common law of the District of Columbia prevails because the ship is owned by the United States Shipping Board domiciled in the District of Columbia.

3.   **From Old Theology to New Sociology.** Concepts of marriage were largely determined by religious ideas identified as such, or under the generic label of "natural law." In the twentieth century, popular theories of sociology and psychology have been influential.

B.   THE CONSTITUTION AS A SHAPING FORCE

1.   **The First Amendment.** Given the historic significance of religion as a factor influencing ideas about the nature of marriage, it should come as no surprise that the First Amendment has been invoked in litigation concerning marriage and its incidents.

a.   **Religious objection to divorce--Sharma v. Sharma,** 667 P.2d 395 (Kan. Ct. App. 1983).

Sharma v. Sharma

    1)   **Facts.** Wife (D) sought revocation of divorce which was granted to her husband. The Sharmas were citizens of India and Hindus of high caste. The Hindu religion does not recognize divorce. According to D, if she were to return to India as a divorced woman, her family and friends would treat her as though she were dead. A divorce decree was granted to Mr. Sharma (P). D appeals.

    2)   **Issue.** Does the First Amendment right to the free exercise of religion require the court to revoke a divorce decree if one party claims her religion does not allow divorce?

    3)   **Held.** No. The decree dissolving the marriage is affirmed.

        a)   Granting a divorce to the husband does not deny the wife her religious beliefs. She may continue to believe that "in the eyes of God, she and her estranged husband are ecclesiastically wedded as one . . . " [Williams v. Williams, 543 P.2d 1401 (Okla. 1975)], even though as a matter of law the civil contract has been dissolved.

        b)   The husband does not share his wife's conviction regarding the prohibition of divorce. To compel him to remain married because of his wife's religious beliefs would be to prefer her religious beliefs over his.

b.   **Religious practice of polygamy--Reynolds v. United States,** 98 U.S. 145 (1878).

Reynolds v. United States

    1)   **Facts.** Reynolds (D) was charged with bigamy, a violation of a federal statute. Evidence showed that he had married a second wife during the lifetime of his first wife. D, a member of the Church of Jesus Christ of Latter-Day Saints (Mormon Church), claimed that he had a religious duty to engage in polygamy, and

asked for a jury instruction that he should be found not guilty if he had violated the law pursuant to his religious beliefs. The court refused to give the instruction. D was convicted and sentenced to two years imprisonment at hard labor, and a $500 fine. D appeals.

2) Issue. Does conviction of a Mormon polygamist, under a law which prohibits bigamy, violate the constitutional doctrine that Congress cannot prohibit the free exercise of religion?

3) Held. No. D's conviction is affirmed.

a) Polygamy has never been acceptable to the northern and western nations of Europe, and was an offense at common law. There has never been a time in any state when polygamy has not been an offense against society, punishable by the courts. These laws against polygamy existed both before and after the passage of the constitutional duty not to interfere with the free exercise of religion.

b) The statute involved in this case is within the legislative power of Congress. Laws are made to govern actions and, while they cannot interfere with beliefs, they can regulate practices.

c) Every act necessary to constitute the crime was knowingly done. Ignorance of the law is not an excuse.

4) Comment. Although polygamy was practiced by Mormons in the nineteenth century, it is estimated that no more than 2% of the men ever engaged in the practice, and the Mormon Church outlawed the practice in 1890. Today, conceptually similar questions arise in connection with international marriage and divorce customs.

2. Constitutional Protection of Property. The Due Process Clauses of the Fifth and Fourteenth Amendments forbid the deprivation of property without due process of law.

Buchholz v. Buchholz

a. Divorce and property consequences--Buchholz v. Buchholz, 248 N.W.2d 21 (Neb. 1976).

1) Facts. Wife (P) sought judgment that Nebraska divorce statutes were unconstitutional. She claimed that the status of marriage includes a property right and that a divorce decree deprived her of a substantial property interest in violation of the Fourteenth Amendment's Due Process Clause. The trial court rejected her argument and she appeals.

2) Issue. Does the marriage contract create a property right in the marital status?

3) Held. No. The trial court's conclusion is affirmed.

a) Although a wife has a legitimate interest in her status as a married woman, this interest does not amount to "property" within the purview of the Fourteenth Amendment. A marriage is not a property interest but is a personal relationship subject to dissolution on terms fixed by state law.

3. **Substantive Due Process.** Despite the rejection of substantive due process in economic regulation, the substantive due process notion of "privacy" is currently the "hottest" source of constitutional influence on marriage regulation.

a. **Intrafamily privacy--Griswold v. Connecticut,** 381 U.S. 479 (1965).

Griswold v.
Connecticut

1) **Facts.** Griswold (D) was executive director of Planned Parenthood in Connecticut, and Buxton (D) was medical director for the group. Ds gave information to married persons regarding contraceptive devices. A state law forbids the use of contraceptives and also assisting others to use contraceptives. Ds were convicted as accessories and were fined $100 each. Ds appeal.

2) **Issue.** Is a state law which prohibits the use of contraceptives by married persons unconstitutional?

3) **Held.** Yes. Ds' convictions are reversed.

a) Penumbras emanating from the First, Third, Fourth, Fifth, Ninth and Fourteenth Amendments to the Constitution create a right of privacy. In fact, this right of privacy is older than the Bill of Rights. Notions of privacy surround the marriage relationship itself, and this statute violates that constitutional right.

b) By forbidding the *use* of contraceptives rather than by banning their manufacture, this law has a maximum destructive impact upon the private relationship of marriage. This statute sweeps unnecessarily broadly, invading an area of protected freedoms.

4) **Concurrence** (Goldberg, Brennan, JJ., Warren, C.J.). The Ninth Amendment, which indicates the retention of other rights by the people, is a sufficient basis for finding a constitutional right of privacy. The Connecticut statutes deal with an especially important area of privacy—the marital home and bedroom. Today's holding does not interfere with the state's proper regulation of sexual misconduct or promiscuity.

5) **Comment.** The opinion of the Court and the concurrence find a right of privacy in the Bill of Rights and apply this right to state regulation through Fourteenth Amendment substantive due process. The fundamental nature of the right of privacy means that any law which infringes upon the private marriage relation must be tested by strict judicial scrutiny, a very difficult standard to satisfy.

b. **Racial discrimination--Loving v. Virginia,** 388 U.S. 1 (1967).

Loving v.
Virginia

1) **Facts.** Mr. Loving (D), a white man, and Mrs. Loving (D), a black woman, both residents of Virginia, were married in 1958 in the District of Columbia and then returned to Virginia to live. They were indicted and convicted of violating a Virginia law which banned interracial marriages between whites and persons of any other race.

Ds' sentence was suspended on the condition that they leave the state, which they did. In 1963, Ds filed a motion to vacate the judgment and to enjoin Virginia from enforcing their convictions. The trial court denied their motion, and the state supreme court of appeals affirmed. Ds appeal to the U.S. Supreme Court.

2) **Issue.** Does a state statute which prohibits interracial marriages violate the Equal Protection and Due Process Clauses of the Fourteenth Amendment?

3) **Held.** Yes. The convictions are reversed.

   a) Marriage is a social relation subject to the state's police power, but the state's power is limited by the Fourteenth Amendment. The Equal Protection Clause demands that racial classifications be subjected to the most rigid scrutiny; and if they are to be upheld, it must be shown to be necessary to the accomplishment of some permissible state objective. Here, there is no legitimate purpose which justifies this classification.

   b) It is true that the statute punishes both white and nonwhite offenders equally. But the statute only punishes interracial marriage when a white is involved. A black person and a Mexican-American may marry without violating the law. The law is an attempt to maintain "white supremacy."

   c) The statute also deprives the Lovings of their fundamental freedom to marry, in violation of the Due Process Clause of the Fourteenth Amendment. Marriage is one of the basic civil rights of society; it is fundamental to our very existence and survival. The Fourteenth Amendment requires that the freedom of choice to marry not be restricted by invidious racial discriminations.

4) **Comment.** With the *Loving* decision, the right to marry became firmly rooted as one of the fundamental rights protected by substantive due process. The decision also spurred substantial legislative abolition of similar antiquated restrictions on marriage.

Zablocki
v. Redhail

c. **Marriage as a fundamental right--Zablocki v. Redhail,** 434 U.S. 374 (1978).

1) **Facts.** A Wisconsin law provided that no resident who has minor issue not in his custody and which he is under an obligation to support may marry without a court order. The order will not be granted unless the applicant submits proof of compliance with the support obligation and demonstrates that the children are not then or are not likely thereafter to become public charges. Redhail (P), the indigent father of one illegitimate child whom he was under order to support but never had, and who was a public charge, filed an application for a marriage license. His application was denied by Zablocki, the Milwaukee County Clerk (D). P brought a class action challenging the statute in the federal district court. The court held the statute violative of equal protection. D appeals.

2) **Issue.** Is a state law that conditions the right of support-obligated persons to marry upon judicial finding of adequate current and probable future support payments unconstitutional?

3) **Held.** Yes. The judgment is affirmed.

   a) The right to marry is a fundamental right. Statutes which significantly interfere with the right to marry, as the statute in the case does, must satisfy critical judicial scrutiny. However, reasonable regulations that do not significantly interfere with the right to enter the marriage relationship may legitimately be imposed.

   b) One rationale for the statute is that it requires an applicant to make support payments to his children. This "collection device" rationale cannot justify the state's broad infringement on the right to marry. The state has numerous other means of exacting compliance with support obligations that are less burdensome of the right to marry.

   c) The statute is both underinclusive and overinclusive with respect to the welfare of supported children—it is underinclusive in that it limits marriage but does not limit any other financial commitments by an applicant that might limit his ability to support existing children, and overinclusive in that a marriage may in fact improve an individual's ability to pay.

4) **Concurrence** (Powell, J.). The Court's decision was correct, but its opinion sweeps too broadly in an area that has long been regarded as a virtually exclusive province of the states. If a compelling state interest test were applied, most marriage restrictions would be of doubtful validity. The law at issue here might be valid if applied to financially capable but delinquent support-obligated persons.

d. **Privacy extended--Eisenstadt v. Baird,** 405 U.S. 438 (1972).

Eisenstadt
v. Baird

1) **Facts.** A Massachusetts law made it a felony for anyone other than a registered physician or pharmacist to dispense an article for the prevention of conception. Under the statute, married persons may obtain contraceptives to prevent pregnancy, but only from doctors or druggists on prescription; single persons may not obtain contraceptives to prevent conception; and both married and single persons may obtain contraceptives from anyone to prevent the spread of disease. William Baird (D) was convicted for giving vaginal foam to a young woman following a lecture at Boston University. His conviction was affirmed by the state supreme court, and he brought a federal habeas corpus petition which the district court dismissed. The court of appeals reversed; Eisenstadt (P), the sheriff of Suffolk County, appeals.

2) **Issue.** Does a state law which allows married persons to obtain contraceptives for the purpose of preventing pregnancy, but does not allow single persons the same right, violate the Equal Protection Clause of the Fourteenth Amendment?

3) **Held.** Yes. The judgment of the court of appeals is affirmed.

   a) Deterrence of premarital sex may not reasonably be regarded as the purpose of this law. It does not deter married persons from using contraceptives in illicit affairs with single persons. And it punishes those who give away contraceptives with a felony, while Massachu-

setts law provides a mere misdemeanor charge for those who forni-
cate.

    b)   Protection of health is not the rationale of this law. **The federal and
          state food and drug acts already regulate the distribution of harmful
          drugs.** The law would prohibit the distribution of safe as well as
          arguably harmful contraceptives.

    c)   *Griswold* held a ban on distribution of contraceptives to married
          persons to be unconstitutional. This law, viewed as a prohibition on
          contraception per se, violates the rights of single persons under the
          Equal Protection Clause. The marital couple is not a real entity, but
          merely an association of two individuals with separate rights and
          attributes.

4)   **Comment.** While the Court squarely based its holding on equal protection
      grounds (the disparate treatment of two classes), the implied substantive
      rationale—of individual sexual privacy—has received the greatest attention.

e.   **Homosexual conduct and the right of privacy--Bowers v. Hardwick, 478
      U.S. 186 (1986).**

1)   **Facts.** Hardwick (P) was charged with violating the Georgia law prohibit-
      ing sodomy by committing that act with an adult consenting male in his
      own home, but the district attorney decided not to present the case to the
      grand jury. P then brought suit to have the sodomy law declared unconsti-
      tutional. The federal district court dismissed for failure to state a claim,
      but the court of appeals reversed, holding that the sodomy law violated
      constitutional rights of privacy and association. The State appeals.

2)   **Issue.** Does a law prohibiting consensual sodomy between consenting
      adults in a private home infringe upon a fundamental constitutional right?

3)   **Held.** No. The judgment is reversed.

    a)   The only issue before the Court is whether the Constitution confers a
          fundamental right to engage in homosexual conduct, not whether laws
          prohibiting such are wise.

    b)   The right of privacy does not extend to homosexual privacy. There is
          no connection between the family, marriage, or procreation, the zones
          of privacy recognized in earlier cases, and homosexual sodomy.

    c)   Homosexual sodomy is neither "implicit in the concept of ordered
          liberty," nor "deeply rooted in this nation's history and tradition."
          Sodomy was a crime at common law, and was forbidden by law in all
          13 states when the Bill of Rights was ratified. Until 1961 all states
          prohibited sodomy, and 24 states and the District of Columbia still do
          so.

    d)   The Court comes closest to illegitimacy when it applies judge-made
          constitutional law that has little or no roots in the language or design
          of the Constitution.

Bowers v.
Hardwick

e) *Stanley v. Georgia*, 394 U.S. 557 (1969), which set aside a conviction for reading obscene material in a private home, is distinguishable because it was firmly grounded in the First Amendment. The home is not a safe haven for criminal activity.

f) The beliefs of Georgia legislators that sodomy is immoral is a rational basis for the criminal proscription.

4) **Concurrence** (Powell, J.). There is no fundamental right to engage in sodomy. But if the punishment for private consensual sodomy were excessive, it might violate the Eighth Amendment.

5) **Dissent** (Blackmun, Brennan, Marshall, Stevens, JJ.). This case is about the right to be let alone. There are two lines of privacy: protected decisions and protected places. Sexual intimacy is a protected decision; the home is a protected place. Intolerance poses a greater threat to our values than sodomy.

6) **Dissent** (Stevens, Brennan, Marshall, JJ.). Sodomy can be heterosexual as well as homosexual. Just because a majority considers a practice immoral is not a sufficient ground for outlawing it. Nonreproductive sexual conduct is protected by *Griswold* and its progeny.

7) **Comment.** Some state courts have invalidated laws criminalizing consensual private homosexual acts on the ground that there is a significant distinction between private and public morality.

f. **Homosexual relations and equal protection--Singer v. Hara,** 522 P.2d 1187 (Wash. Ct. App. 1974).

1) **Facts.** Singer and Barwick, both males, appealed from the trial court's order denying their motion to show cause, by which they sought to compel King County Auditor Hara to issue a marriage license to them. They alleged that the prohibition of same-sex marriages violates the Equal Rights Amendment ("ERA") to the Washington State Constitution and the Equal Protection Clause of the United States Constitution.

2) **Issue.** Does a law which prohibits homosexual marriages violate the state ERA or the Equal Protection Clause of the United States Constitution?

3) **Held.** No. The judgment is affirmed.

a) The appellants argue that by allowing a man and woman to marry but forbidding two men to marry, the state has violated its ERA. But the state bars all same-sex marriages—men may not marry men and women may not marry women. Therefore, men are not treated unequally vis-a-vis women.

b) Approval of the ERA does not reflect the intention to condone same-sex marriages. The primary purpose of the ERA is to overcome discriminatory legal treatment as between men and women. To hold for the appellants would expand the ERA beyond the purpose for which it was intended.

c) Same-sex marriages are outside the proper definition of marriage. Marriage is the union of one man and one woman. Appellants are not denied the right to marry on the basis of their sex, but because they do not meet this time-honored definition.

d) The statute does not violate the Equal Protection Clause of the Fourteenth Amendment. The appellants do not present a case of sexual discrimination; they were denied a marriage license not because of their sex, but because of the nature of marriage itself. To define marriage so as to exclude homosexuals does not create a suspect classification. This categorization is rationally related to many historically rooted and important state interests.

4) Comment. The court based its decision on the nature of marriage itself, defining marriage as the legal union of one man and one woman. Yet, that just defined the legal issue (the permissibility of that classification). The court emphasized the importance of family life and procreation to society. The court read the state ERA as only forbidding discrimination on the basis of sex (identity), not sexuality (orientation).

C. MODERN CONTRACTUAL COHABITATION

1. Contracting to Clarify Shared Expectations. The ability of parties to structure and determine the incidents of their private relationships, "freedom of choice," has become a highly prized notion in recent years. Problems may arise when couples fail to carefully consider the expectations they have prior to beginning a life together—with or without marriage.

Marvin v.
Marvin (I)

a. The economic consequences of nonmarital cohabitation--Marvin v. Marvin (I), 18 Cal. 3d 660 (1976).

1) Facts. Michelle Marvin (P) and Lee Marvin (D) lived together for seven years without marrying. All property acquired during that period was taken in D's name. P sued to enforce an alleged express contract under which she was entitled to half the property and to support payments in exchange for her services as companion, homemaker, housekeeper, and cook to D. The trial court granted D's motion to dismiss. P moved to have the judgment set aside and to amend her complaint. The court denied P's motion, and P appeals.

2) Issue. In the absence of an express contract, can P's complaint be amended to state a cause of action upon theories of implied contract or equitable relief for division of property between nonmarried living partners?

3) Held. Yes. The judgment is reversed and remanded.

a) A court will not enforce a contract if it is based upon services as a paramour. But a contract between nonmarital partners will be enforced unless expressly and inseparably

10 - Domestic Relations

based upon an illicit consideration of sexual services. Adults who voluntarily live together and engage in sexual relations are as competent as anyone else to contract respecting their earnings and property rights.

b)   In addition to an express contract theory, courts may give relief to a nonmarital living partner on the following theories: implied contract, implied agreement of partnership or joint venture, constructive trust, resulting trust, or quantum meruit.

c)   The mores of society have changed. Living together has become an accepted practice. To fail to recognize the reasonable expectations of parties to a nonmarital relationship would be unjust.

4)   Concurring in part, dissenting in part (Clark, J.). The majority properly permits recovery on the basis of express or implied contract, but they should stop there. The majority erred in attempting to determine all anticipated rights and remedies in every meretricious relationship instead of merely deciding the present case.

5)   Comment. In jurisdictions that recognize common law marriages, cases involving nonceremonial unions often fall within the state's legal marriage framework. The number of persons living together outside of formal marriage has significantly increased since 1970; and more and more frequently, courts are having to grapple with the *Marvin* problem.

b.   The difficulty of proving entitlement without a contract--Marvin v. Marvin (III), 176 Cal. Rptr. 555 (Cal. Ct. App. 1981).

Marvin v.
Marvin (III)

1)   Facts. As mentioned in the previous case, Michelle Marvin (P) and Lee Marvin (D) had lived together for seven years without marrying. The cohabitation was ended at D's insistence. P had been employed as a singer before moving in with D. During the cohabitation, she had devoted her time to homemaking, although the parties had never agreed that they would combine their efforts and earnings or share equally in accumulated property. In an action for equitable division of property, P was awarded, among other things, a sum of $104,000 to be used for her economic rehabilitation. D appeals from that portion of the judgment.

2)   Issue. May a party in a nonmarital relationship be awarded support payments for the purpose of learning new job skills after the relationship ends, absent any agreement or equitable entitlement to such payments?

3)   Held. No. The judgment is modified by deleting the rehabilitative award.

a)   While equitable remedies may be devised to protect the expectations of the parties to a nonmarital relationship, there is nothing in the trial court's findings to suggest that such an award is warranted.

b)   Where D was not unjustly enriched during the relationship, P may not expect such an award when the relationship ends.

c)   A court of equity may not create totally new substantive rights under the guise of doing equity.

2. **Procedural Problems.** The federal courts have traditionally refused to exercise jurisdiction in domestic relations cases.

Anastasi v.
Anastasi

    a. **Federal court abstention--Anastasi v. Anastasi,** 544 F. Supp. 866 (D.N.J. 1982).

        1) **Facts.** P instituted an action in state court charging that D had breached his agreement to provide her with financial support for the rest of her life. The parties had lived together without marrying and had separated. D removed the case to federal court on the basis of diversity of citizenship. After briefing and oral argument, the court concluded that since the action was akin to a contract action rather than a domestic action, the domestic relations exception to jurisdiction did not apply. The court here reviews this decision.

        2) **Issue.** Is a federal court the appropriate forum for a "palimony" suit?

        3) **Held.** No. The case is remanded to the superior court of New Jersey.

           a) The domestic relations exception to federal jurisdiction applies when two conditions are met: (i) the state exhibits a significant interest in the nonmarital relationship akin to the state's interest in the marriage relationship; and (ii) in order to protect this interest, the court must make the same kinds of inquiries that have traditionally brought into play the domestic relations exception.

           b) A significant state interest in living relationships established by agreement rather than by formal marriage has been established.

           c) Resolution of the controversy in "palimony" cases requires inquiries and judgments that the state courts are best equipped to handle.

        4) **Comment.** Though often phrased as if it were a jurisdictional limitation, this doctrine is really more akin to abstention than lack of jurisdiction.

3. **Objections to Nonmarital Agreements.** While the *Marvin (I)* decision has had an enormous influence in provoking consideration of the issue of the entitlement of nonmarried cohabitants to property held by their estranged partners, many state courts have refused to adopt the facially broad approach taken by the California Supreme Court.

Hewitt v.
Hewitt

    a. **The effect of statutes abolishing common law marriage--Hewitt v. Hewitt,** 394 N.E.2d 1204 (Ill. 1979).

        1) **Facts.** When Victoria (P) became pregnant in college, Robert Hewitt (D) told her that they were husband and wife and that she would share his life, future, earnings, and property. P and D lived together as husband and wife for 15 years and raised three children. They were never married. P helped put D through professional school.

When P filed a divorce action, it was dismissed. The court also dismissed P's amended complaint, which sought recovery of one-half of the property accumulated during cohabitation upon theories of (i) equitable enforcement of express oral promise, (ii) implied contract, (iii) constructive trust, and (iv) unjust enrichment. The appellate court reversed, finding an express oral contract between unmarried cohabitants regarding property ownership could provide a cause of action if it occurred in a context similar to traditional marriage. D appeals.

2) **Issue.** Does P's complaint seeking recovery of one-half of the property accumulated during unmarried cohabitation state a cause of action for which relief can be granted by the Illinois courts?

3) **Held.** No. The judgment is reversed.

   a) The issue cannot be regarded as merely a problem of the express law of contracts. Realistically, most situations of this type will involve unexpressed understandings and result in substantial litigation.

   b) Because of the sexual services/relations that are inextricably intertwined in such associations, there are (beyond mere contract) many public policy questions involved in deciding whether—or to what extent—such associations should be accorded legal recognition. The implication of recognizing such relationships would be far-reaching.

   c) Illinois public policy has long been that agreements in consideration of illicit cohabitation are void. The real thrust of the plaintiff's argument is that recent changes in social standards regarding unmarried cohabitation make a change in this public policy imperative. Forthright acceptance of that argument would require recognition of common law marriages—which the Illinois legislature abolished in 1905.

   d) The Illinois legislature is a better suited and more appropriate body to make this policy determination than the court. Recent adoption by the legislature of the Marriage and Dissolution of Marriage Act, and rejection of no-fault divorce, evidence a continuing legislative policy that P's claim is not cognizable.

4) **Comment.** The Illinois court avoided the difficult policy question of what to decide by focusing on the threshold issue of who should decide. The California court, in *Marvin (I)*, attempted (with somewhat strained credibility) to stress that their decision did not assume legislative initiative or modify legislative enactment (*i.e.,* abolition of common law marriages).

4. **The Greening of the *Marvin* Doctrine.** Since the *Marvin (I)* decision in 1976, the doctrinal bases for claims for economic consequences flowing from nonmarital cohabitation have matured somewhat. Contract, quasi-contract, quasi-partnership, and equitable theories have been emphasized; quasi-marital theories have not prospered.

a. Wisconsin's version of *Marvin*--Watts v. Watts, 405 N.W.2d 303 (Wis. 1987).

1) **Facts.** In 1969, Sue (P) and James (D) Watts began living together without marriage, although they held themselves out to the public as husband and wife, had two children who were given D's name, filed joint tax returns, had joint bank accounts, and purchased life insurance and real property as husband and wife. P quit nursing training and her job on D's indication that he would provide for her. P contributed childcare and homemaking services, was hostess, worked in D's business, and had her own business. In 1981, P left and D refused to let her return to the business. In 1982, P sued for a share of the wealth accumulated by D. The circuit court dismissed for failure to state a claim. P appeals.

2) **Issue.** Are all claims for recovery of a share of property acquired during nonmarital cohabitation barred in Wisconsin?

3) **Held.** No. The judgment is reversed and remanded.

a) The "property division" statutes do not provide a claim for recovery of a share of property acquired during nonmarital cohabitation. Most courts have rejected or avoided application of marriage dissolution statutes to nonmarital cohabitation. The legislature clearly intended the property division statute to apply to marriage dissolution only, not nonmarital cohabitation breakup.

b) There is no claim for marriage by estoppel either, because the legislature did not intend the property division statutes to govern wealth allocation of unmarried couples.

c) A claim does lie for enforcement of an express or implied contract. Contracts that violate public policy are not enforceable, but courts should be reluctant to frustrate the reasonable expectations of the parties. *Hewitt v. Hewitt, supra*, can be distinguished because Illinois still retains fault divorce, and cohabitation there is illegal. Also, we dispute the inferential leap in *Hewitt's* reasoning. Courts need not await legislative guidance on matters as to which case-by-case judicial development of the law is normal, such as contract and property law. D's attorney agrees that an agreement regarding property division among nonmarital cohabitants is not contrary to public policy; times have changed. So long as property division is independent of any illicit relationship and illicit sex does not constitute part of the consideration bargained for, public policy is not violated. Here, P has pleaded enough to state a claim under the law of contracts. Joint acts of a financial nature can give rise to an inference of intent to share equally.

d) Unjust enrichment claims may also be asserted. Such claims do not arise out of contract but out of the moral principle that one is obligated to make restitution where retention of a benefit would be unjust. Here plaintiff has alleged such a claim.

e) Additionally, nonmarital cohabitants who own property jointly may seek partition.

4) **Comment.** Did D's lawyer "give away the farm" on the issue of violation of public policy? Is nonmarital cohabitation a viable alternative to property division upon dissolution? What if the nonmarriage ends with the intestate death of the wealthier party?

II. GETTING MARRIED

A. COURTSHIP

1. Breach of Promise of Marriage.

a. **State supervision of premarital relations.** State regulation of relations before marriage is not as common as regulation after marriage has occurred. Since the institution of marriage is the major focus of state interest, regulation of premarital relations may not evoke as much state interest. However, the antecedents of marriage have been subject to some legal regulation, such as that pertaining to promises to marry.

Wightman
v. Coates

1) **Promise to marry actions encouraged--Wightman v. Coates, 15 Mass. 1, 8 Am. Dec. 77 (1818).**

a) **Facts.** Coates (D) promised to marry Wightman (P). He then refused to perform his agreement and married another woman. P sued D for breach of promise to marry.

b) **Issue.** In a suit for breach of a contract to marry, can the aggrieved party recover money damages?

c) **Held.** Yes.

(1) Marriage is important to all civilized countries. Breach of the contract to marry is a suitable ground for compensation through the courts.

(2) The delicate and dependent nature of women makes resort to the laws even more justifiable when a woman is injured by such a breach.

d) **Comment.** This opinion reveals much about the paternalistic attitudes of judges in the early nineteenth century.

Stanard
v. Bolin

2) **Changing attitudes about heart balm actions--Stanard v. Bolin, 565 P.2d 94 (Wash. 1977).**

a) **Facts.** Stanard (P) and Bolin (D) were engaged to be married. D promised P that he was wealthy, that P would never have to work again, and that he would provide for P's two children and mother. At D's insistence, P put her home up for sale, sold her furniture, made arrangements to quit her job, engaged a minister to perform the ceremony, planned a reception, and told friends of the betrothal. D then informed P that he would not marry her. P sued D for breach of promise to marry, seeking damages for physical and emotional suffering, and loss of expected financial security. The trial court concluded that the action was contrary to public policy and dismissed P's complaint. P appeals.

b)   **Issue.** Should the common law action for breach of promise to marry be abolished?

c)   **Held.** No. However, the action should be modified so that P cannot recover for loss of expected financial and social position.

     (1)   Because the breach of promise action has its origins in the common law, it is proper for the court to reconsider its propriety as a legal action in modern society.

     (2)   The breach of marriage promise action is a hybrid; although it arises from breach of a contract, its damages more closely resemble a tort action. The plaintiff may recover for loss to reputation, mental anguish, and injury to health, in addition to recovering for expenditures made in preparation for marriage.

     (3)   At common law, a plaintiff could recover for loss of expected financial and social position, but here the court modifies the action not to include such damages because marriage is no longer considered to be a property transaction.

     (4)   It is clearly foreseeable that the jilted party will have expended money and will suffer some forms of mental anguish, loss to reputation, and injury to health. These injuries must be compensated.

d)   **Dissent.** The breach of marriage promise cause of action should be abolished. It allows motive to be considered in assessing damages, while in the divorce area the court must disregard fault in this state.

e)   **Comment.** Quite a number of states have abolished or limited the breach of marriage promise cause of action by legislative enactment. Abuses such as excessive damages, unsavory publicity, and the possibility of extortion have been the main reasons mentioned for abolishing this cause of action.

3)   **Analogous actions.** Analogous heart balm actions have historically existed for alienation of affections, criminal conversation, seduction, etc. The early part of this century saw a widespread movement to repeal such laws because they were difficult to prove, facilitated blackmail, and seemed inconsistent with the "right to choose." However, recently there has been a counter trend of creating heart balm actions for deceived lovers, ex-spouses, etc.

4)   **Criminal actions.** Criminal seduction and fornication laws may be found in many jurisdictions, including some that have abolished "heart balm" civil suits. But the standards of proof are higher and often there are other restrictions.

2.   Recovery of Gifts Made in Anticipation of Marriage.

a. **Failed expectations.** The failure of marriage plans may leave not only wounded feelings but also conflicting claims to property transferred in anticipation of marriage.

Brown v.
Thomas

1) **Conditional gifts in contemplation of marriage may be recovered--Brown v. Thomas,** 379 N.W.2d 868 (Wis. 1985).

  a) **Facts.** In September 1983, Dennis Brown (P) and Terry Thomas (D) became engaged. P gave D an engagement ring. In December 1983, the engagement was terminated. P sued D to recover the ring. At trial both claimed the other broke the engagement. The trial court granted D's motion for directed verdict, holding that a state law prohibiting suits for breach of promise to marry barred P's claim. P appeals.

  b) **Issue.** Does Wisconsin law prohibit suits to recover conditional gifts given in anticipation of marriage?

  c) **Held.** No. The judgment is reversed and remanded.

    (1) In 1959, the legislature abolished breach of promise suits, finding that they bordered on extortion. The trial court's interpretation of this law as barring all common law suits related to breach of contract to marry is inconsistent with precedent. Moreover, nothing in the statute or in accepted rules of statutory construction justifies such a broad reading of the statute. Also, the Wisconsin Constitution provides that every person is entitled to a remedy for all injuries.

    (2) Most jurisdictions recognize that an engagement gift made in contemplation of marriage is a gift conditioned upon the subsequent ceremonial marriage. If a gift is delivered with intent to take effect irrevocably, it is absolute, but a wedding ring is a conditional gift.

    (3) Most jurisdictions allow recovery on conditional engagement gifts only if the giver has not unjustifiably broken the engagement. But that approach breeds difficult litigation over "who broke the engagement." Because Wisconsin has abolished fault upon failure of marriage, that same policy should apply to failure of engagements as well.

    (4) P may not recover interest and damages, unless he alleges fraud.

b. **Other states.** Such factors as the type of property given, fraud, and conditions attached to the gift may be relevant to the determination of whether a gift given in anticipation of marriage is recoverable in other states.

3. **Actions Against Third Parties for Interference with Betrothal.** Generally, actions against third parties for interference with a prospective marriage are not

maintainable because of the policy favoring the liberal availability of advice from friends and family regarding a pending union "before it is too late."

B. ANNULMENTS GENERALLY

1. **Historical Confusion.** Some confusion exists regarding the usage of terminology in this area.

   a. **Divorce and annulment.** Strictly speaking, annulment signifies that no valid marriage ever existed. Divorce signifies the termination of a previously existing valid marriage.

   b. **Voidable and void marriages.** *Voidable* marriages offend some ordinary public policy. Court action to determine the voidability is required; often only the parties to the marriage can attack it, and never after the death of either party to the marriage. *Void* marriages offend extraordinarily strong public policies. Technically, no formal action is necessary to declare the marriage void; third parties can attack the marriage, even after the marriage is terminated by death (or possible divorce).

2. **Modern Approaches.** Some commentators have called for the abolition of "voidable" categories of annulment in states where no-fault divorce laws exist.

   a. **The Uniform Marriage and Divorce Act.** The Uniform Marriage and Divorce Act (1973) modifies many of the traditional rules concerning annulments. It provides the general presumption that declarations of invalidity should be treated the same way as divorces are concerning property division, child custody, etc.

   b. **An alternative to divorce.** Especially in states with strict divorce laws, annulment actions have been used as an alternative means of dissolving marriage. Always conceptually questionable, the practical justification for this is now also being questioned in states that have enacted no-fault divorce laws.

      1) **The effect of voidable marriages on prior alimony obligations--McConkey v. McConkey, 215 S.E.2d 640 (Va. 1975).** McConkey v. McConkey

         a) **Facts.** Clara (P) and Edward (D) McConkey were divorced in 1968. Edward was ordered to pay $200 per month alimony until Clara remarried. In October 1971, P married Sykes; in November 1971, P brought an action against Sykes for annulment, which was granted in 1973. P then petitioned for reinstatement of alimony from D, her first husband.

         b) **Issue.** Should alimony from the first husband be reinstated when the plaintiff receives an annulment from a later voidable marriage?

         c) **Held.** No.

(1)   There is a difference between void and voidable marriages. Alimony might be reinstated after annulment from a void marriage because it is void ab initio. But a voidable marriage is treated as a valid marriage until, at the party's request, it is decreed void. A state statute provides that alimony payments terminate upon the recipient's remarriage, which includes entering into valid, albeit voidable, marriages.

(2)   The former husband has the right to assume the validity of the second marriage and to arrange his affairs accordingly. He should not be held accountable for his former wife's mistake in entering into a voidable marriage.

d)   Comment. While the court in this case stresses the conceptual reasons for its conclusion, the factual circumstances are often as influential as the theoretical concerns. The equities of the situation—fairness to the former spouse who has relied in his financial dealings upon the termination of the alimony obligation, and fairness to a defrauded "double victim" of marital failure—should not be overlooked.

c.   Putative marriages. To provide equitable relief for disadvantaged parties to invalid (annulled) marriages when legislative authorization to do so does not exist, some courts have adopted the putative marriage doctrine. This concept allows courts to supervise the disentanglement of personal and property relations on equitable principles to the extent that the petitioning party was without knowledge of the invalidating defect.

C.   FORMAL REQUIREMENTS

1.   Historical Antecedents. While we are accustomed now to thinking of marriage as a very formal affair (usually with a presiding civil or ecclesiastical officer, witnesses, certificates, etc.), it has not always been so. For centuries, the Christian Church recognized (even if it discouraged) many less formal methods of establishing the marital relationship. Likewise, civil restrictions on the methods of contracting marriage did not exist for the most part until about the middle of the nineteenth century. Until then, formal, clandestine, and informal marriages were all recognized as legitimate in England.

2.   Licensing and Ceremonial Requirements. If a legal prerequisite for formal marriage is deemed to be a "mandatory" requirement, failure to comply therewith may result in an invalid marriage. But if the requirement is deemed to be merely "directory," failure to comply therewith will not affect the validity of the marriage.

a.   Licensing requirements. Licensing requirements, in large part, are developments of the last century. While the purpose of such laws is important (to insure regularity and order), they are often only considered to be directory. Similarly, requirements concerning the qualifications of officials performing marriages are often considered to be directory.

b. **Failure to obtain license prior to marriage--Carabetta v. Carabetta,** 438 A.2d 109 (Conn. 1980).

Carabetta v. Carabetta

1) **Facts.** Wife (P) and Husband (D) exchanged marital vows before a priest according to the rite of the Roman Catholic Church, but did not obtain a marriage license. Thereafter they lived together as husband and wife and reared four children. The birth certificates list D as the father. A state statute prescribes two formalities in order to effectuate a valid marriage: a marriage license, and a solemnization. P brought an action for dissolution of the marriage. D moved to dismiss. The trial court granted the dismissal, having determined that the parties had never been legally married. P appeals.

2) **Issue.** Under Connecticut law, is a marriage void when there has been noncompliance with a statutory requirement of a marriage license?

3) **Held.** No. The trial court erred in granting the motion to dismiss for lack of subject matter jurisdiction. A marriage is dissolvable rather than void in the absence of express language in the governing statute declaring the marriage void for failure to observe a statutory requirement. This statute did not describe as void a marriage celebrated without a license.

4) **Comment.** The good faith formal celebration of marriage according to the solemn rites of the Catholic Church is clearly the critical fact in this case. The failure to obtain a proper license, while significant alone, cannot be considered dispositive without reference to the other facts of the case.

D. COMMON LAW MARRIAGE

1. **Ceremonial Requirements.** Once a popular (and populist) means of creating valid marriages, common law marriage is now recognized in only 13 American jurisdictions.

a. **Common law marriage favored--Meister v. Moore,** 96 U.S. 76 (1877).

Meister v. Moore

1) **Facts.** The trial court judge instructed the jury that, if a minister or magistrate was not present at the alleged marriage of William Mowry and the daughter of Indian Pero, the marriage was invalid under a Michigan statute. This instruction withdrew from jury consideration all evidence of common law marriage. This instruction is alleged to be erroneous.

2) **Issue.** Does a statute that prescribes certain formalities for entering into marriage take away the common law right to marry?

3) Held. No.

    a)   Marriage is a civil contract. Statutes may regulate the mode of entering into the contract, but they do not create the right. It is true that a statute may take away a common law right, but there is a presumption that the legislature has no such intention unless they plainly express it.

    b)   The formal provisions in the Michigan statute may be held to be merely directory. This is because marriage is a thing of common right, because it is the state's policy to encourage marriage, and because to hold otherwise would result in declaring illegitimate the offspring of many parents who are unconscious of a violation of the law.

4) Comment. In contrast to this case, some courts have outlawed common law marriage by holding the statutory solemnization requirement to be mandatory. In other states, the legislature has expressly abolished common law marriages.

Boswell v.
Boswell

b. Presumption of common law marriage upon removal of prior impediment to marriage--Boswell v. Boswell, 497 So. 2d 479 (Ala. 1986).

1) Facts. Marjorie Boswell (P) was ceremonially married to Arthur Fair in 1944 and never divorced. In 1946, P began living in matrimonial co-habitation with S.C. Boswell and lived with him for 37 or 38 years. Mr. Fair died in 1983, and S.C. died the following year. P brought this action to obtain the widow's allotment as S.C.'s widow. The executor of S.C.'s estate (D) opposed. The trial court ruled for P. D appeals.

2) Issue. Upon the death of P's legal husband, was a common law marriage formed between P and her long-time cohabitant?

3) Held. Yes. The judgment is affirmed.

    a)   In Alabama, no ceremony or particular words are necessary to form common law marriage, so long as both parties have capacity to marry and indicate a present, mutual agreement to have an exclusive marriage relationship, and there is public assumption and recognition of a marital relation.

    b)   No common law marriage could be created while P's ceremonial husband was alive and not divorced.

    c)   Upon death of P's ceremonial husband, the impediment to marriage was removed, and continued cohabitation manifested mutual agreement to common law marriage.

4) Comment. About one-fourth of all states still permit common law marriage. But even under the Uniform Marriage and Divorce Act, in the case of a bigamous marriage, parties who otherwise satisfy the marriage requirements and who cohabit after removal of the impediment are lawfully married as of the date of the removal.

2. **Temporary Residence in a Common Law Jurisdiction.** The choice-of-law question often is a significant factor when a party or parties claim the existence of a common law marriage by virtue of satisfying the three requirements while temporarily residing in or visiting a common law marriage jurisdiction. While some courts have used those facts to find marriages in compelling equitable cases, most courts require a significant connection to the jurisdiction before finding a common law marriage. But massaging the facts and finessing the law to do equity may create problems for courts having to apply the precedents thus made.

E. INDIVIDUAL CAPACITY TO MARRY

In addition to complying with the procedures and formalities required by the state, both parties to the marriage must be legally qualified to enter the relationship of marriage.

1. **Marriageable Age.** Age is a factor used in many statutes to qualify the right to marry on personal consent, the right to marry with parental or judicial consent, and the physical/cognitive ability to enter into the marriage relationship.

    a. **Constitutionality of marriage restrictions--Moe v. Dinkins,** 533 F. Supp. 623 (S.D.N.Y. 1981).

    Moe v. Dinkins

    1) **Facts.** A New York statute requires that when applying for marriage licenses, males between the ages of 16 and 18 and females between the ages of 14 and 18 must obtain written consent from both parents of the minor. Maria Moe, Raoul Roe, and Ricardo Roe (Ps) sought a judgment declaring the statute unconstitutional. Raoul, 18, and Maria, 15, have lived together without being married. A son, Ricardo, was born to them. Maria's mother, a widow, refused to consent to their marriage because she wished to continue receiving welfare benefits for Maria. Seventeen-year-old Pedro Doe and 15-year-old Christina Coe, in a similar situation (Christina was eight months pregnant), intervened as plaintiffs. The federal trial court declined to decide the constitutionality of the statute until it had been construed by the New York state courts. The court of appeals reversed and remanded to the district court.

    2) **Issue.** Does the New York Domestic Relations Law requiring parental consent for the marriage of minors deprive Ps of their constitutional rights?

    3) **Held.** No. Ps' motion for summary judgment is denied.

        a) Activities related to marriage and procreation are constitutionally protected rights of individual privacy, and minors are not beyond the protection of the Constitution. However, the state's concern with the unique position of minors allows the state to make some adjustment in the minors' rights. Three reasons justify this conclusion: (i) the vulnerability of children, (ii) their inability to make informed decisions in a mature manner, and (iii) the importance of the parental role in child rearing. The state has an interest in preventing unstable marriages which might be entered into by immature minors.

    b)   The denial of marriage without parental consent is a temporary situation at worst. The couple may subsequently marry when they reach the proper age.

2.   **Consanguinity and Affinity.** Prohibitions against marriage among persons related within certain degrees of kinship are the most ubiquitous form of marriage regulation.

Israel
v. Allen

    a.   **Related by adoption--Israel v. Allen,** 577 P.2d 762 (Colo. 1978).

        1)   **Facts.** Martin Richard Israel and Tammy Lee Bannon Israel (Ps) challenged a Colorado statute forbidding marriage between adopted brother and sister. Martin's father married Tammy's mother when Martin was 18 years old and living in the state of Washington and Tammy was 13 years old and living with her mother. The new stepfather adopted Tammy. Six years after the parents' marriage, Ps wanted to get married, but were denied a marriage license. They sought a declaratory judgment. The district court held the statute unconstitutional as violative of equal protection. The state appeals.

        2)   **Issue.** Does a statute prohibiting the marriage of adopted siblings deny them equal protection under the Constitution?

        3)   **Held.** Yes. The decision of the district court is affirmed.

            a)   Legal regulation of adoptive relationships is strictly statutory. The motive in recent legislation regarding adopted children has been to make their rights equal to those of natural children.

            b)   We disagree with the state's contention that this statute furthers the state interest in family harmony. As this case illustrates, the statute is just as likely to promote family discord.

            c)   Striking the phrase "or by adoption" from the statute will not invalidate the remainder of the statute, because the phrase is independent of the other valid parts.

        4)   **Comment.** While the approach taken by the Colorado Supreme Court has some appeal, it is by no means certain that courts in all other jurisdictions would agree with its decision. In some states, the expectation of family unity which underscores the concept of adoption may be deemed to be threatened by allowing siblings by adoption who have lived as brother and sister to marry.

3.   **Physical and Mental Capacity.** Since marriage is a contract, the ability to comprehend and voluntarily agree is an indispensable requirement for a valid marriage. Since sexual intercourse is deemed to be a universal object and intent of marriage, capacity for sexual intercourse is also a necessary requirement.

a. **Mental incompetence--Edmunds v. Edwards,** 287 N.W.2d 420 (Neb. 1980).

1) **Facts.** Renne Edmunds (P), guardian of the estate of Harold Edwards, brought an action in district court to annul Harold's marriage to Inez Edwards (D). P argued that the marriage was void because Harold did not have the mental capacity to enter into a marriage contract. Harold was 57 years old at the time of his marriage. He had spent 30 years of his life in an institution for the mentally retarded. He first met his wife at this institution, where she was also a resident. At the time of the marriage, both parties had been residing outside the institution and receiving assistance in normalizing their lives from the Eastern Nebraska Community Office of Retardation. Harold was employed and had received wage increases and good reports from his supervisors. P did not bring the action to annul the marriage until two years after the ceremony. The court found the marriage valid under the laws of Nebraska. P appeals.

2) **Issue.** Can a marriage be annulled for the reason of lack of capacity to enter into the marriage contract if the party is classified as mildly mentally retarded?

3) **Held.** No. The district court's dismissal of the petition to annul the marriage is affirmed.

   a) A marriage is presumed valid and the burden of proof is upon the party seeking annulment. P's expert witnesses could not verify Harold's lack of capacity to understand the meaning and the obligations of marriage.

   b) What persons establish by entering into matrimony is not a contractual relation but a social status. The only essential features of the transactions are that the participants are of legal capacity to assume that status, and freely consent to do so. Although statutes provide that marriages are void if either party is insane or mentally incompetent, the degree of mental weakness must be such that the party is incapable of understanding the fundamental meaning of marriage. Expert witnesses in this case tended to agree that Harold was capable of understanding the marriage status.

4) **Comment.** Recognizing that half of all Americans are "below average" in intelligence (whatever that means), the potential for mischief if too strict a mental capacity requirement is imposed should be obvious.

b. **Impotence--Rickards v. Rickards,** 166 A.2d 425 (Del. 1960).

1) **Facts.** Mrs. Rickards (P) brought an action for annulment of her marriage to Mr. Rickards (D) on the ground that he was impotent. Her action was based on a statute that allowed annulment where a party was incurably physically impotent, or was incapable of copulation. At trial, evidence showed that D's incapacity was due to psychic causes and that he suffered no physical defect of a sexually incapacitating nature. The trial court granted the annulment. D appeals.

2) **Issue.** May annulment of a marriage be granted where the cause of impotency is psychic rather than physical in origin?

3) **Held.** Yes. The judgment is affirmed.

    a) The only ground of annulment authorized by the statute is incurable physical impotency. Whether the inability stems from physical or mental defects, the requirement of the statute is met if the condition is incurable.

    b) The fact has been established to a reasonable certainty that D is incurably physically impotent. The psychiatrist who worked with D testified that the possibility of cure was remote.

4) **Comment.** Under the doctrine of triennial cohabitation, if a woman is still a virgin after three years of marital cohabitation, that may give rise to a presumption of the husband's incapacity.

M.T. v.
J.T.

c. **Transsexuals--M.T. v. J.T.,** 355 A.2d 204 (N.J. Super. Ct. App. Div. 1976).

1) **Facts.** M.T. (P) was biologically a male, but always felt like a female. With the help of J.T. (D), P had a sex change operation to become a female. A year later, P and D were married. Following their separation a few years later, P sued D for support and maintenance. D's defense was that P was a male and that their marriage was void. The trial court held for P and ordered D to make support payments. D appeals.

2) **Issue.** Should the marriage between a male and a postoperative transsexual, who has surgically changed her external sexual anatomy from male to female, be regarded as a lawful marriage between a man and a woman?

3) **Held.** Yes. The judgment is affirmed.

    a) The fundamental premise is that a lawful marriage requires the performance of a ceremonial marriage of two persons of the opposite sex, male and female. The court concludes that P qualifies as a female.

    b) For purposes of marriage, sex is not irrevocably cast at the moment of birth. Sex in the biological sense is not the exclusive standard. The psychological gender of an individual may be different from his or her anatomical sex.

    c) Some courts have held that anatomical sex at birth is the only measure for the sex of an individual. This court disagrees. Where an individual's physical sex is harmonized with his or her psychological sex by medical treatment, so that he or she can sexually function as a member of the new sex, that individual becomes a male or female, as the case may be. Here, P became a female when the operation reconciled her physical and psychological sex.

4) **Comment.** Sex change operations may lead to similar questions regarding birth certificate, sex identification, medical welfare entitlements, etc.

4. **Prohibition of Bigamy.** One form of marriage that is historically common and still accepted in many "third world" countries, but which has been the subject of strong public policy objections in most countries, is polygamy.

a. **Constitutionality--*See* Reynolds v. United States, *supra* at p. 3.**

b. **Equitable doctrines used to overcome problems of premature remarriage--*In re* Marriage of Sumners,** 645 S.W.2d 205 (Mo. Ct. App. 1983).

In re Marriage of Sumners

1) **Facts.** Jerry Lee Sumners (D) obtained a Nebraska divorce decree dissolving his third marriage on October 18, 1963. The divorce decree prohibited D from remarrying within six months of the date of the decree. However, three months later D married the plaintiff, who was aware, at least inferentially, of the remarriage restriction. Although P and D were Nebraska residents, they were married in Iowa in order to avoid a Nebraska waiting period requirement. After the marriage the parties lived in Nebraska for four years, then moved to Missouri and lived together for almost 12 years before separating. The parties had four children during this time. P filed an action to dissolve the marriage. D filed a motion to dismiss for lack of subject matter jurisdiction, arguing that his marriage to P was void. The trial court granted his motion.

2) **Issue.** Did the trial court err in dismissing P's action for dissolution on the ground that her marriage to D was void because in violation of the remarriage restriction?

3) **Held.** Yes. The judgment of dismissal is reversed and the action is reinstated.

a) Missouri adheres to the presumption that the latest marriage is valid.

b) Under Nebraska law the divorce decree entered on October 18, 1963, did not operate to terminate D's marital status for six months.

c) However, if D's former wife had died before the date of his marriage to P, he would have been free to marry P when he did, and D has presented no evidence that his former wife was alive on the date he married P.

d) Furthermore, under doctrines of preclusion, estoppel, or quasi-estoppel, a party may be prevented from attacking the validity of his divorce decree if it would be inequitable to allow him to do so, such as when that party caused the misleading situation by relying on the validity of his divorce when marrying a woman, then claiming that it was not a valid divorce when she seeks to dissolve the marriage.

e) The Full Faith and Credit Clause and federal statutes do not prevent application of this equitable doctrine because the doctrine does not validate a void marriage but only prevents raising a defense of invalidity, and Iowa, the place of marriage, would apply forum law (here Missouri) to determine which equitable doctrines can be invoked in a dissolution action.

F. CONSENT TO MARRIAGE

Wolfe v.
Wolfe

1. **Fraud Going to the "Essentials" of the Marriage--Wolfe v. Wolfe,** 389 N.E.2d 1143 (Ill. 1979).

   a. **Facts.** After Judith Wolfe (P) filed a complaint for divorce, James Wolfe (D) counterclaimed for an annulment of the marriage on the basis of fraud. P had been previously married and divorced. D, a Roman Catholic, was forbidden by his religion to marry a divorced woman. P represented to D that she had heard that her former husband had been killed in an auto accident. She converted to Catholicism and executed a Sponsa stating that her former husband was dead. She also produced a purported death certificate of the former husband. The couple were married and had a child, and remained married for eight years. The ex-husband was in fact not dead. During the divorce proceeding, P admitted that she knew that her ex-husband was alive. D claimed that he would not have married her if he had not been convinced she was a widow. The jury returned a verdict in favor of D on his counterclaim. The court vacated the judgment and dismissed D's counterclaim. D appeals.

   b. **Issue.** Does the nature of the fraud perpetrated here go to the "essentials" of marriage, therefore allowing the marriage to be annulled?

   c. **Held.** Yes. D is entitled to an annulment.

      1) Fradulent conduct that would render an ordinary contract void will not render a marriage void unless the nature of the fraud affects the essentials of the marriage. In this case, D was not able to continue to perform the duties and obligations of his marriage within the bounds of his religious convictions once he learned the nature of the fraud. He declared that he would not have entered the marriage except for P's fraudulent representation.

      2) Although lengthy marital cohabitation is a factor militating against the granting of an annulment, it is not necessarily controlling. Similarly, the existence of a child, although a factor, will not bar an annulment.

   d. **Comment.** This relaxed view of "fraud going to the essentials of the marriage" is the most common modern approach to the issue.

G. CHOICE OF LAW

1. **Legislative Rules.** If the state legislature has established a choice of law rule applicable to any controversy, it should be applied.

2. **Judicial Rules.** If no statute applies, a marriage valid where performed should be considered to be valid elsewhere unless it is contrary to a strong

public policy of a state having a more significant relation with the parties and marriage regarding the particular issue or defect involved. However, a marriage invalid where performed should be considered valid if valid under the law of a state having a significant relation with the parties and marriage, unless the interest of the state of performance in enforcing its invalidating rule is of greater significance.

3. **Multi-State Marriages.** In today's mobile society, many marriages involve parties from two different states who may even be marrying in a third state. Since marriage laws differ significantly from state to state, the question of which state laws govern the validity of the marriage is important. [*See In re* Marriage of Sumners, *supra*]

III. THE RELATIONSHIP BETWEEN HUSBAND AND WIFE

A. THE DISABILITIES OF MARRIED WOMEN IN GENERAL

1. **At Common Law.** For centuries, married women were under substantial disabilities at common law. In large part, they were deprived of their property (if not their entire legal identity) during coverture. Many of these disabilities proceeded from (at least were justified by reference to) the Judeo-Christian notion that upon marriage the man and woman became one.

2. **Married Women's Acts.** By the middle of the nineteenth century, a movement was sweeping America to remove the most extreme (and socially antiquated) disabilities of married women. Subsequent movements (*e.g.*, suffrage, prohibition, etc.) removed other disabilities and provided new protections to married women.

3. **Judicial Scrutiny.** Beginning about 1970, a new, strict standard of judicial scrutiny was constitutionally mandated for sex-based distinctions.

4. **Legislative Action.** Responding to a growing women's liberation movement, federal state legislatures enacted substantial legislation during the 1970s abolishing or modifying many sex and marriage-based disabilities and providing new statutory rights for women.

5. **New Attitudes.** Underlying the vast changes that have occurred, not only during the past decade but over the centuries, are significant changes in social, intellectual, and economic conditions.

B. THE FAMILY NAME

1. **Married Women's Surnames.** One result of the women's liberation movement of the last decade is renewed concern over married women's legal names.

Stuart v.
Board of
Supervisors
of Elections

    a. **Retaining maiden name--Stuart v. Board of Supervisors of Elections,** 295 A.2d 223 (Md. 1973).

        1) **Facts.** Mary Emily Stuart (P) married Samuel Austell and, in accordance with the couple's antenuptial agreement, P continued to use her maiden name. She registered to vote in the name of Mary Emily Stuart, but disclosed that she had married Austell. Later, the board (D) informed her that, since by law a woman's legal surname becomes that of her husband upon marriage, she would have to change her name or she would not be allowed to vote. P promptly challenged D's decision. The trial court agreed with D and held that P would have to register in her husband's surname. P appeals.

        2) **Issue.** Does a woman's legal surname automatically change to that of her husband upon marriage as a matter of common law?

        3) **Held.** No. The judgment is reversed.

a)   It is only by custom that a woman, upon marriage, adopts the surname of her husband. The court has previously recognized the right of any person, absent a statute to the contrary, to adopt any name by which he or she shall be known.

b)   There is no statutory requirement that a woman adopt the sur-name of her husband. A married woman's surname does not become that of her husband where, as here, she evidences a clear intent to consistently and nonfraudulently use her birth-given name subsequent to her marriage.

4)   Comment. The jurisdictions are split on this question (the context in which it arises is not insignificant).

2.   **Children's Names.** Initially, one would expect that parents would enjoy as much latitude in selecting their children's names as their own. But different state interests are implicated when children are involved, limiting somewhat parents' latitude in this area.

a.   **Children's surnames--Henne v. Wright,** 904 F.2d 1208 (8th Cir. 1990), *cert. denied,* 498 U.S. 1032 (1991).

Henne v. Wright

1)   Facts. Debra Henne (P1) gave birth to a daughter and listed the child's name on a birth certificate form as Alicia Renee Brinton, using the surname of the father instead of P's husband, from whom she had not yet been officially divorced. Hospital personnel informed her that she could not use "Brinton" because of her marital status, even though neither P1 nor P1's husband objected to the use of the surname Brinton. P1 filled out another form using "Henne," leaving blank the space for the father's name. Separately, Linda Spidell (P2), who was unmarried, gave birth to a daughter and wished to name the child Quintessa McKenzie; P2 had given the surname McKenzie to her other children, even though the name had nothing in common with her own name, or the name of the biological father, Ray Duffer. The hospital personnel informed P2 that she had to use the name Spidell as the girl's surname. P1 and P2 brought a civil rights action challenging the constitutionality of a Nebraska statute that restricted surnames that could be given to children at birth. The district court entered judgment for Ps. The heads of the Nebraska Department of Health and the Nebraska Bureau of Vital Statistics (Ds), appeal.

2)   Issue. Does the Fourteenth Amendment right of privacy give a parent the fundamental right to give a child a surname at birth with which the child has no legally established parental connection?

3)   Held. No. The judgment is reversed.

a)   A "fundamental" right is one "deeply rooted in this Nation's history and tradition."

b)   Two of the earliest right to privacy cases, *Meyer v. Nebraska,* 262 U.S. 390 (1923) (fundamental right to instruct a child in a foreign language), and *Pierce v. Society of Sisters,* 268 U.S. 510 (1925) (fundamental right to send a child to a non-public school), established the right of parents to make child rearing decisions free from unwarranted governmental regulation.

c) In contrast to those cases, which recognized rights and extended constitutional protection to parental decisions which centered primarily around the training and education of children, the subject of this case is not related to the training and education of children.

d) Traditionally, a child born in wedlock receives the father's surname, and a child born out of wedlock receives the mother's surname. While some unmarried mothers give their child the father's surname, and other couples use hyphenated surnames, there is no tradition to support the extension of the right to privacy to cover the right of a parent to give a child a surname to which that child has no legally recognized parental connection.

e) A statute that significantly infringes upon a right deemed fundamental under the Fourteenth Amendment right of privacy merits rigorous scrutiny by a court; otherwise, the statute is reviewed under the highly deferential rational basis standard applicable to meet challenged economic and social legislation.

f) The Nebraska statute bears a rational relationship to that state's legitimate interest in promoting the welfare of children, insuring the names of citizens are not appropriated for improper purposes, and expediting record keeping.

4) **Concurring in part, dissenting in part.** The right being claimed here is well within the principle of *Meyer* and *Pierce* and within our country's early tradition. The state has no interest compelling enough to override such a fundamental right.

C. ECONOMIC RELATIONS BETWEEN SPOUSES

1. **Gender Equality.** At common law, the legal identity of a married woman merged with that of her husband, who was vested with a legal power similar to an unrestricted trusteeship over most of her property. The passage of the Married Women's Property Acts in the mid-nineteenth century began the movement toward economic equality under law. This doctrine of legal "unity" of personhood prevented spouses from contracting with each other.

2. **Spousal Support.** Traditionally, the law expected the husband to support the wife. Modern cases and statutes have imposed like obligations upon both spouses.

McGuire v.
McGuire

a. **Judicial interference to compel support--McGuire v. McGuire, 59** N.W.2d 336 (Neb. 1953).

1) **Facts.** Lydia McGuire (P) and Charles McGuire (D) were married in 1919 and have lived together ever since. The facts showed that D was frugal to a fault. He provided P with food and medical care, but little else. P brought an action to recover suitable maintenance and support money, and for costs and attorney's fees. The trial court declared that P was entitled to use the credit of D and ordered D to do such things as purchase a new car and furniture, give P money to visit her adult children each year, and give P a personal monthly allowance of $50. D appeals.

2) **Issue.** As long as the parties remain living together, will the court order a husband to support his wife in a particular manner?

3) **Held.** No. The judgment is reversed with direction to dismiss.

   a) In order to maintain an action for support and maintenance, the parties must be living apart and the separation must not have been the fault of the plaintiff. Here, the parties still live together.

   b) The living standards of a household are a matter of concern for that household, not for the courts. As long as the home is maintained and the parties are living together as husband and wife, the purpose of the marriage relation is being carried out. Public policy requires this holding.

   c) The couple has lived together for over 30 years with no complaint on P's part until now. P is not devoid of money in her own right. She has a fair-sized bank account and income from property.

4) **Dissent.** A wife should be able to bring an action for support even while she lives with her husband. But the court, in this case, was without power to make any of the awards other than the one for $50 per month.

5) **Comment.** The court recognizes the principle of family autonomy—that a court should not interfere with the inner workings of an ongoing family. But when the family has broken apart (through death, separation, or divorce) or failed (from abuse or neglect), then courts will intervene and exercise their equity power to insure reasonable support.

b. **Necessaries and equal obligations.** Under the common law necessaries doctrine, a husband was liable for necessary goods and services furnished to his wife for her support and maintenance. This gender-based presumption has been modified or abolished by legislative or judicial action in most jurisdictions, and a sex-neutral duty of spousal support widely adopted in its place.

c. **The extent of "necessaries"--State v. Clark,** 563 P.2d 1253 (Wash. 1977).   State v. Clark

1) **Facts.** M'Lissa Clark (D) was charged with one count of possession of a controlled substance and one count of possession of marijuana. Before her trial, she married Jay Daling. D was convicted and asked for appellate review at public expense because she was an indigent. The trial court denied her request because her new husband had sufficient funds to pay for the legal services. D appeals.

2) **Issue.** Are appellate legal services a "necessary" for which a husband is liable, even when the crime his wife is defending occurred before their marriage?

3) **Held.** Yes. The judgment is affirmed.

    a) A state statute makes neither husband nor wife liable for an antenuptial debt. But the cost of D's appeal is not an antenuptial debt. Following her trial, she decided she wanted an appeal. She was married at that time.

    b) A state family-expense statute also requires a husband to pay "necessaries" for his family. Legal expenses fall into the category of "necessaries" when a criminal action is involved and a spouse's liberty is at stake. Thus, Jay Daling's assets may be considered in determining whether D is an indigent.

    c) The same rule would apply if the circumstances were the opposite. A wife may now be liable for failure to support her husband under circumstances where her husband would be liable for failure to support her.

Kirchberg v. Feenstra

d. **Control of property--Kirchberg v. Feenstra,** 450 U.S. 455 (1981).

1) **Facts.** While incarcerated on a criminal charge, Harold Feenstra retained services of attorney Karl Kirchberg (P). As security on a $3,000 promissory note in prepayment for legal services, Feenstra executed a mortgage on the home he owned jointly with his wife Joan (D). D was not informed of the mortgage. Her consent was not required because a Louisiana statute in force at the time of the execution gave husbands exclusive control over the disposition of community property. When the criminal charge against Harold was dropped, he obtained a legal separation from his wife and moved out of the state, leaving D to pay the amount outstanding on the promissory note. P threatened to foreclose on D's home. When D refused to pay the obligation, P obtained an order of executory process directing the sheriff to seize and sell the home. D appealed the court order, seeking a declaratory judgment that the mortgage executed on her home is void as having been executed without her consent pursuant to an unconstitutional state statute. While the appeal was pending, the state legislature revised its community property code, granting spouses equal control over community property. The court of appeals reversed the district court's ruling. P appeals.

2) **Issue.** Is the application of a statute that granted the husband control over community property unconstitutional gender-based discrimination?

3) **Held.** Yes. The judgment is affirmed.

    a) A statute that grants a husband exclusive control over the disposition of community property clearly constitutes unconstitutional gender-based discrimination, absent a showing that the classification furthers an important governmental interest. P does not claim the provision serves any such interest.

b) Although the statute contained a provision whereby Mrs. Feenstra could have made a "declaration by authentic act" prohibiting her husband from executing a mortgage without her consent, this provision does not redeem the statute. The absence of an insurmountable barrier will not redeem an otherwise unconstitutionally discriminatory law.

e. **Community property.** The core concept of community property is that marriage should be treated as an equal partnership for purposes of determining rights with and among spouses. The basic legal principle of community property is that all property acquired during the marriage, other than by gift, bequest, or devise, is community property of which each spouse is full and equal owner, and when the marriage ends because of death or dissolution, each spouse is entitled to keep or dispose of half of such property. Eight states (Arizona, California, Idaho, Louisiana, Nevada, New Mexico, Texas, and Washington) have community property laws. Additionally, the Uniform Marital Property Act is a model law incorporating community law principles. Wisconsin has adopted such community law principles recently by legislation.

D. PRIVILEGES, IMMUNITIES, AND CIVIL AND CRIMINAL REQUIRE-MENTS

1. **Testimonial Privilege.** The special relationship between husband and wife is recognized in the law of evidence.

   a. **The privilege against spousal testimony--Trammel v. United States,** 445 U.S. 40 (1980).

   Trammel v. United States

   1) **Facts.** Otis Trammel (P) was indicted on drug charges. His wife was named an unindicted co-conspirator. She agreed to cooperate with the government and was granted immunity. At trial, over P's objection, she was allowed to testify about any act she had observed during the marriage and all conversations with P that occurred in the presence of third persons; however, she was not permitted to testify about confidential communications with P. P was convicted and that judgment affirmed on appeal. P's petition for writ of certiorari was granted.

   2) **Issue.** Is the voluntary testimony of a spouse against her husband regarding his actions and nonconfidential communications during marriage admissible in federal court criminal cases over the husband's objection?

   3) **Held.** Yes. The judgment is affirmed.

      a) The privilege against adverse spousal testimony is derived from the medieval rule that an accused could not testify in his own behalf and from the notion of absolute spousal unity in the law. These reasons for the rule are no longer valid.

b) The modern justification for the rule is the need to protect marital harmony. This was noted in *Hawkins v. United States* 358 U.S. 74 (1958), upholding the exclusionary privilege.

c) Since the 1958 *Hawkins* decision, seven more states (making a total of 26) have abandoned the rule, and scholars have criticized it.

d) In Rule 501 of the Federal Rules of Evidence, Congress acknowledged the continuing power of federal courts to proceed with the evolutionary development of testimonial privileges.

e) Exclusionary rules should be strictly limited. The privilege against adverse spousal testimony is broader than necessary to protect confidential marital communications. And when one spouse is willing to testify against the other, marital harmony provides a weak justification for exclusion.

f) The exclusionary rule should be modified so that the witness spouse possesses the privilege to refuse to testify adversely against her spouse—the witness can be neither compelled nor prohibited from testifying.

4) Comment. The spousal privilege against the disclosure of confidential marital communications remains intact after (if it has not been strengthened by) this decision.

2. Crimes. In criminal law, the marital relation of the victim and aggressor has seldom been a legally significant factor (rape being one exception), but it has been a practically important consideration.

Warren
v. State

a. Rape of a spouse--Warren v. State, 336 S.E.2d 221 (Ga. 1985).

1) Facts. Daniel Warren (D) was indicted and convicted for the rape and aggravated sodomy of his wife with whom he was living. His defense of an implicit marital exclusion was rejected. D appeals.

2) Issue. Are there implicit marital exclusions for the crimes of rape and sodomy?

3) Held. No. The conviction is affirmed.

a) Lord Hale's 17th century contract theory held that a husband could not be guilty of rape upon his wife because her consent to marriage conveyed irrevocable consent to sex with her husband. The dramatic change in the status and rights of women makes this theory untenable today. Neither wife-as-chattel nor unity-of-husband-and-wife are theories that can be reconciled with modern notions of equality and dignity. The fear of unfounded, vindictive charges of spousal rape has not materialized.

b) There is not and never has been any express marital exemption in the Georgia rape statute. Rape is a reprehensible crime.

c) Since consent of the victim was not a defense to sodomy, even the old marital rape defenses did not apply.

4) Comment. Both gender and marital exemptions to rape and sodomy statutes have been replaced in some jurisdictions.

b. Property crimes committed against a spouse--Cladd v. State, 398 So. 2d 442 (Fla. 1981).

Cladd v. State

1) Facts. Cladd (D) was charged with burglary and attempted burglary after he broke through the locked door of his wife's apartment. Although D and his wife had been separated for six months, there was no formal separation agreement. He had no ownership interest in his wife's apartment nor had he lived there at any time. D not only used a crowbar to break through the door, but he also assaulted his wife after gaining entrance. The trial court granted D's motion to dismiss the charges on the basis that because the victim was D's wife, he was licensed to enter as a matter of law. The State appealed and the court of appeals reversed. D appeals.

2) Issue. Can a husband who is physically but not legally separated from his wife be guilty of burglary when he enters premises, possessed only by the wife and in which he has no ownership interest, without the wife's consent and with the intent to commit an offense?

3) Held. Yes. The judgment is affirmed.

a) Marriage and a right of consortium are not sufficient to give a husband a right of entry, nor do they preclude the state from establishing the nonconsensual entry requisite to the crime of burglary (overruling *Vazquez v. State*, 350 So. 2d 1094 (Fla. Dist. Ct. App. 1977).

b) Since burglary is an invasion of the possessory property rights of another, where premises are in the sole possession of the wife, the husband can be guilty of burglary if he makes a nonconsensual entry into her premises with intent to commit an offense, the same as he can be guilty of larceny of his wife's separate property.

4) Dissent. Consortium is so basic an incident of marriage that it should not be undermined, except by a clear legislative statement of the state's public policy. The legislature has met several times since the *Vasquez* (holding a husband was not guilty of burglary when he broke into his wife's apartment) and *Wilson v. State*, 359 So. 2d 901 (Fla. Dist. Ct. App. 1978) (holding a husband was not guilty of burglary when he broke into his father-in-law's house, where his wife was staying) cases were announced, and the legislature has failed to modify the burglary statute involved.

5) Dissent. This case did not involve spouses who are divorced or legally separated, nor was it ever established that the property was separately owned. The separate residence was merely like a separate bedroom in which one spouse may seek a retreat. Although D may or may not be prosecuted for the assault on his wife, criminal courts should not be involved in domestic disputes which involve an invasion of one spouse's claim of separateness of privacy.

6) **Comment.** The court seemed to be influenced by the fact that D had entered with the intent to commit an offense.

State *ex rel.* c. **Spouse abuse and protective orders--State *ex rel.* Williams v. Marsh,** 626
Williams   S.W.2d 223 (Mo. 1982).
v. Marsh

1) **Facts.** Denise Williams (P) and Edward Williams (D) were married with one child, but had been living separately for five months, with P having custody of the child. During the separation, D provided no substantial support to P or the child. D, a former Golden Gloves boxer, had willfully beaten P on several occasions causing serious injury. P then petitioned the trial court for a protective order restraining her husband from entering her home and an order granting her custody pursuant to the Missouri Adult Abuse Act. The statute provided that the ex parte order could be issued without notice to D and would remain in effect for not more than 15 days, and violation of the order would be declared a class C misdemeanor for which D could be arrested without a warrant. The trial court ruled that the act violated the Missouri Constitution because it contained provisions relating to children rather than exclusively to adults (*i.e.,* it contained more than one subject), and violated the due process guarantees of the Fourteenth Amendment, as well as the Fourth Amendment, because it authorizes warrantless arrests. P petitions the Supreme Court of Missouri to issue a writ of mandamus to compel the trial court to issue an order of protection.

2) **Issues.**

a) Does the Missouri Adult Abuse Act violate the Missouri Constitution because it contains provisions dealing with both children and adults?

b) Does the Missouri Adult Abuse Act violate the Fourteenth Amendment because it allows for the deprivation of constitutionally protected rights without notice to D?

c) Does the Missouri Adult Abuse Act violate the Fourth Amendment because it allows for warrantless arrests?

3) **Held.** a) No. b) No. c) No. The judgment is reversed and the writ is granted.

a) The child custody provisions of the Act fairly relate to the subject of adult abuse and promote its purpose. In a large percentage of families, the children are present when the abuse occurs, and often the abuse also occurs to the children. Abuse appears to be perpetuated through the generations. Adult abuse, therefore, is also a problem affecting the children.

b) The due process guarantee is intended to protect an individual against arbitrary acts of the government, and this is determined by weighing the private interests affected and the government functions involved. Here, the private interests are significant, and the governmental interest is the protection of the citizen's general welfare, health, and safety. In accomplishing this, the government has broad powers. Here, the order is similar to a temporary restraining order; P must satisfy the court that grounds exist to justify granting it. The judge may see for himself evidence of abuse, *e.g.,* bruises. In addition, the 15-day period is only a maximum and D may request an earlier hearing. Therefore, the Act is necessary to secure an important governmental interest, and it is a reasonable means to achieve that goal.

    c) The Act does not authorize unconstitutional arrests, because the police must still have consent or exigent circumstances to arrest D within his home.

    4) Concurrence. The fact that violation of an order issued under this Act is considered a crime makes it a personalized criminal offense and questionable under the Constitution. However, this is not a criminal case and we need not answer that constitutional issue.

    5) Dissent. The Court's decision violates the established rule that penal statutes are to be strictly construed against the state.

    6) Comment. This statute typifies the strong modern trend of providing physical protection for women against violent husbands. All 50 states have enacted laws to respond to domestic violence. Thirty-seven states have included provisions for ex parte preliminary relief.

3. Tort Immunity. Traditionally courts have been reluctant to impose civil liability in suits between spouses for injuries suffered in the family or to family relations. Today, the majority of states allow actions for negligence.

4. Protecting Family Integrity. While courts have traditionally been reluctant to interfere with the family structure by imposing the same duties and rights on spouses as are imposed on strangers, there has been less reluctance to use legal doctrines to protect the family from interference from outsiders. Ironically, the interference often comes from "extended family" members, *e.g.,* grandparents, in-laws, etc., which creates the dilemma of protecting the integrity of the nuclear family by curtailing the legal interests of the extended family.

5. Medical Decisions. Although the law is not clear, it is standard practice for doctors and medical institutions to obtain consent for life-threatening procedures from the spouse of an incapacitated person. In recent years, many states have adopted legislation addressing the medical decisionmaking authority in near-death circumstances. Most effectuate the written instructions of the patient; however, most patients do not sign written decisionmaker instructions before they become incompetent.

IV. PARENT-CHILD RELATIONS IN THE LAW

A. LEGITIMACY

Because of the role the family plays in our social lives, children born to unmarried women occupy a uniquely disadvantaged place in society. In the law, this fact of life is reflected in the concept of "illegitimacy." Historically an invidious label, recently this classification has more frequently been used in remedial or beneficial schemes. The preferred term today is "children born out of wedlock."

1. The Burden of Illegitimacy.

Zepeda v.
Zepeda

    a. **Wrongful life--Zepeda v. Zepeda**, 190 N.E.2d 849 (Ill. App. 1963), *cert. denied*, 379 U.S. 945 (1964).

        1) **Facts.** P is the infant son of D. D induced P's mother to have illicit sexual relations by promising to marry her, a promise D knew he could not keep because he was already married. As a result of the act, P was born and now seeks damages from his father because he is an illegitimate child. The trial court dismissed P's complaint for failure to state a cause of action. P appeals.

        2) **Issue.** Does an illegitimate child have a cause of action in tort against his father for the social disability he suffers as a bastard?

        3) **Held.** No. The judgment is affirmed.

            a) It is true that D may have committed a criminal act (adultery) when he engaged in illicit sexual relations with P's mother. Clearly, D's act was tortious in nature.

            b) D has also committed a tortious act against P. Even though D's wrongful conduct occurred at or before the time of P's conception, D can be held accountable to P. It makes no difference how much time elapses between a wrongful act and a resulting injury if there is a causal connection between them (as there is here). D's act was a criminal and moral wrong when committed, and it became a legal and tortious wrong against P.

            c) Although D has committed a tortious act against P, the act cannot be pigeonholed into an existing tort category. Neither intentional infliction of emotional distress nor defamation is alleged. And, although P may have been deprived of a normal homelife, he cannot maintain an action for lack of affection or failure to provide a normal home, because a legitimate child could bring no such action.

            d) Although a wrong has been committed against P, the court will not create a new tort action for wrongful life. To do so would have staggering social consequences and would open the floodgates of litigation. If we are to have a tort action for wrongful life, it should come after thorough study of the consequences.

4) **Comment.** This case was one of the first to consider whether or not a new cause of action for "wrongful life" could be maintained. The court went out of its way to suggest that other causes of action might lie (*e.g.*, infliction of emotional distress, defamation) but declined to engage in such radical lawmaking "where the results could be as sweeping as here."

b. **Equal protection for illegitimates--Levy v. Louisiana,** 391 U.S. 68 (1968).

1) **Facts.** Louise Levy was the mother of five children born out of wedlock, whom she raised, worked to support, took to church, etc. She died, and P sued the doctor and insurer for wrongful death on behalf of the five surviving children. The Louisiana District Court dismissed the suit, construing the wrongful death statute as applying only to legitimate children and rejecting P's equal protection and due process challenges. The Louisiana Supreme Court affirmed. P appeals.

2) **Issue.** Does the restriction of wrongful death recovery to legitimate children deny children born out of wedlock equal protection of the law?

3) **Held.** Yes. The discrimination is invidious.

a) Illegitimate children are not "nonpersons." They are humans, live, and have their being.

b) State legislation regarding social and economic regulation is given wide latitude, and upheld if it has a rational relation to legitimate state purposes.

c) The rights here involve the intimate, familial relationship between parent and child, and the Court is extremely sensitive when it comes to protecting basic civil rights against invidious classification.

d) Legitimacy bears no relation to the nature of the wrong inflicted on the mother or the children, for which the statute provides the remedy of a cause of action.

4) **Dissent** (Harlan, J.). Admittedly legitimacy (legal relatedness) is an arbitrary classification regarding dependency or family love, but so also is biological relatedness. The state has a right to require marriage or an acknowledgement action to establish family relationships.

c. **Support of illegitimate children--Gomez v. Perez,** 409 U.S. 535 (1973).

1) **Facts.** The mother (P) of an illegitimate child filed a petition in Texas district court seeking support from the child's biological father (D). The district court found that D was the father of P's illegitimate child and that P was in need of support, but concluded that because the child was illegitimate, D had no legal duty of support. P appealed. The court of civil appeals affirmed and the Texas Supreme Court refused application for a writ of error.

2) **Issue.** Does a law that creates a judicially enforceable right on behalf of legitimate children to support from their natural father, but denies such a right to illegitimate children, violate the Equal Protection Clause of the Fourteenth Amendment?

3) **Held.** Yes. The judgment is reversed and remanded.

a) Under Texas law, a natural father has a duty to support his legitimate children. But for the fact that the child in this case is illegitimate, she would be entitled to support from D.

b) Prior decisions have held that illegitimate children cannot be excluded from the right to sue for wrongful death, nor can they be excluded from sharing equally with other children in the recovery of workers' compensation benefits. Once the state creates a right of support in favor of legitimate children, it cannot constitutionally exclude illegitimate children from exercising this right.

c) There will be problems in some cases (although not in this one) with respect to proof of paternity, but such problems cannot be used as a rationale to justify invidious discrimination against illegitimate children.

4) **Comment.** A strong theme in the illegitimacy decisions of the Supreme Court is that benefits made available to legitimate children cannot be denied to illegitimate children *solely* because they are illegitimate.

2. **Effect of Illegitimacy on Parents.** At common law the illegitimate child was "filius nullius," a child of no one. The father had no legal rights or duties toward his illegitimate child.

Stanley v. Illinois

a. **Custody of illegitimate children--Stanley v. Illinois,** 405 U.S. 645 (1972).

1) **Facts.** Joan Stanley lived with Peter Stanley (P) for some 18 years, during which time they had three children. Under Illinois law, the children of unwed fathers become wards of the state upon the death of the mother. Joan Stanley died. P's children were declared wards of the state of Illinois (D). P appealed, but the Illinois courts rejected his equal protection claim. P appeals.

2) **Issue.** Is an irrebuttable statutory presumption that all unwed fathers are unfit to have custody of their children violative of the Due Process and Equal Protection Clauses of the Fourteenth Amendment?

3) **Held.** Yes. The judgment is reversed and remanded.

a) It is immaterial that P might be able to regain custody of his children through guardianship or adoption proceedings. Both of these avenues, while apparently open to P, would seriously prejudice him because of his status. A wrong is not excused simply because it can be undone.

b) The interest of a man in the children he has sired and raised warrants great deference. The rights to conceive and raise one's children have been deemed "essential." The law has not refused to recognize those family rights even when there has been no marriage ceremony.

c) The state's interests—protection of the moral, physical, mental, and emotional welfare of the minor—are clearly legitimate concerns. But the means of effectuating them, by the application of an irrebuttable presumption of unfitness on the part of unwed fathers, is not constitutionally proper. Even though procedure by presumption is cheaper and administratively more convenient, it cannot stand when it rides roughshod over the important interests of parent and child. Here, the procedure operates to "dismember" P's family.

d) Since the court concludes that all parents—even unwed fathers—are entitled to a fitness hearing before they can be deprived of custody of their children, it follows that Illinois's failure to provide such a hearing for P denied him equal protection of the law.

4) **Dissent** (Burger, C.J.). No due process issue was raised in the state courts and therefore P should not have prevailed upon a due process issue in this court. The Equal Protection Clause is not violated when Illinois gives full recognition only to father-child relationships arising in the context of legal family units. The state may distinguish between unwed mothers and unwed fathers based on common human experience that unwed fathers rarely show any interest in or provide any support for their illegitimate children. In addition, P took no action to gain guardianship of the children or to legally adopt them.

5) **Comment.** This decision had a tremendous impact on adoption law.

B. PROVING PARENTHOOD

Much of the burden of illegitimacy can be alleviated if a legal father for the child can be established. Balanced against the humanitarian and remedial policies favoring paternity determinations are the tremendous problems of proof and the need to protect innocent defendants from abuse actions.

1. **The Presumption of Parenthood.** Since the creation of Lord Mansfield's Rule establishing a conclusive presumption that a child born to a married woman is legitimate, there has been a strong presumption in law that a married woman's husband is the father of a child born to her. With the development of reliable means of scientifically proving paternity, this presumption is beginning to be modified.

Michael H.
and
Victoria D.
v. Gerald D.

a. **Irrebuttable presumption of spousal paternity is not unconstitutional--**
Michael H. and Victoria D. v. Gerald D., 491 U.S. 110 (1989).

1) **Facts.** Carole married Gerald (D) in 1976. Two years later she began an adulterous affair with a neighbor, Michael (P). While married to D she became pregnant and gave birth to Victoria. Six months after Victoria was born, Carole and D separated, and during the next two and a half years, Carole and Victoria lived sometimes with D, sometimes with P, and sometimes with a third man. P, Carole, and Victoria had blood tests showing a 98% probability that P was the biological father of Victoria. P filed a suit to obtain visitation with Victoria, and the court appointed a guardian ad litem for Victoria (P2). While living with P, Carole signed a stipulation that P was Victoria's biological father, but they broke up again before it was filed. P and P2 sought visitation rights for P with Victoria, and a psychologist recommended P be allowed limited visitation. D and Carole reconciled, and D intervened in the action, moving for summary judgment because Cal. Evid. Code section 621 provides that the issue of a wife cohabiting with a nonimpotent, nonsterile husband is conclusively presumed to be the child of the husband. The superior court granted the motion. The California Court of Appeals affirmed, and the California Supreme Court declined review. P appeals.

2) **Issue.** Is an irrebuttable presumption that the child born during marriage is the issue of the nonimpotent husband, which bars a putative biological father from obtaining visitation rights, unconstitutional?

3) **Held.** No. The judgment is affirmed. (No majority opinion.)

4) **Opinion** (Scalia, J., Rehnquist, C.J., O'Connor, J., Kennedy, J.). Justice Scalia announced the judgment of the Court and delivered an opinion. (Note that Chief Justice Rehnquist joined in all but note six of of Justice Scalia's opinion.)

a) The California legislature unmistakably intended to absolutely preclude persons outside the marriage to challenge the presumption of spousal paternity. Only the husband or wife, in certain circumstances, is allowed to dispute this presumption. This presumption is actually a substantive rule of law.

b) The law, like nature itself, makes no provision for dual paternity.

c) The Court finds unwritten fundamental liberties (substantive due process) only when they are "so rooted in the traditions and conscience of our people as to be ranked as fundamental." The relationship between P and Victoria (three months full-time common household, and eight months part-time) does not qualify for such constitutional status.

d) The presumption of a husband's paternity of a child born during coverture is long- and well-established. Neither husband nor wife could give evidence to rebut that presumption. Even in modern cases, the ability of a person in P's position to claim paternity has generally been rejected.

e) *Footnote 6:* The Court should consult the most specific tradition available in looking for unwritten fundamental liberties.

f) Prior cases recognizing paternal rights of unmarried men are distinguished because in none of them did the man assert a claim against an intact marriage or family. P's claim to parental rights is in derogation of D's existing parental rights.

g) P2's claim fails also. Even if P2 had rights symmetrical to the parents with respect to association, the claim of multiple fatherhood is insupportable. Victoria is not illegitimate. The Constitution does not require states to allow P2, a stranger to the family, to challenge the family integrity on behalf of the child.

5) **Concurrence** (O'Connor, Kennedy, JJ.). I agree with all of Justice Scalia's opinion except footnote 6.

6) **Concurrence** (Stevens, J.). Even assuming P's relationship with Victoria is entitled to constitutional protection, California already affords him a right to seek custody in the best interests of the child. The trial court found that it was not in the interests of Victoria for P to have visitation.

7) **Dissent** (Brennan, Marshall, Blackmun, JJ.). Five justices refuse to rule out the possibility of a protected relationship between the child born in wedlock and the biological father who is not the mother's spouse. Five justices view the controlling issue as one of procedure. Scalia's narrowest-possible-tradition test is irreconcilable with the precedents, and unworkable. Our precedents have recognized constitutional protection for unwed fathers. The statute's failure to provide even a hearing is unconstitutional.

8) **Comment.** If the *Michael H.* opinion does not establish with any certainty a prevailing legal doctrine, it does at least indicate that certain values may be adopted by states without violating the Constitution. In family law, as this case clearly illustrates, the issues usually are not state vs. individual, *i.e.,* the kind of case in which judicial vigilance for individual rights is especially important, but individual vs. individual, with the state merely setting the balance of the competing individual rights. Thus, less strict scrutiny may be appropriate.

b. **Voluntary bastardization--Cleo A.E. v. Rickie Gene E.,** 438 S.E.2d 886 (W. Va. 1993).

Cleo A.E. v. Rickie Gene E.

1) **Facts.** The Child Advocate Office filed a petition to collect support payments from a divorced father from West Virginia who was then residing in Florida. No child support had been awarded through the final order of divorce based on the fact that the mother (P) had made no request for support. Rickie E. (D) requested blood tests to determine paternity. The Florida court reserved jurisdiction to modify both support and arrears retroactively upon its receipt of a modified final order of divorce from the West Virginia court. A West Virginia circuit court entered an order ruling that D was not the father of the child born during the marriage. The order incorporated an attached stipulation that D was not the father and otherwise provided no reasoning for its decision to approve an amendment to the final order of divorce which had as its primary objective the bastardization

of one of the children born to the parties during their marriage. The Child Advocate Office appeals, seeking to have the order set aside.

2) **Issues.**

    a) May the parties to a domestic proceeding agree by stipulation to bastardize minor children born during the marriage?

    b) Should the guidelines established by this court in *Michael K.T. v. Tina L.T.*, 182 W. Va. 399 (1989), regarding the admission of blood test evidence on the issue of paternity be similarly utilized when making a ruling which has as its effect the bastardization of a minor child?

    c) Should a guardian ad litem be appointed to represent the interests of the minor child whenever an action is initiated to disprove a child's paternity?

3) **Held.** a) No. b) Yes. c) Yes. Reversed and remanded.

    a) Our conclusion disallowing stipulation to bastardize children is not based on the traditional arguments against bastardization, *i.e.,* the social stigma on the children and the financial burden on the state, but on the principle that "the best interests of the child is the polar star by which decisions must be made which affect children."

    b) In *Michael K. T.* we instructed courts to consider the following factors regarding the admissibility of blood test evidence offered to disprove paternity: (i) the length of time following when the putative father first was placed on notice that he might be the biological father before he acted to contest paternity; (ii) the length of time during which the individual desiring to challenge paternity assumed the role of father to the child; (iii) the facts surrounding the putative father's discovery of nonpaternity; (iv) the nature of the father/child relationship; (v) the age of the child; (vi) the harm which may result to the child if paternity were successfully disproved; (vii) the extent to which the passage of time reduced the chances of establishing paternity and a child support obligation in favor of the child; (viii) all other factors which may affect the equities involved in the potential disruption of the parent/child relationship or the chances of undeniable harm to the child. These guidelines should be utilized along with active participation of the court in making a ruling which has as its effect the bastardization of a child.

    c) An adjudication of paternity expressed in a divorce order is res judicata as to the husband and wife in any subsequent proceeding. Absent evidence of fraud, this court will not sanction the disputation of paternity through blood test evidence if there is more than a relatively brief passage of time.

    d) A child has a right to the establishment of paternity and a child support obligation, and a right to independent representation on matters affecting his or her substantial right and interests. A guardian ad litem should be appointed to represent a minor child whenever disproving paternity is involved. If paternity is abrogated, the guardian ad litem should seek to establish paternity and child support.

2. **Resources.** Access to modern technology that may be probative of paternity is critical if truth and justice are the objects of a paternity suit.

    a. **Costs of proving parenthood; blood grouping tests--Little v. Streater,** 452 U.S. 1 (1981).

Little v.
Streater

        1) **Facts.** Streater (P) gave birth to a child while unmarried and, in order to obtain public assistance, she brought a paternity suit against Little (D), alleging that he was the father. At the time of the suit D was in prison and indigent. The trial court granted D's request that a blood grouping test be done, as allowed by Connecticut statute. However, the court denied his request that the State pay for it because D was indigent. The test was never done, and the trial court found that D was the father and entered judgment against him. D appeals that judgment on the grounds that denying his request to pay the expenses for the blood test was a denial of due process.

        2) **Issue.** Is the Connecticut statute an unconstitutional denial of due process because it provides that the cost of making blood grouping tests shall be charged to the party requesting them?

        3) **Held.** Yes. The judgment is reversed and the case is remanded.

            a) The State's involvement in this paternity proceeding was considerable, giving rise to a constitutional duty. The State had required P to bring the action in order for her to gain public assistance. Although these proceedings are generally considered "civil," they do have criminal overtones, in that failure to comply with the court's support order is punishable by imprisonment.

            b) It is also difficult for D to overcome P's prima facie case, and the blood grouping test is the best possible evidence a defendant might offer in his defense. Denying certain individuals such a defense merely because they are indigent is irreconcilable with the Due Process Clause.

            c) The State has a legitimate public policy interest to secure support for the child, as well as its own financial concerns. However, the State's monetary interest is hardly significant enough to overcome the important private interests. The fundamental fairness requirement of the Due Process Clause is not satisfied by the application of the Connecticut statute.

3. **Discrimination on the Basis of Legitimacy.** In the past 20 years, the Supreme Court has wrestled with the question of the extent to which classification on the basis of legitimacy is constitutional.

    a. **Illegitimacy and intestate succession--Lalli v. Lalli,** 439 U.S. 259 (1978).

Lalli v. Lalli

        1) **Facts.** Robert Lalli (P) sued the administrator (D) of the estate of Mario Lalli, who died intestate, claiming a share of the estate as an

illegitimate child. Although P tendered a notarized statement of the decedent referring to P as his "son" and affidavits of several persons showing that the decedent had openly acknowledged P as his son, the surrogate's court ruled that P's claim was barred under a New York statute that allowed illegitimates to share in intestate estates only if they had initiated filiation proceedings before or within two years of birth. The New York Court of Appeals affirmed. P appeals.

2) **Issue.** Does a statute that discriminates against illegitimate children in eligibility to inherit from their fathers by requiring that paternity be established within two years of birth violate the Equal Protection Clause of the Fourteenth Amendment?

3) **Held.** No. The judgment is affirmed.

   a) Illegitimacy classifications will be upheld if substantially related to a permissible state interest.

   b) In *Trimble v. Gordon*, 430 U.S. 762 (1977), the Court acknowledged the special competency and interest of states in regulating intestacy, and that more exacting proof requirements could apply to illegitimates.

   c) Problems of giving notice to unknown illegitimates and problems of protecting deceased putative fathers from spurious claims of paternity justify special treatment of illegitimates.

   d) The New York statute was designed to alleviate the plight of illegitimate children. It provides accuracy and fairness for both the child and the accused father. It is much narrower than the Illinois scheme invalidated in *Trimble*, and has received liberal construction by the courts of New York. Accordingly, while it could be narrower, it is not constitutionally defective.

4) **Concurrence** (Stewart, J.). This statute differs from the Illinois scheme, and *Trimble* is still good law.

5) **Concurrence** (Blackmun, J.). *Trimble* is derelict and should be overruled.

6) **Dissent** (Brennan, White, Marshall, Stevens, JJ.). This case is indistinguishable from *Trimble* and should be governed by that decision. As a practical matter, the statute makes it virtually impossible for illegitimate children to inherit from their intestate fathers. While a stricter standard of proof might be permissible, this form of discrimination ought not to be allowed.

7) **Comment.** As this case illustrates, the cases often turn on the *degree* of exclusion.

Rivera v. Minnich

b. **Preponderance of evidence standard of proof is constitutional in paternity suits--Rivera v. Minnich,** 483 U.S. 574 (1987).

   1) **Facts.** Jean Marie Minnich (P) gave birth to Cory out of wedlock, then sued Gregory Rivera (D) claiming that he was the father of her son. The

judge denied D's request to instruct the jury to apply a clear and convincing evidence standard, and rejected his constitutional challenge to the application of a preponderance of the evidence standard. After the jury found that D was the father, the court granted D's motion for a new trial. The Pennsylvania Supreme Court upheld the preponderance standard and reinstated the jury's verdict. D appeals.

2) **Issue.** Does it violate the Constitution to require a plaintiff to prove paternity allegations by a mere preponderance of the evidence?

3) **Held.** No. The judgment is affirmed.

   a) Preponderance of the evidence is the most common civil standard of proof, and in most states that is the standard applied in paternity suits.

   b) In *Santosky v. Kramer*, 455 U.S. 745 (1982) the Supreme Court held that the Constitution requires clear and convincing evidence before terminating parental rights ("TPR"). But *Santosky* is distinguishable because TPR extinguishes existing parental rights, whereas paternity creates the same. The State is the adverse party in TPR suits, whereas paternity suits are private suits. There is no double jeopardy protection in TPR suits, whereas preclusion applies in paternity suits.

4) **Concurrence** (O'Connor, J.). The flexible concept of due process does not bar Pennsylvania from providing paternity litigants with roughly equal risk of factual error.

5) **Dissent** (Brennan, J.). What is at stake is a life-long relationship with significant legal, financial, and moral dimensions. A clear and convincing evidence standard should be applied, and would only make a practical difference in cases in which blood tests were not introduced into evidence.

6) **Comment.** Both TPR and paternity suits disturb the status quo in a way that has secondary financial consequences for the public. If TPR is granted, a private support obligation will be ended, and the exposure of the public treasury is increased, whereas if paternity is granted, a private support obligation will be created, and the exposure of the public treasury decreased.

c. **Statutes of limitations in paternity suits must be extended--Opinion of the Justices,** 558 A.2d 454 (N.H. 1989).

   Opinion of
   the Justices

   1) **Facts.** The New Hampshire Senate asked for an advisory opinion.

   2) **Issue.** Would a bill authorizing paternity suits where former paternity actions were dismissed based on a statute of limitations of less than 18 years violate the state or federal constitutions?

   3) **Held.** Yes.

      a) The support obligations for a child born out of wedlock are the same as for a legitimate child.

b) Until 1985, the statute of limitations for paternity was one or two years. In 1985, it was extended to 18 years.

c) Once a statute of limitations has run, application of a longer limitations period for the same cause of action would not be allowed, unless the former statute of limitations was unconstitutional.

d) New Hampshire's prior one- and two-year statutes of limitation were unconstitutional, as they could not be tolled until the child was an adult. This was a deliberate policy.

e) Under the doctrine of claim preclusion (res judicata), a final judgment on the merits in one suit absolutely bars a subsequent suit involving the same issues or issues that could have been raised by the parties or their privities.

f) A putative father who obtains a judgment based on the statute of limitations has the defense of res judicata. The proposed law would violate that defense in violation of the state constitution. But it would not violate the *ex post facto* provision of the federal constitution, which applies only to criminal laws.

4) **Comment.** The tolling of statutes of limitation during minority is not infrequently of relevance in domestic litigation.

4. **Jurisdiction.** The constitutional parameters of jurisdiction in paternity suits are not absolutely clear, though as a general principle in personam jurisdiction has been held to be necessary. It must be remembered that the standard for jurisdiction in custody and parental rights litigation is different (higher, essentially) from the standard for litigation regarding spousal rights. Sexual intercourse within the forum state may give personal jurisdiction.

V. PROCREATION

A. CONTRACEPTION

With the development of reliable contraceptive substances, devices, and surgical techniques, couples have the ability to have sexual intercourse without the "risk" of becoming parents. But these new technologies can be misused, *e.g.,* the practice of involuntary sterilization. The limits on the use of technology are set by law; often questions about the necessary and proper limits have been addressed by courts before they have been faced by legislatures.

1. **Constitutional Limits.** The "privacy" doctrine grew out of a series of cases dealing with procreation.

   a. **Contraception by married adults--Griswold v. Connecticut.** (*See* brief of case, *supra* at p. 5.)

   b. **Contraception by single adults and children--Eisenstadt v. Baird.** (*See* brief of case, *supra* at p. 7.)

   c. **Parents' rights vs. minors' rights and state policy.** While advocates of minors' rights and parents' rights have both waged aggressive judicial lobbying campaigns to have their agenda concerning access by teenagers to contraceptives adopted as constitutional law, most courts have refrained from deciding any constitutional questions. There may be merit to the notion that the issue is one of legislative policy, not constitutional mandate. While that insight does not resolve the policy battle, it points the direction toward the proper battlefield.

   d. **Involuntary sterilization--Buck v. Bell,** 274 U.S. 200 (1927). Buck v. Bell

      1) **Facts.** Bell (D) was ordered to perform a sterilization operation on Buck (P). P was an 18-year-old female and considered "feeble-minded." P was the child of a "feeble-minded" mother and the mother of a "feeble-minded" illegitimate child. P brought this action contending that the Virginia statute that authorized the sterilization was a violation of the Due Process and the Equal Protection Clauses. The state supreme court affirmed the order and P appeals.

      2) **Issue.** Is the Virginia statute authorizing the sterilization of certain "mental defectives" unconstitutional?

      3) **Held.** No. The judgment is affirmed.

         a) Many defective persons if now discharged would be a menace to society, but if incapable of procreating might be discharged with safety and become self-supporting with benefit to themselves and to society. It is better for the world if society can prevent those who are manifestly unfit from continuing their kind. The principle that sustains compulsory vaccination is broad enough to cover cutting the fallopian tubes.

4) **Comment.** The Virginia statute on eugenic sterilization was repealed in 1974; however, there are still circumstances where involuntary sterilization is allowed by statute. Justice Holmes's infamous dictum in this case that "three generations of imbeciles is enough" reflected the popular "eugenic" movement of the time. Within a decade of this opinion, the movement had begun to fall out of favor.

2. **Wrongful Life and Wrongful Birth.** Recently many states have recognized "preconception torts" (outgrowths of medical malpractice) arising from procreation of unwanted children.

B.   ABORTION RESTRICTIONS

1. **Political Controversy.** During the late 1960s and early 1970s, no more controversial a domestic social issue faced legislators than the abortion reform movement. From 1967 to 1972, more than one-third of the states adopted liberalizing abortion reform laws patterned after the Model Penal Code.

2. **Judicial Entanglement.** Moving on a wave of recent privacy decisions dealing with contraception restrictions, the Supreme Court took over the fray by constitutionalizing the question in 1973.

Roe v. Wade

a. **Abortion--Roe v. Wade,** 410 U.S. 113 (1973).

1) **Facts.** Texas statutes made it a crime to procure or perform an abortion except for the purpose of saving the life of the mother. Jane Roe (P), an unmarried pregnant woman who desired an abortion, sought a declaratory judgment, on behalf of herself and others similarly situated, that the Texas criminal abortion statutes were unconstitutional on their face, and an injunction prohibiting their enforcement. The district court held that the statutes were unconstitutional, but did not grant the injunctive relief. (A husband and wife, John and Mary Doe, filed a companion complaint, but were held to lack standing.) Both P and Wade (D), a county district attorney, appeal.

2) **Issue.** Does a criminal abortion statute that makes it a crime to procure or perform an abortion except to save the life of the mother violate an abortion-seeking woman's right to privacy?

3) **Held.** Yes. The judgment is affirmed. The Texas authorities must not enforce the statute.

a) At common law, an abortion performed before quickening was not an offense. The United States followed the common law rule until about the middle of the 19th century when states began passing laws prohibiting abortions. Recently, there has been a trend toward liberalizing abortion laws.

b) A woman has a fundamental right of privacy from the Fourteenth Amendment's concept of personal liberty, which is sufficiently broad to encompass her decision whether or not to terminate her pregnancy. State regulations that infringe upon or unduly burden this right can be sustained only if narrowly drafted to effectuate compelling state interests.

c) Three reasons or purposes have been advanced to support laws restricting abortions: (i) to discourage illicit sexual relations; (ii) to protect the woman from the abortion procedure; and (iii) to protect prenatal life. The first reason is too speculative and attenuated to justify an abortion prohibition. Medical techniques have altered the situation with respect to protection of the woman—it is now safer to have an abortion during the first trimester than to go through childbirth. And the Fourteenth Amendment does not protect the fetus, because the term "person" is applied only postnatally.

d) Thus, during the first trimester, the decision whether or not to have an abortion must be left to the woman and her physician. After the first trimester, the state may regulate the abortion procedure (but not the decision) to protect maternal health. Subsequent to viability of the fetus, the state may proscribe abortion except when necessary to protect the life or health of the mother.

4) Comment. This opinion has been severely criticized because the author went far outside the record and attempted to "legislate" instead of adjudicate. The judgment has been vigorously defended, but almost always with an apology for the way it was reached. The effect of this case was to invalidate, totally or in part, the abortion laws then in effect in all 50 states, including the liberalized abortion laws patterned after the Model Penal Code provisions.

C. ARTIFICIAL CONCEPTION

Not only is it possible to have sex without procreation (with contraceptives) but it is also possible to have procreation without sex (artificial conception)—which makes it possible for thousands of infertile couples to have the children they desire.

1. **Artificial Insemination.** Artificial insemination involves inseminating a woman mechanically with the sperm of her husband or of another donor.

   a. **Artificial insemination and child support--R.S. v. R.S.,** 670 P.2d 923 (Kan. Ct. App. 1983).

   R.S. v. R.S.

   1) **Facts.** This appeal arises out of a divorce action in which the husband (D) argues that he should not be ordered to support a child conceived during the marriage by artificial insemination from a donor. A state statute required the written consent of both husband and wife for artificial insemination. The statute also provided that any child conceived by artificial insemination

was a natural child at law. No written consent was obtained by the doctor. However, D orally consented to the procedure a number of times, was aware of the procedure, and never objected. The trial court found for the mother and held D responsible for payment of child support. D appeals.

2) **Issue.** Does the Kansas statute require written consent before a child conceived by artificial insemination can be considered the same as a naturally conceived child of the husband?

3) **Held.** No. The judgment is affirmed.

   a) There is nothing in the statute that would express a legislative intent that a husband who orally consents to artificial insemination cannot be held responsible on an equitable estoppel or implied contract theory. A husband so consenting is estopped from denying that he is the father of the child unless he can establish by clear and convincing evidence that he had withdrawn his consent.

4) **Comment.** The court's opinion followed a number of other jurisdictions applying the implied contract and equitable estoppel theories.

Jhordan C. v. Mary K.

b. **Parental rights of semen donors--Jhordan C. v. Mary K.,** 224 Cal. Rptr. 530 (Cal Ct. App. 1986).

1) **Facts.** In 1978, Mary (D) decided to bear a child by artificial insemination and raise it with Victoria (P2). Jhordan (P1) agreed to donate his semen. D apparently inseminated herself. After D became pregnant, P1 started a trust fund. The child, Devin, was born March 30, 1980. P1 was listed as the father. P1 visited D and Devin at the hospital, and afterward once a month with D's agreement, until five months later D refused to let P1 see Devin anymore. P1 sued to establish paternity and get visitation, and was awarded weekly visitation. In another case, P1 stipulated to a support judgment in a suit by the county to recover public assistance given to support Devin. P2 jointly raised Devin, and joined the suit seeking joint custody. The trial court awarded D sole custody and P2 visitation. P1 was found to be Devin's legal parent and was awarded visitation. D and P2 appeal.

2) **Issue.** Can a sperm donor be determined to be the legal father of a child conceived by artificial insemination?

3) **Held.** Yes. The judgment is affirmed.

   a) California Civil Code section 7005 provides that the donor of semen provided to a licensed doctor for use in artificial insemination is treated in law as if not the natural father of the child. Here D did not take advantage of this provision and did not use a physician.

   b) That provision comes from the Uniform Parentage Act ("UPA"), and the legislative history indicates conscious adoption of the physician requirement. The health benefits and independent judgment of a physician support the physician requirement.

   c) The California legislature has apparently embraced the UCC drafters' decision to limit application of donor nonpaternity to use of a physician.

d) This provision itself applies equally to married and unmarried women. While the paternity statutes give an advantage to married women, the social policy of preserving the integrity of the family justifies the protection of spousal paternity rights.

e) Family autonomy is not violated by the artificial insemination provision because P1 was part of the family.

f) Rights of procreative choice are not infringed because the provision does not forbid self-insemination.

g) P2 has obtained sufficient recognition of her rights, so consideration of her de facto parent claim is unnecessary.

h) Public policy on artificial insemination is best made by the legislature.

c. **Parental responsibilities of the consenting spouse--Karin T. v. Michael T.,** 484 N.Y.S.2d 780 (N.Y. Fam. Ct. 1985).

Karin T. v. Michael T.

1) **Facts.** Michael T. (D) was born a female named Marlene A.T., but in her twenties she began to dress and behave like a man. When she was 29, she began a relationship with Karin T. They got a marriage license and were married. Thereafter, Karin gave birth to two children by artificial insemination, after D signed an agreement to support the children. D lived with and helped support Karin and the children until 1983, when D left and moved away. Now, the County Department of Social Services (P), as assignee of Karin T., seeks support from D for the two children. D claims that she is not the father and not responsible for support of the children.

2) **Issue.** Is a woman who "marries" another woman, consents to the artificial insemination of that woman, and lives with and supports the mother and children, liable for child support of the children born?

3) **Held.** Yes. Support is ordered.

a) Family court has limited jurisdiction and cannot answer all the fascinating questions this case presents, but it has jurisdiction to determine whether D is liable for child support.

b) Generally, only biological or adoptive parents are liable for child support.

c) But here, D specifically agreed in writing to treat the children conceived by artificial insemination as her own.

d) Prior cases have recognized that parental support obligations can be imposed on one whose conduct leads others to assume parental responsibilities in reliance on the parental support commitment. The doctrine of equitable estoppel may be invoked to prevent such a party from denying parental duties.

e) In exceptional circumstances children may enforce such support agreements as third-party beneficiaries.

f) While New York domestic relations law imposes parental support duties only on "parents," D is a "parent" for purposes of the statute because by her action she did "bring forth offspring."

4) Comment. One of the keys to this opinion is the first point—the carefully focused analytical approach taken by the court.

2. In Vitro Fertilization. In vitro fertilization involves the ex utero fertilization of a human ovum, followed by embryo implantation (usually in the uterus of the ovum donor).

Davis v.
Davis

a. Disposition of frozen embryos--Davis v. Davis, 842 S.W.2d 588 (Tenn. 1992).

1) Facts. Mary Sue Davis and Junior Davis, a married couple, discovered that they were unable to have children through a normal pregnancy and decided to try in vitro fertilization. Nine of Mary Sue's ova were fertilized, two were unsuccessfully implanted, and the remaining seven were cryogenically frozen. Subsequently, Junior filed for divorce. Trial court granted divorce and, on the basis of a determination that the embryos were human beings from the moment of fertilization, awarded custody of seven "frozen embryos" to Mary Sue, who intended to have the embryos transferred to her own uterus in an effort to become pregnant. Junior preferred that the embryos remain in their frozen state until he decided whether he wanted to become a parent outside of marriage. Junior appealed and the court of appeals reversed, holding that Junior had a "constitutionally protected right not to beget a child" where there had not been a pregnancy and there was no compelling state interest to justify ordering implantation against the will of either party. Mary Sue appeals, although she is now remarried and no longer wishes to utilize the embryos herself, but wishes to donate them to a childless couple.

2) Issue. Does the right to procreational autonomy dictate that the authority to decide the disposition of preembryos taken for in vitro fertilization rests with the gamete providers to the extent that their decisions have impact upon their individual reproductive status?

3) Held. Yes.

a) With respect to the state's public policy and its constitutional right to privacy, the state's interest in potential human life, as embodied in these four- to eight-cell preembryos (which may or may not ultimately be able to develop into fetuses) is slight at best, especially when weighed against the interests of the gamete-providers and the burdens inherent in parenthood.

b) Junior has a greater interest in the preembryos than Mary Sue and should be awarded custody because she wishes only to donate them and he is vehemently opposed to fathering a child that would not live with both parents.

    c)   Disputes of this nature should be resolved first by looking at the progenitors' preferences, and if these cannot be ascertained or if there is a dispute, then their prior agreement should be carried out. If there is no prior agreement, then the parties' interests must be balanced and in ordinary circumstances, the party wishing to avoid procreation should prevail, assuming the other party has a reasonable possibility of becoming a parent by means other than the frozen embryos. If no other reasonable alternatives exist, then the argument of using the preembryos should be considered. Where a party seeks only to donate the embryos, the objecting party should prevail.

3.   **Surrogate Parenting.** Surrogate mothering involves artificial insemination of a "carrier" woman with the sperm of a man who is married to another woman. Under a contract, the carrier will bear a child for the couple and deliver the child to them upon birth.

    a.   **Surrogate parenting vs. baby-selling prohibitions--Surrogate Parenting Associates, Inc. v. Commonwealth *ex rel.* Armstrong, 704 S.W.2d 209 (Ky. 1986).**

Surrogate Parenting Associates, Inc. v. Common- wealth *ex rel.* Armstrong

        1)   **Facts.** Surrogate Parenting Associates (D) operates a clinic where couples (with infertile wives) desiring children and surrogate mothers may contract for childbearing and the surrogate mothers are artificially inseminated. The surrogate mothers agree to surrender the child to the couple. The husband's semen is used, and he pays a fee to the surrogate mother as well as her medical and related expenses. The Kentucky attorney general (P) sued to revoke D's charter for violating the Kentucky laws prohibiting baby selling for adoption, prohibiting filing a petition for termination of rights in adoption before five days following the birth of the child, and invalidating consent to adoption if given before the fifth day after the birth of the child. The circuit court dismissed the complaint; the Kentucky Court of Appeals reversed. D appeals.

        2)   **Issue.** Do surrogate parenting contracts violate Kentucky baby-selling and adoption restrictions?

        3)   **Held.** No. The judgment is reversed.

            a)   The baby-selling prohibition is intended to keep baby brokers from overwhelming an expectant mother with financial inducements, but the surrogacy contract is entered into before the surrogate is even pregnant.

            b)   The decision to bear or beget a child is at the very heart of the constitutionally protected right of choice.

            c)   When the baby-selling prohibition was amended in 1984 the legislature explicitly added that nothing in it should be construed to prohibit artificial insemination.

d)   Dealings between the surrogate and biological father cannot be characterized as adoption.

e)   As between surrogate and biological father, custody is determined according to the best interests of the child. The contract between the parties must give way to the public policy. The statutes prohibiting adoption petitions or consent before the fifth day after birth would supersede the contract, if there was a conflict. Custody contracts are voidable, but not void.

f)   The public policy regarding surrogate parenting should be decided by the legislature.

4)   **Dissent.** A portion of the surrogacy fee is paid for surrendering the child, and that is what the baby-selling statute prohibits.

5)   **Dissent.** The surrogacy contract is a pure commercial transaction in human flesh. The legislature has not been silent; a bill that would legalize surrogate parenting was rejected by the legislature. Safeguarding marriage and the family is ample justification for prohibiting surrogacy contracts.

b.   **Surrogacy may illegally exploit poor women--Matter of Baby M,** 537 A.2d 1227 (N.J. 1988).

1)   **Facts.** After William Stern's (P's) wife learned that she might have multiple sclerosis, and that her health might be endangered by pregnancy, P and Mary Beth Whitehead (D) entered into a surrogacy contract in February 1985 with the permission of D's husband. P's wife, who was to adopt the child, did not sign the contract to avoid violating the baby-selling law. D agreed to be artificially inseminated and bear P's child, and P agreed to pay D $10,000 on delivery of the child to him for adoption by his wife. D was inseminated with P's sperm and gave birth to Baby M on March 27, 1986. D realized from the moment of birth that she could not part with Baby M, yet on March 30, she delivered Baby M to P. The next day she went back to P and begged to have the baby back for a week. Fearful that D might commit suicide, P let her take the child. D refused to return Baby M to P. P filed suit to enforce the contract and for custody and got an ex parte order because of the risk that D would flee the jurisdiction, which she did when served with the papers. D and Baby M fled to Florida. In a telephone conversation with P, D threatened to kill herself and Baby M and to accuse P of sexually molesting D's other daughter. P commenced enforcement proceedings in Florida, and the Florida court ordered D to give custody of Baby M to P and his wife. Back in New Jersey, the earlier temporary order granting custody pendente lite was confirmed and D was granted visitation. P asked the court to terminate D's parental rights and allow P's wife to adopt Baby M. A guardian ad litem was appointed, who recommended P and his wife have custody and D have limited visitation (later). After 32 days of trial, the court held the surrogacy contract was valid, found that it was in the best interests of Baby M that P be awarded custody, and approved the adoption of Baby M by P's wife.

2)   **Issue.** Is a surrogate motherhood contract valid in New Jersey?

3) **Held.** No. The judgment is affirmed on other grounds.

   a)   Private placement adoption is highly disfavored in New Jersey. The use of money in connection with adoption is illegal and perhaps criminal. The irrevocable agreement prior to birth (even before conception) to surrender a child for adoption is unenforceable.

   b)   New Jersey forbids giving or receiving money for placement of a child for adoption. Here it is clear that money was paid and accepted for precisely that reason. That the money was for delivery of a live human being is shown by the contract term reducing payment to $1,000 if the child were stillborn.

   c)   Public policy behind the baby-selling proscription is strong. The natural mother in surrogacy is denied counseling, and the adoptive parents may be uninformed of the medical history of the mother. Baby-selling exploits all involved.

   d)   New Jersey law strictly regulates the abandonment of parental rights, and a contract to do so outside the scope of the statutory scheme is clearly illegal.

   e)   New Jersey public policy puts the best interests of the child as the prime concern; surrogacy carries inevitably the risk of a tug-of-war over the infant, as this case illustrates. Here, the profit motive got the better of the Infertility Center that set up this surrogacy arrangement.

   f)   In civilized society, some things cannot be for sale. Surrogacy risks exploitation of the poor, especially poor women. It may totally degrade the surrogate mother.

   g)   The Constitution protects certain rights of personal intimacy, but the right of surrogate procreation is not one of them. One's exercise of privacy rights is qualified by the effect it has on innocent third persons. There is no denial of equal protection because a sperm donor cannot be equated with a surrogate mother.

   h)   The award of custody to P or D must be based on the interests of Baby M, not on a surrogacy deterrence policy. There is credible evidence to support the trial court's finding that P and his wife are the more suitable parents for Baby M. D's family stability is doubtful because of economic uncertainties, alcoholism, and stubborn contempt for professional help. P's family is economically secure and stable, and P's wife is a pediatrician.

   i)   Award of custody ex parte should be done only in rare circumstances involving a substantial showing of threat to the health or welfare of the child. D's threats to flee the jurisdiction were not enough.

   j)   D should be awarded some visitation, but the trial court should decide that on remand. It is desirable for a child to have contact with both parents.

k)   The legislature remains free to deal with this sensitive issue as it deems proper within constitutional constraints.

4)   Comment. On remand the trial court awarded D one eight-hour visitation period weekly, increasing to two days weekly as the child grows older. Was there any economic bias in the opinion of the New Jersey Supreme Court? If so, was it inappropriate or just realistic?

c.   **Determination of disputed parentage--Johnson v. Calvert,** 851 P.2d 776 (Cal. 1993)(en banc).

1)   Facts. The Calverts, a married couple, entered into a surrogacy argeement with Anna Johnson, who was subsequently artificially impregnated with the Calverts' embryo. The Calverts brought suit seeking a declaration that they were the legal parents of a child born of Johnson. Johnson filed her own action to be declared mother of the child and the actions were consolidated. It was determined by blood tests that Johnson was not the genetic mother. The trial court ruled in favor of the Calverts, ruling that they were the child's "genetic, biological, and natural" parents, and that Johnson had no parental rights. The court also terminated a court order allowing Johnson's visitation. Johnson appealed. The appeal court affirmed. Johnson appeals.

2)   Issue. When, pursuant to a surrogacy agreement, a zygote formed of the gametes of a husband and wife is implanted in the uterus of another woman, who carries the resulting fetus to term and gives birth to a child not genetically related to her, is the wife the child's "natural mother" under California law?

3)   Held. Yes. The judgment is affirmed.

a)   Even though the Uniform Parenting Act, which applies to any parentage determination, recognizes both genetic consanguinity and giving birth as a means of establishing the mother and child relationship, when the two means do not coincide in one woman, the "natural mother" is she who intended to procreate the child, *i.e.,* bring about the birth of the child she intended to raise as her own. (Thus, in a true "egg donation" situation, where a woman gestates and gives birth to a child formed from the egg of another woman with the intent to raise the child as her own, the birth mother is the natural mother.)

b)   A contract for gestational surrogacy does not violate public policies embodied in adoption statutes, statutes governing termination of parental rights, or those making it a violation of the law to pay money for consent to adoption, nor does it constitute involuntary servitude or exploit or dehumanize women.

c)   A surrogate has no protected liberty interest in the companionship of the child. A surrogate is not exercising her own right to make procreative choices, but is agreeing to provide necessary and important services without any expectation that she will raise the resulting child as her own.

4) **Dissent.** The majority's resort to intent to break the "tie" in this case is without statutory support. I would apply the best interests of the child standard.

VI. PARENT-CHILD RELATIONS

A. EDUCATION

The essence of the parent-child relationship is the right and responsibility of parents to raise their children—to teach, direct, socialize, and protect persons who have not acquired the physical, cognitive, and judgmental ability to be self-sufficient. Directing the formal and informal education of children is the primary function of parenting.

1. **Formal Education.** The desires of some parents and children to avoid formal education in public schools (or public-standard private schools) have provoked many difficult legal challenges.

Wisconsin
v. Yoder

    a. **Compulsory education--Wisconsin v. Yoder,** 406 U.S. 205 (1972).

        1) **Facts.** Wisconsin (P) prosecuted Yoder and others (Ds), members of the Old Order Amish religion, for failing to comply with a compulsory education law requiring that their children attend public high school. Amish parents did not believe in sending their children to school after the eighth grade, while Wisconsin required all children to attend school until at least age 16. Ds resisted the prosecution on the ground that the compulsory education statute unconstitutionally violated their right to the free exercise of their religion.

        2) **Issue.** Is a compulsory education statute which compels Amish parents, against their religious beliefs, to send their children to public school violative of the Free Exercise Clause of the First and Fourteenth Amendments?

        3) **Held.** Yes. The state must recognize an exception where the Amish are involved.

           a) In order to be protected by the religion clauses, a practice must be rooted in religious belief. The unchallenged testimony of experts in this case shows that Ds' aversion to public high school education is based upon their historic religious beliefs and practices.

           b) The Amish have shown the sincerity of their beliefs and the hazards to their religion and way of life that compulsory high school attendance would have, and have shown that they provide the children with an alternative mode of vocational education.

           c) This case does not involve a claim by an Amish child wanting to attend public school. The state is prosecuting the parents; they are the parties whose religious rights are being infringed upon. Past decisions have recognized the traditional concepts of parental control over the religious upbringing of their children.

4) **Concurrence** (Stewart, Brennan, JJ.). Wisconsin cannot constitutionally brand as criminals Amish parents for their religiously based refusal to send their children to public high school. This case does not involve the right of Amish children to attend public high school or any other schools if they wish to do so.

5) **Concurrence** (White, Brennan, Stewart, JJ.). The state's valid interest in education has been satisfied by the eight years the children have been in school. The state has not demonstrated that Amish children will be unable to acquire new academic skills later in life.

6) **Dissent** (Douglas, J.). The children should have the right to be heard. Although the parents usually speak for the entire family, the education of the child is something upon which the child's own views should be heard. The Court's decision imperils the future of the student, not the parents, and the Wisconsin courts should have given the students an opportunity to be heard.

7) **Comment.** *Yoder* is, above all else, a First Amendment freedom of religion case. The Court carefully limited its holding so that the spurious "religious" defenses to legitimate prosecutions would not be encouraged. The family relationship impact of the case was minimal since the Court presumed (not unreasonably in the context) that no disagreement between the parents and children on this issue.

b. **Sex education--Smith v. Ricci,** 446 A.2d 501 (N.J. 1982)   Smith v. Ricci

1) **Facts.** The State Board of Education adopted a regulation requiring local school districts to develop and implement a family life education program in public elementary and secondary school curricula. The definition of the program included in the regulation states that family life program means "instruction to develop an understanding of the physical, mental, emotional, social, economic, and psychological aspects of interpersonal relationships; the physiological, psychological and cultural foundations of human development, sexuality, and reproduction . . . [and] development of responsible personal behavior . . . ." The regulation includes an excusal clause whereby any student may be excused, without academic penalty, from any parts of the program that a parent or guardian finds morally, conscientiously, or religiously objectionable. Upon adoption of the regulation, Smith and other parents sought review in appellate court. Before argument was heard, the appellate court certified the matter directly to the state supreme court.

2) **Issues.**

    a) Does the regulation violate the Free Exercise Clause or the Establishment Clause of the First Amendment?

    b) Did the Board's action in adopting the regulation violate the Due Process Clause of the Fourteenth Amendment?

3) **Held.** a) No. b) No. The judgment is affirmed.

a) The Board regulation required the inclusion of an excusal clause whereby anyone could be excused from the program without penalties as to credit or graduation. Where there is no compulsion to participate in a program, there can be no infringement in the free exercise of religion.

b) The regulation withstands constitutional scrutiny under the Establishment Clause. It has a secular purpose, its primary effect neither advances nor inhibits religion, and it does not create excessive governmental entanglement with religion. There is nothing in the regulation or its accompanying guidelines that indicates that the program favors a "secular" view of its subject matter over a "religious" one.

c) The presumption of reasonableness attaches to the actions of an administrative agency and the burden of proving unreasonableness falls on the challengers of the validity of the action. Appellants' bare assertion that there is no data that proves that the program will have an effect on the social ills it is intended to address does not satisfy appellants' burden of proving that the regulation is unreasonable. Furthermore, there is a factual basis for the Board's conclusion that the program is a reasonable, desirable, and necessary way of dealing with identifiable educational and social problems.

Board of Education, Plainfield v. Cooperman

c. **AIDS does not automatically justify expulsion--Board of Education, Plainfield v. Cooperman, 523 A.2d 655 (N.J. 1987).**

1) **Facts.** In August 1985, the State Commissioners of Health and Education jointly announced the adoption of guidelines on admission to schools of children with AIDS, ARC, or HTLV-III antibodies. They provided for admission of such children unless incontinent, not toilet trained, unable to control drooling, or exceptionally aggressive with a history of biting or harming others. They established a Medical Advisory Panel ("MAP") to review local school board decisions. In September, the Plainfield Board of Education (P) excluded from kindergarten a female child ("I.C.") under state guardianship who had AIDS, even though both doctors P consulted recommended that I.C. be admitted. The MAP reversed the exclusion. P requested 30 days to determine appropriate placement, but the Commissioner of Education ordered I.C. placed in regular kindergarten. The state filed suit for immediate enforcement of the MAP decision, and P appealed the Commissioner's decision and guidelines. Another child denied admission to kindergarten by P despite a decision by the MAP and Commissioner to admit her joined the action. The appellate division held that the rules were invalid because they had been promulgated without formal rulemaking procedures and denied the excluded children a right to a hearing before the decision. The State Board of Education proposed new regulations and they are now reviewed.

2) **Issue.** Are the New Jersey regulations regarding exclusion of children from school legal?

3) **Held.** Yes. The regulations are upheld.

a) The power to admit or exclude school children does not reside exclusively with the local school boards. The legislature has granted the Commissioner power to promulgate regulations.

b) The new regulations satisfy notions of due process. Under *Mathews v. Eldridge*, 424 U.S. 319 (1976), the private interests at stake include the pupil's interest in receiving an education; the government has an interest in protecting its citizens from dangerous diseases.

c) The regulations adequately protect the right of the parties to produce and cross-examine witnesses before an impartial tribunal. A degree of discretion is necessary and appropriate.

B. DIRECT STATE SUPERVISION OF CHILDREN

1. **Parental Control.** One reason for direct state supervision of children is to provide quasi-parental control for children without adequate parental guidance (because of extreme parental failures, extreme disobedience of children, or a combination of parental and juvenile failings).

   a. **Runaways--L.A.M. v. State,** 547 P.2d 827 (Alaska 1976).

   L.A.M. v. State

   1) **Facts.** L.A.M. (D) was born in 1958 and adopted shortly afterwards. Her adoptive parents were soon divorced and her mother moved to Alaska. In 1971, her mother remarried and quit her job so as to spend more time with D. D began staying away from home with friends. In 1972, she began to run away. In November, a petition to have her declared a person in need of supervision was filed. The hearing was continued and she was released to her parents, but she ran away within a week. The court again released her to her parents. Again she ran away. This time she was placed in a foster home and counseling was initiated. Despite a court order that she not leave the foster home without approval, she ran away two days after placement and was not found for a month. A delinquency petition based upon D's criminal contempt was filed. Pending hearing, D was placed in a receiving home and was directed to stay there. She ran away four times. The court directed that D be institutionalized. D appeals.

   2) **Issues.**

      a) Does a minor have a constitutional right of privacy that forbids state institutionalization for noncriminal conduct?

      b) May a child be prosecuted for criminal contempt and institutionalized for violating a court order that she not run away?

   3) **Held.** a) No. b) Yes. The judgment is affirmed.

a) Runaways of D's age are incapable of providing for or protecting themselves. The state has a legitimate interest in protecting children from venereal disease, exposure to drugs, attempted rape, and physical injury, all of which occurred to D while she was a runaway. State constitutional privacy guarantees protect the interests of parents and the state, as well as the interests of children. D's right of privacy would be violated only if her parents did not have a right to her custody. D did not show that neglect, abuse, or unfitness was involved, so her parents have a right of custody superior to her right to "do her own thing."

b) Failure of an adult to abide by the order would be a crime. Hence, criminal contempt is a valid basis for a delinquency proceeding. The court resorted to all available less drastic alternatives before ordering D's institutionalization. The institution to which D has been committed is not a training school for children hardened in delinquency, so additional process was not "due."

4) Concurrence. Protection of parental rights is not a sound basis for institutionalizing children. The state's interest in the welfare of the child is sufficient to justify the order.

b. Child's rejection of parents--*In re* Welfare of Snyder, 532 P.2d 278 (Wash. 1975).

1) Facts. When Cynthia (P) became a teenager, her relations with her parents (Ds) deteriorated. Hostility developed and communications broke down. Her father delivered her to the state-run Youth Service Center ("YSC") and she was placed in a receiving home. To avoid being sent back to her home, P filed a petition in juvenile court alleging that she was a dependent child. Although temporary custody was given to the state, the court concluded that the allegations of parental unfitness were erroneous, and P was returned to her parents. After further family difficulties, P went to the YSC which, on her behalf, filed a petition to have P declared an incorrigible child and to deprive the parents of custody. The court found that P was incorrigible, placed P in a foster home, and directed that counseling continue. P is now 16 and has done well in school. Her parents appeal.

2) Issue. Does a Washington juvenile court have power to deprive parents of custody of a teenage daughter on grounds of incorrigibility at the girl's own request simply because she will not obey her parents?

3) Held. Yes. The judgment is affirmed.

a) By statute, a child is "incorrigible" when she is beyond the power and control of her parents by reason of her own conduct. In determining whether a child is incorrigible, the sole issue is whether the parent-child relationship has deteriorated to the point that parental control is lost.

b) P testified that she absolutely refused to go back to live with her parents and obey them. The parents admitted that a difficult situation existed in the home, and a psychologist also testified that counseling would not help until the family cooled down.

    c)   The several attempts of the court and state agencies to reconcile the differences between P and her parents had failed. Under these circumstances, a finding of incorrigibility depriving parents of custody but directing continuing counseling for all, with continuing review by the juvenile court, was not error.

c. **Minor does not have the unilateral right to select his own foreign residence-- Polovchak v. Meese, 774 F.2d 731 (7th Cir. 1985).**

Polovchak
v. Meese

    1)   **Facts.** Michael and Anna Polovchak (Ps) are citizens of the U.S.S.R. who immigrated with their children to Chicago in 1980. After several months they decided to return to Russia, but 12-year-old Walter and 17-year-old Nataly decided to stay in the United States. When P sought police assistance to force Walter to leave with them, the police placed Walter in state custody as a child in need of supervision. Later, Walter (without parental approval) applied for asylum, claiming persecution risk in Russia. The request was granted and Walter became a permanent resident alien. An Illinois court found Walter and his sister to be in need of supervision. The appellate court reversed, and the Illinois Supreme Court affirmed. Ps, who had returned to Russia without their children, sued in federal court claiming that the grant of asylum was improper. Walter intervened and counterclaimed against his parents asserting they denied him his constitutional rights. The district court ruled for Ps, finding that the departure control order violated due process. The government appeals. Walter will turn 18 within a few days.

    2)   **Issue.** Did the issuance of a departure control order on petition of a minor without parental approval and without an opportunity to be heard violate Ps' due process rights?

    3)   **Held.** Yes. The judgment is affirmed as modified.

        a)   Here the minor's rights are pitted against parental rights, with the state supporting the minor.

        b)   The Constitution protects the right of parents to exercise authority in their home in the rearing of their children. State intervention must strictly adhere to procedural due process. Ps have a very strong interest in protecting their parental authority and their children. Yet they were never notified that Walter was applying for asylum and no provision was made for a hearing.

        c)   Under the *Mathews v. Eldridge* test, the private interests, state interests, and risk of error must be balanced. In this case, the parents deserve more protection than they received. Also, the court needs to adequately weigh Walter's interest in avoiding the sanctions imposed by the Soviet Union.

        d)   The district court did not abuse its discretion in deciding to invalidate the departure control order, but now an equitable remedy must be fashioned (before Walter turns 18).

4) **Comment.** Did the court of appeals cop out by directing the district court to pull a rabbit out of a hat?

Matter of Andrew R.

d. **Constitutional rights of children and parental control--Matter of Andrew R., 454 N.Y.S.2d 820 (N.Y. Fam. Ct. 1982).**

1) **Facts.** The father of 13-year-old Andrew R. brought a "Person in Need of Supervision" ("PINS") proceeding in order to return Andrew to foster care against his will. Andrew had for seven months been placed in foster care at Hawthorne under a so-called voluntary placement, without any review by a neutral factfinder. Andrew ran away from the center and returned home, where he threatened his father's life if he was made to go back. Andrew had also been truant while at Hawthorne. The father now alleges his child is a PINS.

2) **Issues.**

a) Is Andrew a "Person in Need of Supervision" because he has resisted his parents' efforts to return him to foster care against his will?

b) Did Andrew suffer a constitutionally infirm deprivation of liberty by being kept at Hawthorne for seven months against his will and without review?

3) **Held.** a) No. b) Yes. Case dismissed.

a) The statutory provision evidences a clear legislative intent to accord a PINS respondent adequate notice of the charges. A PINS proceeding is quasi-criminal in nature and requires due process. No petition can stand unless the acts complained of are set forth in specific terms.

b) It is apparent that the father is using the PINS procedure to compel his son's return to Hawthorne. Andrew was not "voluntarily" placed in Hawthorne in the first place, but was tricked into going under the promise that it would only be for a month. Andrew's placement at Hawthorne, without review and against his will, was a substantial deprivation of his liberty.

c) New York has virtually ignored the feelings of children who are placed in foster care against their will. It is apparent that the protection afforded a child under the voluntary placement statute is minimal to nonexistent. A child may not be adjudicated a PINS for refusing to comply with a directive that violates his constitutional rights.

d) Andrew's threats against his father are understandable under the circumstances, and evidence of his truancy was not substantial enough to sustain a PINS finding. The petition is dismissed and a final order of protection is issued to the child directing the father to cease and desist his efforts to have Andrew returned to Hawthorne. The father is warned that any violation of this protection order may result in a six-month jail term.

C. NEGLECTED AND DEPENDENT CHILDREN

1. **Protection of Children.** Under the historic concept of *parens patriae*, the state has a duty to act to protect those who are incapable of protecting themselves, including children whose natural guardians (*i.e.,* parents) are failing to provide them with the physical and intangible necessities for ordinary growth and development.

   a. **Statutes defining child neglect and dependency--*In re* Juvenile Appeal (83-CD),** 455 A.2d 1313 (Conn. 1983).

      1) **Facts.** The superior court for juvenile matters granted temporary custody of D's five children to the Department of Children and Youth Services ("DCYS"). D and her six children were receiving support and services from DCYS. The DCYS caseworker felt that the children had a very warm relationship with their mother. In September 1979, D's youngest child died and, because of his unexplained death (and unexplained superficial marks on his body), DCYS seized custody of the five remaining children. This summary seizure is allowed by statute if the DCYS commissioner has reasonable cause to believe that it is necessary to insure a child's safety. A hearing on the matter was later held and still there was no explanation of the child's death; however, the pediatrician doing the autopsy testified that marks found on the child's body were not the cause of death and the child may have died from "sudden infant death syndrome." The court found the requisite reasonable cause and ordered that custody of the children was to remain with the DCYS. D appealed to the Connecticut Supreme Court, claiming that the statute allowing DCYS to seize her children was unconstitutional and that probable cause is not the standard of proof in a temporary custody proceeding.

      2) **Issues.**

         a) Is the neglect statute unconstitutional because it allows for the temporary seizure of children if the DCYS has probable cause that it is necessary to insure the child's safety?

         b) Is the standard of proof in a temporary custody proceeding "probable cause"?

      3) **Held.** a) No. b) No. The judgment is reversed and custody is returned to the parent.

         a) The statute must be read together with other neglect proceedings statutes even though they might not be found in the same sections. The statute is constitutional because when it is read together with the other sections, as it must be, it is justified by a compelling state interest and is narrowly drawn to express only that legitimate state interest.

b) The standard of proof is a preponderance of the evidence. No substantial showing was made at the temporary custody hearing that the defendant's children were suffering from either serious physical illness or injury, or that they would be in immediate physical danger if they were returned to the defendant's home.

c) In this situation, the state cannot constitutionally sit back and wait for the parent to institute judicial proceedings. The state had a duty to seek the best interests of the child even after adversary proceedings with the parent had begun. The state bears the burden of showing the necessity to continue the commitment. It is shocking that the defendant's children have been in "temporary" custody for more than three years; the DCYS must make continuing review of temporary custody cases imperative.

4) Comment. The court follows the test for determining constitutionality that was set forth in *Roe v. Wade*. This underscores the idea that the right of parents to custody of their children is a fundamental, but not an absolute, right.

D. CHILD ABUSE

1. Beyond Neglect. When injury suffered by a child results from parental activity, not passive neglect, stronger state interest is generated. However, sometimes this well-meaning state interest is misdirected.

Johnson
v. State

a. Passing illegal substances in utero--Johnson v. State, 602 So.2d 1288 (Fla. 1992).

1) Facts. Johnson (D) delivered a healthy son in 1987. D admitted to a pediatrician that she had used cocaine the night before she delivered, and a basic toxicology test performed on her son was positive for a "breakdown" product of cocaine. D also delivered a healthy daughter in 1989. D told the obstetrician that she had used rock cocaine the morning she was hospitalized, while she was in labor. D was convicted of delivery of a controlled substance to her two minor children, via the umbilical cord in the 30 to 90 seconds after they were born, but before their umbilical cord were severed. D appealed. The appeals court affirmed and certified the question for review.

2) Issue. Does cocaine passing through the umbilical cord after birth, but before cutting the cord, violate the Florida statutory prohibition against adult delivery of a controlled substance to a minor?

3) Held. No. The decision below is quashed, the certified question is answered in the negative, and the case is remanded with directions that the conviction be reversed.

a)   We adopt Judge Sharp's analysis concerning the insufficiency of the evidence to support D's conviction and her analysis concerning legislative intent.

b)   Criminal statutes are strictly construed, and when the language is ambiguous, the statute is to be construed most favorably to the accused.

c)   There is no indication in the legislative history that the legislature intended that the word "delivery" to be used in the context of criminal prosecution of mothers for delivery of a controlled substance to a minor through the umbilical cord.

d)   There can be no doubt that drug abuse is one of the most serious problems confronting society today, and the effects of cocaine use by pregnant women is well-established. However, prosecuting women for using drugs and "delivering" them to their newborns appears to be the least effective response to this crisis.

b.   Battering parent syndrome--Sanders v. State, 303 S.E.2d 13 (Ga. 1983).

1)   Facts. Sanders (D) was convicted and given a life prison sentence for the murder of her infant daughter. The baby had been born three months premature and was often sick after she was released from the hospital. An autopsy showed that the baby had died of a severe crushing head injury, and that she also had numerous bruises on her body which seemed to have been caused by an adult's knuckles, a split liver which was the result of a day-old blow to the front of her chest, and a broken arm. When questioned by police, D stated that she did not know what had happened, but later testified that she had dropped the child and may have smashed her head while picking her up. She also testified that she had been upset, was pregnant, and did not want another baby. During trial, the prosecution introduced testimony of a clinical psychologist concerning the battering parent syndrome. After introduction of this testimony, the defendant moved for a mistrial. The motion was denied. D appeals.

2)   Issues.

a)   Is introduction, by the prosecution, of testimony concerning the battering parent syndrome proper when the defendant has not placed her character in issue or raised some defense which the battering parent syndrome is relevant to rebut?

b)   Was there sufficient evidence of guilt without the battering parent syndrome testimony to support the jury's guilty verdict?

3)   Held. a) No. b) Yes. The judgment is affirmed.

a)   The testimony clearly implicated D's character. D possessed many characteristics which the testimony identified as being shared by the typical battering parent and it could lead a reasonable juror to no other inference than that the state was implying that this parent fit within the syndrome. The state may not introduce testimony demonstrating the parent has the characteristics of a typical battering parent unless the defendant has placed her character in issue.

b) It is highly probable that the error did not contribute to the verdict, and the evidence of guilt was otherwise overwhelming.

4) **Comment.** The court discussed other areas where the defense had used similar syndromes to show character types, *e.g.,* "battered woman syndrome" and "battered child syndrome." The court had never been faced with the question of allowing the prosecution to introduce such evidence. To come to their decision above, the court adopted the reasoning of the similar Minnesota case of *Loebach v. State*, 310 N.W.2d 58 (Minn. 1981). Wyoming, however, does allow admissibility of such testimony. [*See* Grabill v. State, 621 P.2d 802 (Wyo. 1982)]

People v. Jennings

c. **Definitions of child abuse--People v. Jennings,** 641 P.2d 276 (Colo. 1982).

1) **Facts.** Jennings (D) was convicted of child abuse resulting in serious bodily injury. D had returned home from work early because he felt ill. His four-month-old daughter was being fussy and he tried to give her a bottle but she continued to cry. He then was going to pick her up, but instead struck her on the head with his hand; this caused her to stop breathing. Brain damage occurred and resulted in blindness and arrested mental development. After the trial the baby died. D testified that he did not mean to hurt the baby and was not trying to punish her. After his conviction, D moved to dismiss the charges because the statute was unconstitutionally vague. The trial court granted D's motion. The state appeals.

2) **Issue.** Is the language of the child abuse statute unconstitutionally vague because of the subjective nature of the words "cruel" and "punish"?

3) **Held.** No. The case is reversed and remanded for a new trial.

a) A penal statute is unconstitutionally vague if it forbids or requires the doing of an act in terms so vague that persons of common intelligence must necessarily guess as to its meaning and differ as to its application. Criminal statutes should inform persons subject to them of the standards of conduct imposed and should give fair warning of which acts are forbidden.

b) Common law allowed for moderate and reasonable force in light of the child's age and condition, the misconduct being punished, the kind of punishment inflicted, the degree of harm done to the child, and other relevant circumstances. This general rule is codified throughout our statutes and evidences the legislative intent to protect children from unwarranted abuse.

c) Scientific exactitude in statutory language is not required as long as the statute meets the minimal requirements of due process. Given the statutory and common law context in which the "cruelly punished" language is set, we are satisfied that it is intelligible and capable of nonarbitrary enforcement.

4) **Comment.** The court also stated that the inclusion of "negligently" as a state of mind within the statute did not render it unconstitutional.

d. **Fifth Amendment does not excuse failure of court-supervised parent to disclose location of missing child--Baltimore City Department of Social Services v. Bouknight,** 493 U.S. 549 (1990).

Baltimore City Department of Social Services v. Bouknight

1) **Facts.** Bouknight (D) is the mother of Maurice. Maurice was hospitalized with a fractured left femur at age three months. D was seen shaking and dropping the casted infant, and a child abuse report was filed. The Baltimore City Department of Social Services (P) got a shelter care order. Several months later, Maurice was declared a child in need of assistance and put in the care of P, who returned custody to D subject to extensive, court-ordered supervision. Eight months later, P petitioned to remove Maurice from D's custody for foster care placement because D had refused to abide by the supervision conditions, the father had died in a shooting incident, none of the relatives had seen Maurice recently, and D refused to produce him. The juvenile court ordered D to produce Maurice or be subject to contempt. D did not produce Maurice, but said he was with a relative; the relative denied having seen the child. D was ordered held in prison for contempt until she produced Maurice or revealed where he was. The Maryland Court of Appeals vacated, holding that it violated the privilege against self-incrimination to imprison for failure to produce a child whose production could give evidence of child abuse or worse.

2) **Issue.** May a custodial mother invoke the Fifth Amendment privilege against self-incrimination to resist an order of a juvenile court to produce a child?

3) **Held.** No. The judgment is reversed and the case is remanded.

   a) The Fifth Amendment privilege against self-incrimination applies only to testimonial communication. When the government demands production, communication is not required. The possibility that production may also provide testimonial assertions does not necessarily mean that the Fifth Amendment applies.

   b) Once Maurice was adjudicated a child in need of assistance, his care and safety became a specific concern of the state. By accepting custody of Maurice subject to substantial conditions, D submitted to the supervision of P. P's efforts to gain access to Maurice do not focus especially on D's criminal conduct, but on Maurice's welfare. In such circumstances, D may not invoke the Fifth Amendment.

4) **Dissent** (Marshall, Brennan, JJ.). D could face criminal abuse and neglect charges as well as be charged with causing Maurice's death. D is not merely a state-appointed custodian; she is Maurice's mother. When the conduct at which the civil child abuse statutes are aimed is the same as the criminal child abuse laws, it is problematic to deny application of the Fifth Amendment.

In re
Michael C.

e. **Denial of direct confrontation for protection of child witnesses is permissible--*In re* Michael C., 557 A.2d 1219 (R.I. 1989).**

1) **Facts.** The parents (Ds) of 13-year-old Michael C. were charged with neglect stemming from charges that the father sexually abused him. The mother testified that the boy told her that his father was "after his body." The father denied ever having any sexual activity with Michael. Michael had expressed great anxiety about testifying in court. The judge ruled that Michael could testify in camera before him and a stenographer. The testimony would then be read to Ds and their attorneys, and the attorneys could submit written questions for the judge to ask Michael. Michael told the judge about various incidents of his father stripping him and sexually molesting him, of telling his mother, and of her disbelieving him. Michael denied that he was retaliating against his father for various punishments or for not getting a motorcycle. The court found that Michael had been abused by his father and neglected by his mother, and awarded his custody to the state. Ds appeal.

2) **Issue.** Is the denial of Ds' right to confront their son while he testified against them unconstitutional?

3) **Held.** No. The judgment is affirmed.

a) In a previous case, this court approved the steps taken by the trial court in this case. There, this court found no violation of the constitutional right to confrontation because that was a noncriminal case, and that constitutional right only applies in criminal cases.

b) In this case, the child witness was 13, while in the earlier case the child was only five, but a similar trauma exists for the teenager who must testify against an adult accused of molesting him.

c) It is best to leave such matters to the discretion of the trial judge, who sees and hears the witnesses personally, and can weigh the interests of the child as against the interests of the parents and the state.

d) Michael's father admitted threatening to strangle, kill, or put Michael "through the wall" if he ever tried to hit his mother or another family member again. Such shocking remarks justified the judge's decision to use the procedure he used in this case.

4) **Comment.** In *Coy v. Iowa*, 487 U.S. 1012 (1988), the U.S. Supreme Court upheld a conviction for committing lascivious acts with a child in a case where the child had testified with a screen separating him from the accused. In *Maryland v. Craig*, 110 S. Ct. 3157 (1990), the Supreme Court upheld the use of video cameras to protect child witnesses in abuse cases. In both cases, the Court indicated that the Sixth Amendment guarantee of a right to confrontation would not be abandoned, however, even for the sake of protecting child witnesses. The tension between protecting the rights of defendants and protecting the vulnerabilities of children creates a major dilemma about which there will doubtless be further litigation.

f. **Incompetence or inaction by state child protection agencies does not alone constitute state action--DeShaney v. Winnebago County Department of Social Services, 489 U.S. 189 (1989).**

1) **Facts.** Joshua DeShaney was born in 1979. In 1980, his parents divorced and his father, Randy DeShaney, was awarded custody. Randy moved to Wisconsin, married and divorced again. In 1982 the Winnebago County Department of Social Services (D) investigated possible child abuse when Randy's second wife complained to police at the time of their divorce that he hit the boy. D interviewed the father, who denied the allegation. In 1983, D investigated again when Joshua was admitted to a local hospital with multiple bruises symptomatic of child abuse. D immediately got a temporary custody order. D's child protection team decided there was insufficient evidence of child abuse to convince a court, but recommended protective measures. The juvenile court dismissed the case and returned Joshua to his father's custody. A month later, hospital emergency personnel reported that Joshua again had been treated for suspicious injuries. For the next six months, D's caseworker made monthly visits and observed many suspicious injuries on Joshua's head. In November 1983, hospital emergency personnel again reported treating Joshua for suspicious injuries. D's caseworker was unable to see Joshua on the next two visits allegedly because he was too ill. In March 1984, Randy DeShaney beat Joshua so severely that he suffered permanent brain damage, leaving him profoundly retarded. Randy was tried and convicted of child abuse. Joshua and his mother (Ps) then filed suit against D, alleging that D's failure to intervene to protect him had deprived him of liberty without due process of law. The district court granted summary judgment for D. The court of appeals affirmed.

2) **Issue.** Is the failure of a government agency to protect an individual against abuse by his or her parents a violation of the Fifth or Fourteenth Amendment?

3) **Held.** No. The judgment is affirmed.

a) The Due Process Clause of the Fourteenth (and Fifth) Amendment provides that "[n]o State shall . . . deprive any person of life, liberty or property without due process of law." Nothing in this language requires the state to protect the life, liberty, or property of persons against private action, only improper public deprivation. The history of the amendment shows that it was intended to protect individuals against government action, not private conduct. Our cases hold that there is no affirmative right to government aid, even when necessary to preserve life.

b) In certain narrow circumstances, the Constitution requires the government to undertake affirmative duties of care and protection of persons whose care or control the government has assumed and who are unable to care for themselves, *e.g.,* prisoners and involuntarily committed mental patients.

c) The affirmative duty of the government to protect does not arise because of mere knowledge of the need of the individual for protection. The fact that the state once took temporary custody of

Joshua does not mean it undertook a continuing duty of care or protection, because the state returned Joshua to the custody of his father.

d) Our sympathy for Joshua must not lead us to ignore the consequences of creating constitutional liability for welfare agencies here. Premature or overzealous action by the state would intrude upon the constitutional rights of parents and families.

e) The state is free to impose a common law duty of care and protection upon its agencies, by statute or common law tort, but the Constitution does not compel such action.

4) **Dissent** (Brennan, Marshall, Blackmun, JJ.). I would approach this case from the opposite direction, focusing on the action the State has taken instead of the action it has not taken. Wisconsin's system of child protection is designed to help children like Joshua, and the agency did not just stand by and do nothing, but it acted and that action and system created liability.

5) **Dissent** (Blackmun, J.). "Poor Joshua!" He is victim not only of his cowardly, bullying father, but also of D, who abandoned its responsibilities.

6) **Comment.** If Ps were allowed to maintain their action, would D have a "clean hands" defense with respect to Joshua's mother on the ground that if she retained enough responsibility for Joshua to bring this suit, she also should bear responsibility for the injuries caused by her parental failure? The last point of the majority is significant: the decision in no way precludes the creation of liability by statute or state common law. Only a constitutional tort is disallowed.

E. MEDICAL CARE

The line between "therapeutic" and "elective" medicine is not always clear.

1. **Medical Treatment for Children.** The basic principle appears to be that the state may intervene to prevent irremediable injuries (*e.g.,* death) to children.

Hermanson
v. State

a. **Unclear statutory language--Hermanson v. State,** 604 So.2d 775 (Fla. 1992).

1) **Facts.** The Hermanson's (Ds) daughter, Amy, died of untreated juvenile diabetes. A month before her death, Amy experienced marked weigh loss and lethargy, had a bluish tint to her skin, and complained of not feeling well and being unable to sleep. Ds, members of the First Church of Christ, Scientist, sought help from a Christian Science practitioner and nurse. The pathologist who examined Amy's body stated that if the disease could have been diagnosed by a physician, Amy's death could have been prevented, even up to several hours before her death. Ds

were convicted of felony child abuse and third-degree murder for providing spiritual treatment instead of conventional medical treatment for Amy. Ds appealed. The appeal court affirmed. Ds petition for review.

2) **Issue.** Did the Florida statutes under which Ds were convicted deny them due process by not giving them fair warning of the consequences of practicing their religious beliefs?

3) **Held.** Yes. The decision of the district court of appeals is quashed; the case is remanded with directions that the trial court's finding of guilt be vacated.

   a) The evidence and the stipulated facts establish that Ds treated Amy in accordance with their Christian Science beliefs.

   b) Section 827.04(1)-(2) of Florida's child abuse statutes makes it a third-degree felony for one to willfully or by culpable negligence deprive a child of necessary medical treatment.

   c) Section 415.503, the third-degee murder provision of Florida's statutes, defines an abused or neglected child and defines harm as the result of a parent or other person failing to supply a child with adequate health care. The statute continues: "however, a parent or other person responsible for the child's welfare legitimately practicing his religious beliefs, who by reason thereof does not provide specified medical treatment for a child, may not be considered abusive or neglectful for that reason alone. . . ."

   d) The Supreme Court in *Mourning v. Family Publications Serv., Inc.*, 411 U.S. 356 (1973), stated that one of the purposes of due process is to insure that no person will be convicted unless a fair warning has first been "given to the world in language that the common world will understand, of what the law intends to do if a certain line is passed."

   e) The statutes, when considered together, are ambiguous and result in a denial of due process because they fail to give parents notice of the point at which the parents' reliance on spiritual treatment loses statutory approval and becomes culpably negligent.

   f) To hold that the statutes in question establish a line at which a person of "common intelligence" would know that his or her conduct is or is not criminally negligent ignores the fact that not only did the judges of both the circuit court and the district court of appeal have difficulty with the interrelationship of the statutes, but the jurors also had problems understanding what was required.

b. **State intervention fails--Newmark v. Williams**, 588 A.2d 1108 (Del. 1991).

Newmark v. Williams

1) **Facts.** The Division of Child Protective Services ("DCPS") petitioned for temporary custody of Colin Newmark in order to authorize a hospital to treat his deadly and advanced form of pediatric cancer with an extremely intensive six-month regimen of chemotherapy. If the treatment was not itself fatal, it offered only a 40% chance of "curing" Colin; a physician had opined that without the treatment, Colin would die within six to eight

months. The Newmarks, Christian Scientists, had rejected this proposed medical treatment for Colin, relying on Delaware's statute exempting those who treat their children's illnesses "solely by spiritual means" from the state's abuse and neglect statutes. The family court awarded custody to DCPS. The Newmarks appeal.

2) **Issue.** Was the child abused or neglected under Delaware law when his parents refused to accede to medical demands that he receive a radical form of chemotherapy having only a 40% chance of success?

3) **Held.** No. The judgment is reversed.

    a) Delaware's exemption statute provides that "no child who in good faith is under treatment solely by spiritual means through prayer in accordance with the tenants and practices of a recognized church or religious denomination by a duly accredited practitioner thereof shall for that reason alone be considered a neglected child. . . ."

    b) The legislative history of this chapter reflects the intention to provide a safe harbor for parents like the Newmarks.

    c) The trial court erred in not considering the competing interests at stake, the primacy of the family relationship, including the autonomy of parental decision-making authority over minor children, and the gravity of Colin's illness in conjunction with the invasiveness of the proposed treatment and its likelihood of failure. Here, the factors stongly militate against government intrusion.

    d) Parental autonomy over minor children is not an absolute right. The state can intervene only under compelling conditions, where the health and safety of the child and the public at large are in jeopardy.

    e) Because Colin was too young to reach a detached, informed decision regarding his own treatment, we must substitute our objective judgment to determine what is in his best interest. The proposed treatment was highly invasive, could have independently caused Colin's death, would have removed Colin from his parents' home during treatment, and would have caused him to be placed in a foster home because of the intensive care required.

    f) Under the "best interests standard," DCPS's petition must be denied because the state's authority to intervene cannot outweigh the Newmarks' parental prerogatives and Colin's right to enjoy at least a modicum of human dignity in the short time left to him. Parents must have the right at some point to reject medical treatment for their child.

2. **The Right of Children to Refuse Treatment.** Because parents represent their children, they have the legal authority to give consent for their children. But at some point, as children become adolescents, they may assert their own interests,

sometimes in opposition to parental decisions made for them. Determining when the desires of a minor should be legally recognized instead of the contrary decision of a parent is a difficult (and unavoidably subjective) task.

a. **Commitment for mental treatment--Parham v. J.R.**, 442 U.S. 584 (1979).

1) **Facts.** J.R. (P), a minor, brought a class action seeking an injunction and declaratory judgment that Georgia's procedures for commitment of minors for mental treatment violates the Due Process Clause of the Fourteenth Amendment. At three months, P had been declared a neglected child, and custody was given to the state. P was placed in seven different foster homes. After his disruptive behavior caused his last foster parents to request his removal, the state agency sought his admission to a state mental hospital. Previously, he had received outpatient treatment. He was diagnosed as "borderline retarded" with aggressive reactions to childhood. It was unanimously agreed by the hospital admission team that he would benefit from the structured hospital environment and enjoy the peer relations there. After commitment, J.R.'s condition was periodically reexamined. Unsuccessful attempts to find another foster home for him were made. The Georgia statutes provide that any parent or guardian of a child may apply to have that child admitted to a state mental hospital. The hospital superintendent may admit the child temporarily for observation and diagnosis. If there is evidence of mental illness in a child suitable for treatment, the child may be admitted. The child can be discharged by parental request at any time and, even without parental request, the superintendent is required to release any child who has "sufficiently improved" so that "hospitalization is no longer desirable." The district court granted the relief sought. The state (D) appeals.

2) **Issue.** Did the district court err in holding the Georgia commitment procedures unconstitutional because they failed to provide for an adversarial hearing before an administrative or judicial officer before commitment of a minor at the voluntary request of the parent or guardian of the minor?

3) **Held.** Yes. The judgment is reversed and the case is remanded.

    a) Historically, the treatment of mentally disturbed children was left entirely to the family. State efforts to provide treatment of mentally disturbed children is a recent humanitarian development.

    b) Due process inquiry requires (i) determination of the private interests that will be affected, (ii) balancing the risk of erroneous deprivation, and (iii) evaluating the governmental interest and the burden thereto of alternative procedures.

    c) A child has a liberty interest in not being unnecessarily confined and in avoiding the stigma of commitment for mental problems. (But more profound adverse social consequences result from untreated mental problems than from treatment of them.)

    d) Parents have a valid interest in obtaining necessary treatment for a disturbed child—even if the child objects to the treatment. The law presumes that parents have what the child lacks in maturity, experience, and judgment. Historically, parental affection for their children has caused parents to act in the best interests of their children. That some parents do not is no reason to discard the well-founded presumption that most parents do. Furthermore, neither state officials nor federal courts are equipped to review ordinary parental decisions about hospitalization.

e) Absent abuse or neglect, parents have a substantial, if not dominant, role in deciding their child's treatment; but they cannot have an absolute and unreviewable discretion in the commitment context. The independent medical judgment of the hospital superintendent is also required.

f) The state has a legitimate interest in restricting the use of its facilities to genuine cases, without creating unnecessary and costly obstacles to access that would discourage parents from seeking available services for their children.

g) Due process requires (i) a thorough precommitment investigation by a neutral fact finder, including (ii) a personal interview with the child, and, if the child is committed, (iii) periodic review including the same type of inquiry.

h) Investigation by a hospital staff physician is sufficient; no judge or administrative officer is required. (The issue is essentially medical, not judicial, in nature.) A formal adversary hearing is not necessary. (The detriment resulting from such significant intrusion into parent-child relations outweighs any benefit.)

i) Georgia's procedural requirements are not per se unconstitutional.

j) For wards of the state, the balance of interests is somewhat different, and on remand the court should examine the postcommitment review procedures applicable to state wards.

4) **Concurring in part, dissenting in part** (Brennan, Marshall, Stevens, JJ.). The postadmission review procedures are generally inadequate, and the preadmission procedures for wards of the state are unnecessarily lax.

5) **Comment.** Here, the Court sustained the right of parents to force a child to undergo treatment, while in *Belotti v. Baird*, 443 U.S. 622 (1979), decided less than two weeks later, it refused to allow parents to prevent a child from obtaining controversial treatment (an abortion) despite the parents' objections. Some commentators have suggested that, from the perspective of coercion and access to possible dangerous treatment, the Court decided the cases exactly backwards.

b. **States may uphold parents' right to counsel their minor children regarding contemplated abortion.**

1) In *H.L. v. Matheson*, 450 U.S. 398 (1981), the Supreme Court upheld a Utah statute requiring parental notification. While a state may not give a third party, even a parent, an absolute veto, the Court distinguished mere notification from parental consent. Parental participation not only pre-

serves family integrity, but it also may promote the health interests of the minor. The fact that some minors may be discouraged from getting an abortion does not make the statute invalid.

2) In *Ohio v. Akron Center for Reproductive Health, Inc.*, 497 U.S. 502 (1990), the Court (by a vote of 6-3) upheld a law requiring notification of one parent at least 24 hours before an abortion could be performed on a minor. The statute had a judicial bypass provision. In *Hodgson v. Minnesota*, 497 U.S. 417 (1990), the Court upheld another statute that required notification of **both** parents before an abortion could be performed, when coupled with a judicial bypass provision, but held that without the judicial bypass provision it would bc unconstitutional.

c. **Judicial immunity for deprivation of fundamental rights--Stump v. Sparkman,** 435 U.S. 349 (1978).

Stump v.
Sparkman

1) **Facts.** Sparkman (P) was a "somewhat retarded" child; however, she attended public schools and was promoted each year. Her mother became concerned for her well-being when she began associating with young men and occasionally staying out overnight with them. The mother asked Judge Stump (D), a circuit court judge in Indiana, to sign a petition allowing her to have P sterilized by having her tubes tied. The petition also indemnified the doctor and hospital from any wrongdoing. The judge signed it and P was tricked into the operation. In later years P was married and could not have children. After realizing what had been done to her, she sued D for violating her constitutional rights and sued the doctors, the hospital, and her mother for various torts. D moved to dismiss under the doctrine of judicial immunity. The court of appeals denied the motion and D appealed. P asserts that D acted outside his judicial role and in the clear absence of jurisdiction, therefore judicial immunity does not apply.

2) **Issues.**

a) Does a circuit judge have jurisdiction over a parent's petition to sterilize a minor child?

b) Is D's act so totally devoid of judicial concern for the interests and well-being of the young girl involved as to disqualify it as a judicial act?

3) **Held.** a) Yes. b) No. The judgment is reversed and the case is remanded.

a) A judge will be subject to liability only when he has acted in the "clear absence of all jurisdiction." The statutory authority for the sterilization of institutionalized persons in the custody of the state does not warrant the inference that a court of general jurisdiction has no power to act on a petition for sterilization of a minor in the custody of her parents, particularly where the parents have authority to consent to medical care or treatment, including surgery. State judges are often called upon to approve petitions relating to the affairs of minors. Although it was error to sign the petition, the judge did have jurisdiction to hear it and therefore is immune from liability.

b) Despite the unfairness to the litigants that sometimes results, the doctrine of judicial immunity allows a judicial officer to be free to act upon his own convictions without apprehension of personal consequences to himself.

4) **Comment.** Under the majority's opinion, it is questionable if any judge's decision—no matter how repulsive—would ever leave him or her open to liability for malpractice if the subject matter of the decision was within the competence of the court in any circumstances.

In re Green   **d. Non-lifesaving treatment--*In re* Green,** 292 A.2d 387 (Pa. 1972).

1) **Facts.** Ricky Green, age 15, suffered from paralytic scoliosis (94% curvature of the spine). His doctors recommended spinal fusion, an inherently dangerous operation which, if successful, would relieve his bent condition. His mother (D), a Jehovah's Witness, would consent to the operation only if no blood transfusion were performed. Although Ricky's life was not in danger, a neglect petition was filed seeking appointment of a guardian who would authorize surgery. The petition was dismissed but was reversed by the superior court. D appeals.

2) **Issue.** May a state interfere with a parent's decision not to allow dangerous, non-lifesaving surgery for a 15-year-old minor?

3) **Held.** No. The judgment is reversed and the case is remanded.

a) D's rights of free exercise are implicated. While interferences with religious practices such as polygamy, antivaccination, child labor, etc. may be justified, Ricky's condition is not a threat to society of the same magnitude. If Ricky's life were at stake, the court could overrule his mother's religion-based decision to prohibit treatment.

b) The court is very reluctant to assume the responsibility for deciding when non-lifesaving treatment is "necessary." On such subjective questions of value judgment, the parents' decision ought not to be set aside.

c) Because of Ricky's age and maturity, he should be consulted. The case is remanded for an evidentiary hearing on Ricky's wishes.

4) **Dissent.** Too little consideration has been given to Ricky's health interests. Merely asking Ricky's opinion is inadequate. Under the control and guidance of his parents, he probably cannot make a truly independent decision.

5) **Comment.** On such inherently subjective questions as this, the "best interests" of a child are largely indeterminate; the real question is who decides what is in the best interest of the child.

3. **Parental Authorization of Medical Treatment.** The flip side of parental refusal to authorize necessary medical treatment is parental approval for recommended but life-endangering medical procedures.

a. **Kidney transplant--Hart v. Brown,** 289 A.2d 386 (Conn. Supp. Ct. 1972).

1) **Facts.** Peter and Eleanor Hart (Ps) were parents of identical twins, Katheleen and Margaret, age seven. Katheleen's kidneys were removed and she required dialysis treatments twice a week to survive. A kidney transplant was recommended; because of rejection problems, a kidney from her twin would have been best, with a close to 100% chance that both twins would have normal, full lives. With her parent's kidney, the likelihood of success would have been about 50%, and many undesirable side effects might have accompanied use of the drugs necessary to prevent rejection of the organ. A psychiatrist, a clergyman, and the parents all testified that Margaret wanted to give her kidney and might suffer if her sister died because she was not allowed to give her kidney. The hospital and surgeons involved would not perform the operation unless the court ruled that the parents could consent to the operation for the children.

2) **Issue.** Can the court judicially authorize parental consent to a kidney transplant between identical twins?

3) **Held.** Yes. An order is entered approving parental consent.

a) The equity powers of the court should be cautiously exercised. But the court has the inherent power to grant the relief sought here.

b) Parents have the authority to consent to nontherapeutic operations; thus, the parents can consent for Margaret to give up her kidney.

c) Since the operation is essential for the donee, negligible risk is involved for both children, prognosis is excellent for both donor and donee, and the donor would benefit from giving the kidney, Ps can consent.

4) **Comment.** Although an "advisory opinion," this opinion illustrates the considerations affecting disputes over informed consent to medical treatment on minors.

b. **Parents disagree--*In re* Doe,** 418 S.E.2d 3 (Ga. 1992).

1) **Facts.** Jane Doe suffered from a condition causing her to vacillate between stupor and coma; her brain stem was shrinking and the doctors agreed she suffered from a degenerative neurological disease,

but none could make a definitive diagnosis. When the doctors found it necessary to surgically insert feeding and breathing tubes, they discussed with Jane's parents the possibility of a "Do Not Resuscitate" ("DNR") order in the event Jane suffered cardiac arrest during the procedure. Mrs. Doe agreed to the order; Mr. Doe did not. The hospital brought a declaratory judgment action seeking guidance as to which parent's wishes to follow. The court entered an order enjoining the hospital from deescalating treatment or from enforcing the DNR order unless both parents agreed. The state appealed; even though Jane died several weeks after the final order was entered in the declaratory judgment action, the appeal is not moot because it is among those capable of repetition yet evading review.

2) **Issues.**

   a)   Did the hospital have standing to bring a declaratory judgment action?

   b)   Could the parents legally decide to deescalate the child's medical treatment?

   c)   Could the hospital enter a DNR order?

3) **Held.** a) Yes. b) Yes. c) No.

   a)   The hospital could not determine its legal obligation to its patient without guidance as to which parent's wishes to follow. Jane's condition continued to deteriorate and the likelihood of cardiac arrest increased daily. The hospital was an interested party seeking a judgment to direct further action.

   b)   Even though Jane did not meet the criteria for withdrawal of life support established in *L.R.H.*, 253 Ga. 439 (1984) (requiring a diagnosis that an infant is terminal with no hope of recovery, and that the infant exists in a chronic vegetative state, with no reasonable possibility of attaining cognitive function), that opinion set up guidelines to protect the rights of incompetent patients and did not preclude the propriety of deescalation under other circumstances. The legislature has enacted or amended several statutes governing the legal propriety of proxy health care decisions, and we cannot mandate a single, static formula for deciding when deescalation may be appropriate.

   c)   The parents could legally have decided to deescalate treatment without seeking prior judicial approval. The doctors agreed that Jane was in the final stages of a terminal disease, she vacillated between stupor and coma, she required artificial life support of all bodily functions, and that no known treatment could improve her condition or halt neurological deterioration.

   d)   Under the state statute which allows "any parent" to consent to a DNR order for a minor child and the statute that allows "any parent" to revoke consent, the hospital could not enter the order when the parents disagreed. One parent's consent could be effectively revoked by the other parent.

4) **Concurrence.** This opinion should not be read to confer standing for a hospital under circumstances other than those presented here.

4. **Parental Malpractice.** While a majority of states have modified or abandoned the doctrine of intrafamily immunity for intentional torts, parental malpractice claims have not been accepted. Emotional neglect, in serious cases, may constitute a basis for state intervention but the concept of inadequate parenting is so ambiguous that courts are very cautious about that failing.

5. **The Law of Emancipation.** At common law, emancipation resulted from some act or omission of the parent(s). Some advocates of children's rights in recent years have suggested that children should be able to "divorce" their parents. In fact, there is not much that judges, police, or parents can do to restrain a head-strong, willful teenager who is intent on throwing off parental supervision. But this unwritten fact has not generally been given the endorsement of legal policy.

VII. CUSTODY OF CHILDREN

A. THE "BEST INTERESTS OF THE CHILD" STANDARD

The traditional practice in child custody adjudication has been to award custody to the person who would most likely provide for the child's best interests. Recently this standard has been criticized for being unavoidably subjective.

1. **Presumption Favoring Biological Parents.** The law traditionally has presumed that, as between biological parents and others, the biological parents would be the best custodians of their offspring.

2. **Age of Children and Sex of Parent.** During the last century, the "tender years doctrine," a presumption that mothers are the best custodians of young children, gained widespread acceptance. The doctrine is no longer an irrebuttable presumption, but survives in many jurisdictions as a "common sense" consideration.

Johnson v. Johnson

   a. **Tender years doctrine--Johnson v. Johnson,** 564 P.2d 71 (Alaska 1977), *cert. denied,* 434 U.S. 1048 (1978).

   1) **Facts.** Rudy Johnson (P) and Linda Johnson (D) were married and had two children. The parties joined the Jehovah's Witnesses, and both were active for a time. P was removed from the congregation, which lead to marital difficulties. P sued D for divorce and for custody of the children. P was granted a divorce, but custody was granted to D primarily on the basis of the tender years doctrine (*i.e.,* that all things being equal, where the children are of tender age, the presumption will favor granting custody to the mother). P appeals.

   2) **Issue.** In determining custody of children, is the tender years doctrine inconsistent with the statutory requirement that the best interests of the child be considered?

   3) **Held.** Yes. The case is remanded to the district court for decision based on proper criteria.

      a) Trial courts have great discretion in determining custody, but their discretion is not unlimited. The ages of the children should have been considered as but one factor in determining who should be awarded custody. Recent decisions have rejected the use of the tender years doctrine as a presumption.

      b) In addition to considering the age of the children, the court, on remand, should also consider the moral fitness of the two parties, the home environment each would offer the child, the emotional ties between the child and the parties, the sex and health of the child, and the preference of the child.

      c) P's argument that the trial court abused its discretion in awarding custody to a Jehovah's Witness cannot be accepted. His entire argument centers around the fact that he can provide a more stimulating environment for the children than D because she is a Jehovah's Witness. To use D's religious affiliation as a basis for instructing the trial court to award custody to P would violate the Free Exercise Clause of the First Amendment.

3. **Race.** Race is a suspect classification in constitutional analysis, and is thus subject to strict scrutiny, but inasmuch as it is relevant to the best interests of the child, it may be a factor in a custody proceeding.

   a. **Application--Palmore v. Sidoti,** 466 U.S. 429 (1984).

   Palmore
v. Sidoti

   1) **Facts.** Linda Sidoti Palmore (D) and Anthony Sidoti (P) were divorced, and custody of their three-year-old daughter was awarded to D. A year later, P sought custody of the child because D was cohabiting with an African-American man, whom she later married. Both P and D are white. The trial court made a finding that there is no issue as to either party's devotion to the child, adequacy of housing facilities, or respectability of the new spouse of either parent. The trial court held, however, that because of the social consequences of an interracial marriage, the best interests of the child would be to award custody to P. The court of appeals affirmed and D appeals.

   2) **Issue.** Can the custody of a child be taken away from the mother and awarded to the father merely because the mother has chosen to marry outside her race and because of concern over such racially mixed households?

   3) **Held.** No. The judgment is reversed.

      a) The Florida court did not focus directly on the qualifications of any of the parties or their spouses. It is clear that the outcome would have been different had the mother married a Caucasian of similar respectability. Any such discrimination based on race must be justified by a compelling governmental interest.

      b) There may be private biases against racially mixed households that may inflict possible injury to the children. The Constitution cannot control these prejudices, but neither can it tolerate them. Whatever problems racially mixed households may pose for children can no more support a denial of constitutional rights than could the stress that residential integration was thought to entail. The effects of racial prejudice cannot justify a racial classification that removes an infant child from the custody of its natural mother who is found to be an appropriate person to have such custody.

   4) **Comment.** This decision does not mean that racial, ethnic, or cultural factors may not be considered; rather, the best interests of the child are the paramount consideration and the racial preferences of the court or community are not dispositive in making child custody determinations.

4.   Lifestyle. Parental lifestyle may be validly considered in custody proceedings to assess its impact on the child's development.

a.   Stability--Painter v. Bannister, 140 N.W.2d 152 (Iowa 1966).

1)   **Facts.** Harold Painter (P) married Dwight and Margaret Bannister's (Ds') daughter (against Ds' wishes), and a son, Mark, was born to the couple. Later, Mark's mother was killed in an accident and P asked her parents (Ds) to take care of Mark for a while. In this action, P petitioned for a writ of habeas corpus to cause Ds to return the child to him, because Ds had earlier refused to do so upon his request. The evidence at trial showed that P and Ds would provide entirely different environments for Mark. Ds are well-educated, well-respected members of the community who live on a farm in Iowa. They would provide Mark with a stable environment, a college education, and an excellent moral upbringing. While not unfit as a parent, P was found to be a romantic who had held at least seven jobs in 10 years since he left college, quitting or being fired from them because they did not suit his unique tastes. He was a poor financial manager and had relied on his deceased spouse (and did rely on his present spouse) as a stabilizing influence. P was found to be an intellectual, a liberal, and either an atheist or an agnostic. At trial, an eminent psychologist testified that under Ds' custody, Mark had become secure and well-adjusted, and that Mark should remain with Ds. The trial court ordered that Mark be returned to P. Ds appeal.

2)   **Issue.** In a custody action between a natural parent and the maternal grandparents, may parental preference be overcome where the best interests of the child in a stable, secure home life would best be provided by the grandparents?

3)   **Held.** Yes. The judgment is reversed.

a)   The presumption of parental preference has been weakened in recent times. Where the return of the child to his natural parent is likely to disrupt and disturb the child's development, as in this case, the presumption must give way to the best interest of the child.

b)   The mother's will named P as guardian; and if he failed to qualify, then Ds. Therefore, the maternal grandparents' interests are entitled to consideration.

c)   Before Mark came into Ds' home, he was not well-adjusted, was aggressive toward younger children and cruel to animals. He was not liked by his classmates. After two years with Ds, he appears well-disciplined, well-adjusted, secure, and popular with his classmates.

d)   The trial court erred in lightly dismissing the convincing testimony of an eminent child psychologist who had studied Mark in depth. His conclusion, which the court now relies upon, was that it would not be in Mark's psychological and developmental best interest to be removed from Ds' home.

4) Comment. This celebrated case illustrates the weight and dispositive impact that professional testimony has enjoyed in many courts in custody cases. This case also stimulated much discussion about the psychological parent concept. Subsequently, Mark expressed a desire to live with P, and Ds acquiesced.

B. PSYCHOLOGICAL PARENTING

1. Continuity. Since the publication of the influential book by Goldstein, Freud, and Solnit, courts and commentators have recognized that the child's perspective should not be ignored and that parenting involves far more than biological relatedness.

a. Rebuttal of biological preference--Bennett v. Jeffreys, 40 N.Y.2d 543 (1976).

Bennett v. Jeffreys

1) Facts. Bennett (P), the natural mother of an eight-year-old child, brought an action against Jeffreys (D), the nonparent custodian of the child with whom the child has lived since just after birth, to regain custody. When the child was born, P was only 15 years old, and she was induced by her parents into giving custody to D. There was no finding of neglect or abandonment on P's part, and the trial court specifically found that P is a fit parent. Nevertheless, the trial court held that the child should remain with D. The appellate court reversed and awarded custody to P. D appeals.

2) Issue. In a custody dispute between a natural parent and a nonparent custodian with whom the child has lived for a long period of time, should custody be determined by the best interest of the child standard?

3) Held. Yes. The order is reversed and the case is remanded for a new hearing.

a) The general rule is that the natural parent has the right to rear his or her child. However, the state may intervene and deprive a parent of this right where extraordinary circumstances exist (*i.e.,* abandonment, neglect, surrender, unfitness, extended disruption of custody, etc.). Thus, parental custodial rights are not absolute.

b) In this case, the natural mother and child have been separated for a prolonged period of time. This special circumstance overcomes the usual presumption that the best interest of the child requires custody by the natural parent. Thus, the decision of whether P or D shall be given custody should be based on the best interest of the child.

c) Neither the trial court nor the appellate court, in reaching opposite conclusions, applied this standard properly. The trial court gave undue weight to the fact that the child had lived with D for a long time and the appellate court gave undue weight to the fact that P is the natural parent. On remand, the court must carefully examine all the facts and circumstances to determine what would be in the best interest of the child.

4) Concurrence. The court correctly determined that circumstances other than just the statutory ones (*i.e.,* abandonment, surrender, neglect, and unfitness) would justify a court in terminating natural parental rights. However, the court should not give any weight to the natural mother's status in determining the best interest of the child where she has voluntarily given up custody for a prolonged period. Also, the application of the best interest standard should not have to await a judicial determination of "extraordinary circumstances," as the court's opinion suggests.

Bennett
v. Marrow

b. Application of best interests of the child rule--Bennett v. Marrow, 399 N.Y.S.2d 697 (N.Y. 1977).

1) Facts. This appeal was taken from the new hearing ordered in the case of *Bennett v. Jeffreys*, above. It involves the continuing dispute over the custody of a child between the natural mother, Bennett (P), and the foster mother, Marrow (D). At the end of the new hearing the family court awarded custody to D, noting the psychological parent-child relationship that had been established to the child's benefit. P appeals.

2) Issue. Did the family court err in finding that the best interests of the child justify awarding custody to the foster mother?

3) Held. No. The judgment is affirmed.

a) The family court clearly and closely observed for a second time the conduct and deportment of the natural mother, the foster mother, and the child. For the past 15 months the daughter had been living with P and she has still not emotionally settled into the household. She continues her unswerving request to be restored to the custody of Mrs. Marrow. Although P has been an adequate parent with respect to the child's physical needs, she has not begun to respond to the child's emotional needs. Expert testimony has also supported this finding.

4) Comment. The court continued to note that the long-term custodial relationship made this case one of extraordinary circumstances.

Guardianship
of Phillip B.

2. De Facto or Psychological Parents--Guardianship of Phillip B., 188 Cal. Rptr. 781 (Cal. Ct. App. 1983).

a. Facts. Herbert and Patsy H. (Ps) filed a petition for appointment as guardians of Phillip B., then 14 years old. Phillip's parents (Ds) opposed the petition. Phillip was born with Down's syndrome and Ds decided to place Phillip in an institution. Ds initially visited Phillip frequently, but they soon became detached. Phillip also had a congenital heart defect which could be corrected by surgery; however, Ds would not consent to the operation. At the age of five, Phillip was in very poor physical condition (due to poor care) and his motor skills were very poor. At that time he was transferred to a care center where, through the volunteer work of Ps, he progressed very well. Eventually, Phillip began to spend the weekends at Ps' home, and continued his day-to-day relationship with them at the care center. Phillip subsequently attended a school for the trainable mentally retarded, and his I.Q. was tested as being only mildly retarded. Phillip was openly accepted as a member of Ps' family, whom he came to love and trust. Ds continued their physical and emotional detachment from their son. When Phillip reached age 11, it was again recommended by doctors that Phillip undergo corrective surgery of his heart or his lifestyle in the future would be limited to a bed or chair. Ds still would not give their consent to the operation. When Ds found out about Phillip's weekend stays with Ps and their family, they forbade his removal from the care facility. The abrupt cessation of home visits produced regressive changes in Phillip's behavior. Ps then instituted a petition for guardianship. The trial court granted the petition with the authority to permit the heart operation.

b. **Issue.** Was there clear and convincing evidence to support the trial court's decision that it would be in Phillip's best interest to grant the petition awarding guardianship to Ps rather than leave guardianship in his natural parents?

c. **Held.** Yes. The judgment is affirmed.

1) The right of the parents to retain custody of a child is fundamental and may be disturbed only in extreme cases of persons acting in a fashion incompatible with parenthood. In order to disturb that right, the court must find that an award of custody to the parent would be detrimental to the child and that the award to a nonparent is required to serve the best interests of the child.

2) A person who assumes the role of parent, raising the child in his own home, may in time acquire an interest in the companionship, care, custody, and management of that child. Persons who assume such responsibility have been characterized as de facto or psychological parents and their interest in the child becomes a substantial one. It is not an absolute requirement that residency with the child on a 24-hour basis be had before such a relationship can be developed. Ps have provided an adequate foundation to establish this crucial parent-child relationship with Phillip.

3) There must be clear and convincing evidence that D's retention of custody would cause Phillip profound emotional harm, and the record is abundant with such evidence. There is uncontroverted expert testimony that Phillip would sustain further emotional trauma in the event of total separation from Ps and that parental custody would have resulted in harmful deprivation of essential human needs, contrary to Phillip's best interests.

4) It must be strongly emphasized that this decision is not just based on the fact that the biological parents would keep the child institutionalized and that the nonparents are willing to offer the child the advantages of their home. But the totality of the evidence permits no other rational conclusion than that Phillip's best interests are with Ps.

d.   **Comment.** In an earlier action, Phillip's parents had succeeded in defeating an attempt to have him declared a temporary ward of the court so that the surgery could be performed. The court had refused to override the decision of his parents refusing surgery, because Phillip's life was not in imminent danger at the time.

C.   ALTERNATIVE PRESUMPTIONS

1.   **Sex-Neutral Custodial Presumption.** To move away from the facial gender discrimination of a maternal/tender years presumption, some states have adopted a "primary caretaker" presumption. At present, the practical effects of both presumptions (custody to mothers in most cases) are about the same.

Garska v.
McCoy

a.   **Presumption in favor of the "primary caretaker"--Garska v. McCoy,** 278 S.E.2d 357 (W. Va. 1981).

1)   **Facts.** Garska (P) brought this action to gain custody of his child. McCoy (D) was the natural mother of the child; however, P and D had never been married. D received no support from P during the pregnancy and very little support after. After being born, the child needed considerable medical attention; in order to pay for it, D's grandparents began adoption proceedings so that the child would receive the grandparent's insurance benefits. D signed a consent for adoption. P then brought this action to gain custody and began sending $15 a week for support of the child. A recently adopted state statute had abolished the tender years doctrine in favor of the mother, so the trial court held that the father was in better financial position to take care of the child. D appeals.

2)   **Issue.** Should a presumption in favor of the primary caretaker be used to help determine who shall gain custody of a child when a state statute has recently abolished the tender years presumption in favor of the mother?

3)   **Held.** Yes. The judgment is reversed.

a)   The recent state statute abolishes all gender-based presumptions and establishes a "best interest of the child" standard. There is no evidence before us to indicate that the mother was an unfit parent and, consequently, there was no justification for the trial court to remove custody from the primary caretaker parent and vest it in a parent who had had no previous emotional interaction with the child.

b)   The loss of a child is terrifying, and particularly so to the primary caretaker, who is closest to the child. The primary caretaker may be either parent in any given case. The best interests of the children are usually best served in awarding them to the primary caretaker parent, regardless of sex.

c) Judges cannot measure minute gradations of psychological capacity between two fit parents. The legislature has concluded that private settlements are preferable to judicial ordering. Uncertainty of the outcome is very destructive of the position of the primary caretaker parent because he or she will be willing to sacrifice everything else in order to avoid the possibility of losing the child.

d) We hold there is a presumption in favor of the primary caretaker parent if he or she meets the minimum objective standard for being a fit parent. The first thing a court must do in a custody case is to determine who the primary caretaker is by considering who had the care and nurturing duties. Where the care and custody of the child is equal, no presumption arises. If the primary caretaker qualifies as a fit parent, the trial court must award custody to that parent. In the case at hand D is the primary caretaker; she is a fit parent and should be awarded custody.

4) **Comment.** This is a good example of how the courts can compromise between their prior opinions and legislative rules.

D. MODERN CUSTODIAL ARRANGEMENTS

1. **"Split" Custody.** A popular modern form of custody is called "joint" or "split" custody, whereby both parents are given legal and alternating physical custody of children. Inasmuch as this approach encourages continued paternal involvement with the children, it is a positive approach. However, inasmuch as it replaces realistic assessment of the actual situation with an idealistic model, it may backfire in some cases.

   a. **Determining "joint" or "shared" custody--*In re* Marriage of Weidner,** 338 N.W.2d 351 (Iowa 1983).

   In re
   Marriage
   of Weidner

      1) **Facts.** Marvin Weidner (P) and Betsy Weidner (D) were married for more than 10 years. Two children were born from the marriage. Disagreements and separations began after only five years of marriage, and the strife between the parties continued until the divorce. During the separation before the initial divorce proceeding, both parties spent about an equal amount of time with the children; however, the mother was the primary physical custodian and took care of the children's day-to-day activities. Neither party trusted the other and there was much tension and disagreement concerning the separation and custody of the children. The Iowa Code allowed for joint custody on the application of either parent and if the court determined it was in the best interest of the children after weighing several factors. P petitioned the court to grant joint custody to both parties, but the trial court denied the petition, and granted sole custody of the children to D. P appeals.

      2) **Issue.** Should the trial court have granted joint custody of the children in accordance with the husband's request?

3) **Held.** No. The judgment is affirmed.

a) There is solid support in the record for the trial court's findings about the feasibility of joint custody for these parents. The parents' general inability to communicate and to make shared child-raising decisions wreaked havoc in the lives of the parents and, more importantly, in the lives of their children.

b) The post-separation period of living with one and then the other parent was confusing to the children and created loyalty conflicts with the older child. Although the legislature had listed eight factors for the trial court to consider when determining joint custody, there is no magic number of these factors that will mandate a decision for or against such custody. In the last analysis, the determination must reflect the best interests of the children.

c) Joint custody is preferred because, properly tailored to the parties' circumstances, joint custodial arrangements will often encourage both parents to share the rights and responsibilities, as well as the joyful and meaningful experiences of raising their children.

d) Although a therapist recommended joint custody, it was on the condition that both parties would change their recent pattern of behavior. Those preconditions to successful joint custody arrangements are unlikely to be satisfactorily met based on the parties' demonstrated antagonism toward each other.

4) **Comment.** The court followed the school of thought that child custody should be settled once and thereafter not disturbed unless absolutely necessary.

E. ALTERNATIVE MEANS OF DISPUTE RESOLUTION

1. **The Need for a Better System.** In the past decade, a powerful movement toward alternative means of dispute resolution in domestic relations disputes—particularly in custody disputes—has developed. This reflects the growing recognition that the system for resolving disputes over individual rights among "strangers" living in the same society is not the best or most efficient system for resolving disputes over overlapping "family rights" among persons who have (or at least have had) very intimate relations with each other.

2. **Mediation and Arbitration.** Mediation and arbitration appear to offer hope for more just and effective, as well as less expensive, resolution of family legal disputes. Statutes in a number of states now provide for this alternative in custody disputes. [*See, e.g.,* Conn. Gen. Stat. §46b-54]

F. VISITATION

1. **Temporary and Limited Custody.** It is common for one parent to be designated the primary custodian of a child or children, and for the other parent to be allowed "visitation" rights—regular, temporary periods of time to associate and interact with the child. Conceptually these are periods of shifting custodianship. When the parents are quarreling over other matters (*e.g.*, property division, alimony, child support), it is not uncommon for the visitation relationship to be affected.

   a. **Parent's obligation to noncustodial parent--Schutz v. Schutz,** 581 So. 2d 1290 (Fla. 1991).

      1) **Facts.** Laurel and Richard Schutz were divorced. Under a modified judgment, Laurel was awarded sole custody of the children, and Richard was given visitation rights and ordered to pay child support. The mother moved the children from Miami to Georgia without initially notifying the father. Richard tried to visit his children three times, but found an empty house because he had not been told that Laurel and the children had moved back to Miami. He found them four years later, visited the children, and discovered they "hated, despised, and feared him" because of his lack of child support payments and visitation. After this incident, various motions for custody, support, and visitation were filed by both parties. The trial court found that Laurel had nurtured the children's belligerence toward Richard and breached every duty she owed as the custodial parent. The court ordered Laurel to do everything in her power to create in the minds of her children a loving feeling toward her former husband, and found that she was not protected by the First Amendment from the requirement that she undo the harm that she had already caused. Laurel appealed, and the appeals court affirmed. Laurel appeals.

      2) **Issue.** Is a mother protected by the First Amendment from the requirement that she fulfill her legal obligation to undo the harm she had already caused by nurturing the belligerence of her children toward her former husband?

      3) **Held.** No. Although we do not approve the district court's construction or analysis, the result reached is approved.

         a) A custodial parent has an affirmative obligation to both the child and the noncustodial parent to encourage and nurture the relationship between the child and the noncustodial parent. The obligation may be met by encouraging the child to interact with the noncustodial parent, acting in good faith regarding visitation, and refraining from doing anything likely to undermine the relationship fostered by parent-child interaction.

         b) There is no abuse of discretion in requiring the mother to do everything in her power to create in the minds of her children a loving feeling toward her former husband. The state's interest in restoring a meaningful relationship between the parties' children and their father, thereby promoting the best interests of the children, is substantial. There is no requirement that the mother express opinions she does not hold, a practice disallowed by the First Amendment.

Matter of Marriage of Cabalquinto

b. **Homosexuality--Matter of Marriage of Cabalquinto,** 669 P.2d 886 (Wash. 1983).

1) **Facts.** Ernest (P) and Cheryll (D) Cabalquinto were divorced in 1976, two years after the birth of their son, Michael. The Colorado divorce decree awarded custody to D, with "liberal" visitation during the summer months and alternate major holidays to P. After the divorce, D and Michael moved to Washington, and P moved to San Francisco. For four years after the divorce, P visited Michael once or twice a year in Washington. In 1980, when Michael was six years old, D refused P's request that Michael be allowed to go with P to California to visit him for several weeks. P filed a petition in Washington state court seeking a clarifying or modifying order compelling D to allow Michael to go to California for a lengthy summer visit with P. D objected, stating that P is a homosexual, that P's homosexuality was a cause of the breakup of the marriage, and that P is living with a homosexual companion in California. The trial court denied P's petition, finding that reasonable visitation in Washington fulfilled the Colorado visitation decree and was in the best interests of the child.

2) **Issue.** Did the trial court err in denying P's petition that D be ordered to send Michael to California to visit him when it is unclear whether the trial court considered P's homosexuality to be a substantial reason for denying the petition?

3) **Held.** Yes. The case is remanded.

   a) Trial courts are accorded substantial discretion in determining custody and visitation disputes, and will ordinarily only be reversed if there is a manifest abuse of discretion.

   b) While the written record shows no erroneous overreliance on P's homosexuality, the trial judge expressed strong antipathy to homosexual living arrangements.

   c) P's witnesses testified that visitation in California would not be harmful to Michael, and there was no evidence to the contrary.

   d) In *Schuster v. Schuster*, 585 P.2d 130 (Wash. 1978), we held that homosexuality in and of itself is not a bar to custody or reasonable visitation. The best interests of the child must be the paramount consideration.

4) **Concurring in part, dissenting in part** (Scalia, J.).

   a) In making P's homosexuality the primary consideration, the trial court ignored not only the best interests of the child but also the parental rights of P.

b) The trial court's finding that Michael might be harmed by exposure to the homosexual environment of P's residence is not supported by any evidence in the record. P is a loving father with a "stable home environment."

c. **No parental rights for former live-in partner--Alison D. v. Virginia M.,** 572 N.E.2d 27 (N.Y. 1991).

1) **Facts.** Alison D. (P) and Virginia M. (D) had lived together and agreed that D would be artificially inseminated. P shared all birthing expenses, provided support, and cared for the child jointly with D. When the parties terminated their relationship two years after the birth of the child, P moved out of their jointly owned home and both parties agreed to a visitation schedule. P agreed to pay half of the mortgage and household expenses. Three years later, R bought out P's interest in the home and began to restrict P's visitation. One year later, P moved to Ireland but continued to attempt to communicate with the child. D terminated all contact between the child and P. P brought a habeas corpus petition to obtain visitation rights. The supreme court dismissed. P appealed and the supreme court, appellate division, affirmed. P appeals.

2) **Issue.** Is a woman who had a live-in relationship with a child's mother a "parent" within the meaning of a statute allowing "either parent" to apply for a writ of habeas corpus to determine the issue of visitation rights following the termination of the parties' relationship?

3) **Held.** No. The order is affirmed.

   a) It has long been recognized in this state that, as between a parent and a third person, parental custody of a child may not be displaced absent grievous cause or necessity.

   b) P concedes that (i) she is not the child's parent in that she is not the biological mother of the child nor a legal parent by virtue of adoption, and (ii) respondent is a fit parent.

   c) Where the legislature deemed it appropriate, it gave other categories (*e.g.*, siblings and grandparents) of persons standing to seek visitation and gave the courts the power to determine whether visitation would be in the child's best interests. We decline P's invitation to read the term parent in the relevant statute to include categories of nonparents who have developed a relationship with a child, or who have had prior relationships with a child's parents and who wish to continue visitation with the child.

4) **Dissent.** Our holding firmly closes the door on all consideration of the child's best interest in visitation proceedings such as the one before us, unless petitioner is a biological parent. The parties explicitly planned to raise the child together. I would remand the matter for an exercise of the court's discretion in determining whether P stands in loco parentis to the child and whether it is in the child's best interest to allow P the visitation rights she claims.

G. FOSTER PARENT-CHILD RELATIONS

1. **The Status of Foster Parents.** As previously noted, there is a strong presumption in law that biological parents make the "best" child raisers of their offspring. Adoptive parents are, by statute, treated much like biological parents. However, foster parents traditionally have not enjoyed the same legal status or parental rights that natural parents have been accorded.

2. **The Rights of Foster Parents vs. Natural Parents.** One of the most important social developments of this century was the change in state practice from institutional care (*e.g.*, orphanages, workhouses, correctional facilities) to foster home care for abused or neglected children. Yet, even this success has had its excesses. During the last decade, there has been much concern that foster homes have become dumping grounds for unwanted children, and that foster care has been used to find "better" homes for children of fit and loving, but unconventional, parents.

Smith v.
Organization
of Foster
Families for
Equality &
Reform

a. **Removal from foster homes--Smith v. Organization of Foster Families for Equality & Reform,** 431 U.S. 816 (1977).

   1) **Facts.** The Organization of Foster Families for Equality & Reform (P), an organization of foster parents, filed a section 1983 action on behalf of foster parents and foster children who have lived together for a year or more, seeking declarative and injunctive relief against the laws of New York (D) governing removal of foster children from foster homes. The policy of the New York system is for children to remain with, or be returned to, the natural parents. Most New York foster care placements are voluntary, occurring when family crises make it impossible for the natural parents to provide stable home lives for their children for some temporary period. The natural parents sign a written agreement transferring care and custody of the child to an authorized child welfare agency. The agreement may provide for the return of the child on a certain date, or when conditions are met; if not, the child must be returned by the agency within 20 days of notice from the parent. By court order, children may be transferred to the custody of such agencies upon finding, after full adversary hearing, that the child has been abused or neglected or is in need of supervision. Return of the child to the natural parents then occurs only upon court order.

   Foster parents who are licensed by the state or an authorized agency provide child care under contract for pay. Such contracts usually reserve the right of the agency to remove the child; the foster parent may cancel the contract at will. Thus, the agency assumes legal "care and custody" of the child. The foster parents have the day-to-day supervision of the child, and the parent retains some authority (*e.g.*, in granting permission for marriage, military enlistment, etc.).

   Removal procedures are established in the law. Except in emergencies, the agency must notify the foster parents in writing

10 days before removal. The foster parents may request a conference if they object, and the conference must be scheduled within 10 days of receipt of such request. Counsel may be present at the conference; reasons for the removal will be explained; and objections of the foster parents will be heard. Within five days after the conference, the official must render a written decision and notify the foster parents. Removal is stayed up to this point. If removal is still determined, the foster parents may appeal and obtain a full adversary administrative hearing, but removal is not automatically stayed. In New York City, a full adversary hearing is provided before removal on request. State family courts have jurisdiction to review removal orders involving any child who has been in foster care 18 months or longer. The district court held that these procedures were inadequate, and that a full adversary hearing involving all concerned persons, including natural parents, constitutionally must precede removal of children in foster care for one year or more.

2) Issues.

    a)   Do foster parents have a fundamental liberty interest in the continuity of their relations with foster children?

    b)   Is a full adversary hearing involving all persons claiming any interest in a foster child required before a child welfare agency removes a child from its foster parents?

3) Held. a) Probably not. b) No. The judgment is reversed.

    a)   Foster care involves care in a family other than the natural family of a child for a planned, nonpermanent period, and it is a sensitive and emotion-laden subject.

            Foster care has been condemned by natural parents and others as a class-based intrusion into the lives of poor families. Female-headed and minority families are most frequently affected. Many "voluntary" foster care placements are coerced by threat of neglect proceedings. There is evidence that middle-class social workers favor continued foster care rather than return of the children to the poorer, less conventional natural parents. The median time spent in "temporary" foster care was over four years. The longer a child remains in foster care, the less likely that he will ever return to his natural parents. Nearly 60% of children in foster care in New York City experience more than one placement; more than 25% go through three or more.

            The first inquiry is whether the interest asserted by the foster families is protected by the Fourteenth Amendment. P asserts that a psychological tie is created between foster parents and children who live with them for a year or more, and that family privacy protects that relationship. But the usual understanding of "family" implies biological relations that are absent here. Yet the importance of family relations stems from emotional attachments, not unlike those claimed by P. But, there are distinctions between family ties that have been protected by the Fourteenth Amendment and those asserted by P. Natural family relations have their origins entirely apart from the power of the state, while foster family relations are state-created. Also, any recognition of the "family" interests of foster parents would be at the expense of the established constitutional rights of the natural parents. Because other grounds exist for reversing the lower court, however, it is unnecessary to resolve this issue.

b) Even if P's assertion about a protectible interest were true, the New York laws provide "what process is due" to protect that interest. Due process requires considering the private interest that will be affected, the risk of erroneous deprivation of a protected interest, and the government's interest, including the burden that additional procedures will impose. Joinder of the foster child and the natural parents in the New York City hearing is not required in light of the nature of the interests at stake and the minimal additional information they could provide. Nor is a hearing required to return the child to the natural parents. The setting of judicial review at 18 months of foster care, instead of at 12 months, is not error.

4) **Concurrence** (Stewart, J., Burger, C.J., Rehnquist, J.). The state has deprived no one of liberty or property. New York law provides no basis for a justifiable expectation by foster families that their relations will continue indefinitely. If "psychological ties" develop, that is a failure of the system designed for temporary care and preparation of the child for return to his natural or adoptive parents.

H. ENFORCEMENT OF CUSTODY DEGREES

1. Continued Court Involvement.

Griffin v.
Griffin

a. **Joint agreement provisions are practically unenforceable--Griffin v. Griffin,** 699 P.2d 407 (Colo. 1985) (en banc).

1) **Facts.** Clarence (P) and Mary (D) Griffin were divorced in September 1979. The divorce decree incorporated a separation agreement providing D would have custody of their son, Hardy, but P would have certain full legal rights, and both parties would fully and equally participate in the education of Hardy. Eleven months later, P filed a motion in the state district court to enforce the agreement, alleging that D was planning to enroll Hardy in the Vidya School, run by the Tibetan Buddhist Community, which he believed would hamper Hardy's development. Because P had declined an opportunity to investigate the school personally, the court denied his motion and Hardy attended the Vidya School that year. In May 1981, P again filed a motion to enforce the separation agreement, asserting that D refused to discuss the child's schooling or allow P to participate in the school selection. P asked the court to order P and D to meet to select a school, and, if the parties could not agree, to select a school for them. The court denied the motion. The court of appeals reversed. D appeals.

2) **Issue.** Is a "joint selection of schools" provision enforceable in court?

3) Held. No. The court of appeals judgment is reversed.

   a) Colo. Rev. Stat. section 14-10-130 provides that the custodian is vested with the power to make decisions regarding education, unless the parents agree otherwise, in writing, at the time the custody decree is entered.

   b) Ordinarily, "agreements to agree" are judicially unenforceable because the court cannot force the parties to agree.

   c) Joint agreement provisions are especially inappropriate in custody matters because they are vulnerable to provoking discord between parents, and that is contrary to the best interests of minors.

   d) The court is ill-equipped to determine which school is best for a particular child; parents are in a better position to do this. Resort to the courts to make that decision would foster parental discord.

   e) P has not demonstrated any connection between attendance at Vidya School and the physical or mental health of Hardy—just because it is a Buddhist school, outside the "mainstream" of American life, does not mean it will be harmful to the child. Evidence of religious beliefs is admissible in custody disputes only as it reasonably relates to potential physical or mental harm or benefit to the child.

b. Tort remedies for custodial interference. Some courts have recognized a cause of action for intentional infliction of emotional distress resulting from wrongful denial or interference with custody. Theoretically, the same cause of action could be asserted by a parent denied visitation. Courts are not anxious to embrace such causes of action, but damage remedies may be more practical than perpetual judicial supervision of custody and visitation.

2. Interstate Custody Battles.

a. A move out of state may significantly impair visitation rights, but courts should prevent moving only when avoidable abuse is proven-- Holder v. Polanski, 544 A.2d 852 (N.J. 1988).

Holder v. Polanski

1) Facts. Virginia Holder (P) and Benjamin Polanski (D) separated in 1985, and P was given custody of the two children of the parties, with liberal visitation for D. P wanted to move to Connecticut before the divorce was granted in September 1986. She wanted to live near family there, attend school there, and leave behind bad old memories in New Jersey. D opposed the move because it would make visitation more difficult. P leased a house in Connecticut and planned to move there before school began. The trial court denied the request to remove the children from New Jersey to prevent alienation of the children from D and because P did not establish that the out-of-state move would be in the best interests of the children. P appealed the decision, but moved to Connecticut as planned. She then moved to change custody, and the court granted D residential custody in New Jersey. D has now had custody of the children for nearly two years.

2) **Issue.** Must a custodial parent wishing to move out of state over objections of the noncustodial parent prove that the move is in the best interests of the children?

3) **Held.** No. The judgment is reversed and the case is remanded.

a) Implicit upon granting custody to one parent and visitation to another is the right of the noncustodial parent to move out of state. The custodial parent should be as free to move as the noncustodial parent, as men and women approach parity in society.

b) N.J. Stat. Rev. section 9-2-2 provides that children below the age of discretion shall not be moved out of state without the consent of both parents or a court. That provision is designed to protect the visitation rights of noncustodial parents.

c) Formerly this court ruled that an out-of-state move by a custodial parent could be approved upon a showing of the advantages of the move, motives of the moving parent, and opportunity for visitation. We modify that rule and authorize out-of-state moves unless they are shown to be contrary to the best interests of the child or the visitation rights of the noncustodial parent. The issue is not potential benefit to the child but possible detriment to the child.

d) P's reasons to move to Connecticut are sufficient to justify the move. Connecticut is not so far from New Jersey that it will substantially change the visitation rights.

e) We are confronted with a living record. In the time that has passed, the children have lived with D, so the court will have to make a new decision on remand based on the facts as they now exist.

4) **Comment.** The idea that a custodial parent should be just as free to move as the noncustodial parent appears to ignore the fact that custodial and noncustodial parents are not similarly situated. It might be more accurate to say that the custodial parent should be just as free to move without disturbing the residence of the children as the noncustodial parent is. Or, it might be more accurate to say that the custodial parent should be just as free to disrupt children's visitation with the noncustodial parent as the noncustodial parent is. But the "why not" approach is remarkably injudicious.

3. **Child Snatching.** The problem of "child snatching" and manipulative forum shopping has led to enactment of the Uniform Child Custody Jurisdiction Act in all states and the federal enactment of the Parental Kidnapping Prevention Act.

a. **Jurisdiction of custody matters involving different states--Shute v. Shute,** 607 A.2d 890 (Vt. 1992).

1) **Facts.** The parties were married in Vermont. The wife (W) and son moved to Connecticut and nine months later in 1983, W filed for divorce in Vermont. The complaint stated that W's residence had been Connecticut but did not state the residence of the child. At the time of the final order, the court made no findings as to subject matter jurisdiction over child custody. The final order incorporated the parties' stipulation that child custody would be awarded to the wife, subject to reasonable visitation by the husband (H). The parties also agreed that the Vermont courts would have continuing jurisdiction of all issues, including custody, support, and visitation. In 1986, H filed a motion for contempt of the court order granting the divorce and the incorporated stipulation. After two and one-half years of litigation, in 1988, H filed a second motion for contempt and enforcement and W filed a motion to dismiss, claiming lack of subject matter jurisdiction under the Uniform Child Custody Jurisdiction Act ("UCCJA") and inconvenient forum. The court relinquished jurisdiction to Connecticut because Vermont was an inconvenient forum and Connecticut had closer connections to the child. H appeals.

2) **Issue.** Do the jurisdictional requirements of the Parental Kidnapping Prevention Act ("PKPA") preempt the UCCJA when those acts are in conflict?

3) **Held.** Yes. The judgment is affirmed.

    a) The language of the PKPA indicates that Congress intended to pre-empt the field of custody jurisdiction. Therefore, under the Supremacy Clause, the PKPA takes precedence of state law when the two laws conflict.

    b) Under the Vermont UCCJA, there is no preference for one jurisdictional ground over another. It permits the trial court to exercise subject matter jurisdiction if Vermont is a child's home state at the time of commencement of a proceeding, or if it is in the child's best interest that Vermont have jurisdiction.

    c) The Vermont alternate ground provisions conflict with the home state preference of the PKPA when it appears that the child has a home state other than Vermont. We hold that the PKPA preempts that Vermont statute that conflicts with the PKPA.

    d) A Vermont court had jurisdiction under the PKPA if: (i) Vermont was the child's home state and the child lived there, (ii) it appeared no other state had jurisdiction and it was in the best interest of the child to assume jurisdiction, or (iii) another state had declined to exercise jurisdiction in favor of Vermont, or (iv) the original decree was in compliance with the PKPA and Vermont continued to be the residence of the child or any contestant.

    e) In this case, Connecticut was the child's home state; that state has jurisdiction under its own laws and the PKPA, and it has exercised jurisdiction over child custody issues in this case. Moreover, the

Connecticut court will not be bound by the original Vermont decree under the full faith and credit provisions of the PKPA.

f) Subject matter jurisdiction cannot be conferred by the agreement or consent of the parties if it is not given by law.

b. Jurisdiction to modify custody orders--E.E.B. v. D.A., 446 A.2d 871 (N.J. 1982).

1) **Facts.** Prospective adoptive parents (E.E.B.) seek to retain custody of a three and one-half-year-old girl who had lived with them since six days after birth. The natural mother (D.A.) and father, who were not married, signed a sworn "Permanent Surrender of Child" form three days after the child's birth, and three days later the Ohio Welfare Department gave the child to E.E.B. Both E.E.B. and D.A. resided in Ohio until the girl was one year old, whereupon E.E.B. moved to New Jersey for the husband's new job assignment. One week after signing the surrender form, D.A. appeared at the Department and orally revoked the surrender. Thereafter she instituted a habeas corpus proceeding to obtain custody of the child. The Ohio courts denied the writ, but almost two years later the Ohio Supreme Court reversed and the juvenile court then approved the surrender of the child. E.E.B. had moved to conduct a best interest hearing prior to any decision as to whether the writ of habeas corpus should issue. The Ohio court never conducted the best interest hearing, so E.E.B. instituted an action for custody in the New Jersey court where they lived. D.A. did not show up for the hearing. The New Jersey court held that it was in the best interests of the child to remain with her prospective adoptive parents. D.A. appealed the decision of the New Jersey court, arguing that the New Jersey court did not have jurisdiction to modify the Ohio court's order to surrender the child.

2) **Issue.** Did the New Jersey trial court give proper effect to the Ohio determination in light of the Full Faith and Credit Clause, the Federal Parental Kidnapping Prevention Act ("PKPA"), and the Uniform Child Custody Jurisdiction Act ("UCCJA")?

3) **Held.** Yes. The judgment is affirmed.

a) Both the UCCJA and the PKPA permit the courts of the forum state to modify the custody determination of another state on two conditions: the forum has jurisdiction over the matter, and the other state either lost jurisdiction or has declined to exercise it. New Jersey has jurisdiction because it is the home state of the child as defined by UCCJA and because of the significant connection to the forum. Also, Ohio's failure to conduct a best interest hearing at the request of E.E.B. constitutes a refusal to exercise jurisdiction under the PKPA. Therefore New Jersey is free to modify the Ohio decree.

b) In exercising its discretion within the confines of the UCCJA and the PKPA, a court should consider not only the literal wording of the statutes, but their purpose: to define and stabilize the right to custody in the best interest of the child. D.A. did not dispute the New Jersey court's determination that the best interests of the child would be best served by allowing E.E.B. to retain custody. Therefore that finding is affirmed.

4) Note. Another case involving substantially the same issues as *E.E.B.* is *In re Clausen,* 502 N.W.2d 649 (Mich. 1993). Clara Clausen gave birth to a daughter in Iowa. She and the man named as the child's father signed release of custody forms. The DeBoer's filed a petition for adoption in Iowa, were given custody, and took the child to their home in Michigan. Clausen then filed a motion to revoke her release of custody, and Daniel Schmidt, the child's actual father, filed a petition seeking to intervene in the adoption. An Iowa district court held that the petition for adoption should be denied without having considering the best interests of the child. The DeBoers' rights were terminated when they failed to produce the child in court.

The DeBoer's filed a petition in a Michigan court, asking it to assume jurisdiction under the UCCJA. Schmidt and Jessica DeBoer, the child in issue, also filed in Michigan. The circuit court entered an order maintaining the status quo. The Michigan Supreme Court, which granted the DeBoer's application for leave to appeal before an appellate decision was rendered, held that because the Iowa custody determination was made consistent with the terms of the PKPA, the Iowa court's order must be enforced. The United States Supreme Court denied an application for stay. Justices Blackmun and O'Connor dissented, stating that they were not willing to "wash [their] hands of the case" when a child is at risk and the supreme courts of New Jersey (in *E.E.B.*) and Michigan are in fundamental disagreement over the duty and authority of state courts to consider the best interests of the child.

c. No private cause of action under Parental Kidnapping Prevention Act-- **Thompson v. Thompson,** 484 U.S. 174 (1988).

Thompson v. Thompson

1) Facts. David (P) and Susan (D) Thompson were divorced in California in 1978. The parties were awarded joint custody. When D took a job in Louisiana, the court awarded her temporary sole custody pending custody investigation. Three months after moving to Louisiana, D filed a petition for sole custody, and the Louisiana court granted the petition. Two months later, the California court awarded P sole custody based on the custody investigation. P filed an action in federal court to declare the Louisiana decree invalid, the California decree valid, and to enjoin the Louisiana decree under the Parental Kidnapping Prevention Act ("PKPA"). The federal court dismissed the action for lack of subject matter and personal jurisdiction. The ninth circuit affirmed. P appeals.

2) Issue. Does the PKPA create a private cause of action for injunction of custody decrees that violate its terms?

3) Held. No. The judgment is affirmed.

a) The PKPA imposes a duty on states to enforce a child custody determination of a sister state if the court that entered the decree had jurisdiction under the standards of the Act. The purpose of the PKPA is to prevent jurisdiction competition between disputing parents.

b)   Prior to the PKPA, the degree of full faith and credit a state had to give a custody decree entered in another state was unclear. Some courts held that modifiable custody decrees were not final and thus not entitled to full faith and credit. Other courts exercised the power to modify the decrees to the same extent they were modifiable by the courts that entered them. This lack of out-of-state enforceability of custody decrees led to child snatching (an estimated 25,000 to 100,000 per year), forum shopping, and repetitive custody litigation and modification.

c)   Neither the text nor history of the PKPA suggests that Congress intended to create a private cause of action. Congress was concerned about full faith and credit, and the PKPA speaks directly to the states. The legislative history indicates that Congress did not intend federal courts to decide which of two or more state custody decrees was valid. The Department of Justice strongly opposed the creation of a federal forum for resolving custody disputes.

4)   **Comment.** The Uniform Child Custody Jurisdiction Act ("UCCJA") and its parallel federal counterpart, the PKPA, have done much to reduce child snatching in custody disputes. But even the definitions of possible jurisdiction in the UCCJA and PKPA are susceptible of manipulation. Perhaps some discretion is unavoidable in this area of law.

Friedrich v. Friedrich

d.   **Wrongful removal of child from one country to another--Friedrich v. Friedrich,** 983 F.2d 1396 (6th Cir. 1993).

1)   **Facts.** The Friedrichs' were married in Germany and their son was born there. Mrs. Friedrich (W) is a U.S. citizen and a member of the U.S. Army. The couple lived off the base. When they separated after an argument on July 27, 1991, (W) and child moved into the visitors' quarters on the army base. W claimed that this was expensive, that she had no other place to live in Germany, and that her only option was to go back to the United States. She talked with and met with her husband (H) on July 29 and August 1, and H had planned to visit his son during the following week. On August 1, 1991, W returned to the United States with her son without H's knowledge, permission, or consent. W initiated a divorce action in Ohio on August 9; H claims he never received notice of these proceedings. W returned to Germany without her son and sought an emergency discharge from the Army. On August 28, the Ohio court issued a temporary order in favor of W and ordered that her son not be removed from Ohio until further order of the court. H filed a claim in Germany seeking custody. On August 22, a German court granted H custody. W did not receive notice of the proceeding. H filed a petition for return of his son to Germany, alleging W had wrongfully removed her son from Germany in violation of the Hague Convention on Civil Aspects of International Child Abduction ("Convention"). The district court denied the petition. H appeals.

2)   **Issues.**

a)   Was the child a "habitual resident" of Germany rather than the United States?

b) Must the district court determine, under German law, whether Mr. Friedrich was exercising his custody rights at the time of removal or if he would have exercised his rights but for the removal?

3) **Held.** a) Yes. b) Yes. The decision is reversed and the case is remanded.

a) Under the International Child Abductions Remedies Act ("Act"), the parent challenging removal from Germany has the burden of showing by a preponderance of the evidence that the removal was wrongful. The burden then shifts to the other parent to show: (i) by clear and convincing evidence, that there was a grave risk that return would expose the child to physical or psychological harm; (ii) by clear and convincing evidence, that return would not be permitted by fundamental principles relating to protection of human rights and fundamental freedoms; (iii) by a preponderance of the evidence, that the proceeding was commenced more than one year after abduction; or (iv) by a preponderance of the evidence, that the father was not actually exercising his custody right at the time of removal, or had consented to or acquiesced in the removal.

b) Under the Convention, it is wrongful to remove a child from one country to another when "it is a breach of rights of custody attributed to a person . . . under the law of the state in which the child was habitually resident immediately before the removal. . . ." To determine "habitual residence," the court must focus on the child, not the parents, and examine past experience, not future intentions. Habitual residence must not be confused with domicile.

c) For purposes of the Convention and the Act, Germany is the habitual residence of a child who was born in Germany of a German father, and lived exclusively in Germany except for a few short vacations before removal, even though the child has U.S. citizenship, has Ohio as his permanent address for purposes of U.S. documentation, and his mother intended to return to the U.S. when she was discharged.

d) The child's short stay on the base did not alter his habitual residence, nor did it shift when his mother assumed the role of primary caretaker.

e) The mother's removal without the father's knowledge does not alter the child's status, even if the father forced the mother to leave their apartment. A change in geography that could be the basis of such change in status had to occur before the challenged removal.

f) The district court must first determine whether the father was exercising his custody rights at time of removal, such that removal would not violate the Convention and the Act. Expelling the mother and child from the apartment is not sufficiently extraordinary to terminate the father's custody rights in the absence of judicial action.

g) The Convention was intended to address situations where a parent attempts to settle a difficult family situation, and obtain an advantage in any possible future custody struggle, by returning to the parent's native country, or country of preferred residence. Under such circumstances, the Convention is designed to insure that a custody struggle must be carried out, in the first instance, under the laws of the country of habitual residence.

4) Dissent. Absent a finding of clearly erroneous, the trial judge's determination that the father terminated actual exercise of his parental custody rights over the child when the expelled his wife and son from the apartment should be affirmed.

I. INVOLUNTARY TERMINATION OF PARENTAL RIGHTS

1. Due process. For over half a century American courts have maintained that the rights of parents to raise their children are fundamental interests protected by the United States Constitution. Thus, parents must be accorded due process before their child-raising rights are terminated.

Santosky
v. Kramer

    a. Standards of proof in termination hearings--Santosky v. Kramer, 455 U.S. 745 (1982).

        1) Facts. Kramer (P), the Commissioner to the County Department of Social Services, initiated a neglect proceeding against Mr. and Mrs. Santosky (Ds) and removed Ds' three children from the home and placed them in foster homes. This was done on the ground that immediate removal was necessary to avoid imminent danger to the children's life and health. The department then reduced to writing a plan designed to solve the problems at Ds' home and reunite the family. Ds gave little support to the continued and extensive four-year effort, so pursuant to statute P petitioned the family court to terminate Ds' parental rights in the three children. According to the termination statute, in order to terminate parental rights the state had to show by a "fair preponderance of the evidence" that the child is permanently neglected. At the initial hearing, Ds challenged the constitutionality of the fair preponderance of the evidence standard of proof. The trial court rejected the challenge and Ds' parental rights were terminated. The court of appeals affirmed and Ds appeal.

        2) Issue. Does the Due Process Clause of the Fourteenth Amendment require a higher standard of proof in a parental termination hearing than the fair preponderance of the evidence standard set out in the New York statute?

        3) Held. Yes. The judgment is set aside and the case is remanded.

            a) This Court in *Mathews v. Eldridge* specified that the nature of the process due in parental rights termination proceedings turns on a balancing of three distinct factors: the private interests affected by the proceeding, the risk of error created by the State's chosen procedure, and the countervailing governmental interest supporting use of the challenged procedure.

            b) The natural parent's right to care and custody of his or her children is an interest far more precious than any property right. Once affirmed on appeal, a New York decision terminating parental rights is final and irrevocable.

c) Permanent neglect proceedings employ imprecise substantive standards that leave determinations open to the subjective values of the judge. The department has no limits to the sums it may spend prosecuting a given termination proceeding and the State's attorney usually will be an expert. The chance and social cost of even occasional error are sizable.

d) The State's interest in the welfare of the child favors preservation, not severance, of natural familiar bonds.

e) In parental rights termination proceedings, the private interest affected is commanding; the risk of error from using a preponderance standard is substantial; and the countervailing governmental interest favoring that standard is comparatively slight. Therefore the State must support its allegations by at least clear and convincing evidence.

4) **Dissent** (Rehnquist, J., Burger, C.J., White, J., O'Connor, J.). The facts of this case showed the continued unwillingness of Ds to improve their circumstances sufficiently to permit a return of their children, while the State made an extraordinary four-year effort to help them. It is inconceivable that these procedures were fundamentally unfair to Ds. Only by its obsessive focus on the standard of proof and its almost complete disregard of the facts of this case does the majority find otherwise. Because proof by a preponderance of the evidence requires that the litigants share the risk of error in a roughly equal fashion, it rationally should be applied only when the interests at stake are of roughly equal societal importance. The interests at stake in this case (the parents' and the child's) demonstrate that New York has selected a constitutionally permissible standard of proof.

2. Justifying Peremptory Intervention.

a. **Maintaining contact with children is required even of incarcerated parents who wish to maintain their parental rights--Matter of Gregory B., 74 N.Y.2d 77 (1989).**   Matter of Gregory B.

1) **Facts.** D1 is serving a 10- to 20-year felony conviction. His two children, born in 1979 and 1980, are now nine and eight years old. They have resided in foster care with the same family since November 1981. In 1986 the state social services agency petitioned the family court to terminate the rights of both parents. Evidence showed the encouraged parent-child relations to have been of no avail. D1 initially planned to have his children live with his mother until he was released from prison, but the court determined that she was neither physically nor emotionally capable of raising the children. D1 then suggested that the children remain in foster care until he was out of prison. The court found that D1 had permanently neglected the children and terminated parental rights. The appellate division affirmed. D1 appeals.

D2 is serving two concurrent sentences of 25 years to life for murder. His children are 13 and 11 years old. One has been in foster care for 12 years and his foster parents wish to adopt him; the other has been in foster care for nine years and her foster parents wish to adopt her. The agency brought an action to terminate the parental rights of D2. The court found the agency had tried to foster a parent-child relationship by bringing the children to the prison to visit D2 and by contacting relatives who might care for the children, but those efforts were futile. D2 suggested keeping the children in foster care until he was released from prison. With respect to the younger child, the family court dismissed the petition, but granted the petition to terminate parental rights of the older child. The appellate division reversed the order regarding the younger child, and affirmed the order regarding the older child. D2 appeals.

2) **Issue.** Was the termination of parental rights because of Ds' permanent failure to plan for the children justified in these cases?

3) **Held.** Yes. The judgments are affirmed.

a) The threshold determination that must be made in a termination of parental rights ("TPR") action is whether the agency has been diligent in attempting to foster parent-child relations. Here the evidence amply supports the conclusion that the agency was diligent.

b) The TPR statute allows a finding of permanent neglect if there is proof that the parent failed to maintain contact with, or plan for the future of, his or her child. Both Ds here satisfied the minimal contact standard, so the cases turn on whether they adequately planned for the future of their children.

c) The legislature has determined that parental rights will not be terminated solely because a parent is incarcerated. But the legislature also indicated that an incarcerated parent is expected to plan for his or her child's future.

d) Permanence and stability are important to the welfare of children. They cannot simply be "put on hold" in foster care indefinitely. Foster care should not be of permanent or long duration.

In re
Jeffrey E.

b. **Unwillingness to provide parenting responsibilities may justify termination of parental rights--*In re* Jeffrey E., 557 A.2d 954 (Maine 1989).**

1) **Facts.** Jeffrey E. was hospitalized with pneumonia several times in the first year or so of his life. His parents (Ds) were unable to follow through with providing him with the medications and therapies necessary for his health and recovery. In July 1985, Jeffrey was placed in foster care. At that time, he was 17 months old, spoke only two words, could not walk, and was unable to understand simple sentences or use a cup or spoon. Within a few days he was using a cup, and within six weeks he was walking and his vocabulary included 30 words. The following year, he was adjudicated in jeopardy and custody was awarded to the state agency. The agency tried three reunification plans, but Ds did not comply with any of them, nor did they improve their parenting skills. In 1987, the agency petitioned for TPR, and the court granted it. Ds appeal.

2) **Issue.** Does developmental neglect justify termination of parental rights?

3) Held. Yes. The judgment is affirmed.

   a) A finding of jeopardy that justifies TPR may be based on parents' inability to meet a child's special needs. A present medical emergency need not exist.

   b) Jeffrey was susceptible to medical problems, and his parents were unable to improve their parenting skills enough to meet Jeffrey's needs.

   c) There was testimony that the parents did not appropriately discipline their children, and that Jeffrey's mother would scream and swear in response to the children's yelling, kicking, screaming, and hitting.

   d) There was substantial evidence on the record of the inability of Jeffrey's parents to care for him and that TPR was best for Jeffrey.

4) Comment. There is the risk of cultural discrimination when upper middle class professionals judge whether parents from a different background are fit to raise their children.

VIII. ADOPTION

A. HISTORY

Unknown at common law and used to further the interests of adults in Roman law, adoption as a means of providing loving parents for needy children is a uniquely American legal invention.

1. **Defined.** Adoption is a legal proceeding whereby the legal relationship between natural parents and child is terminated, if not previously extinguished, and a new legal relationship of parent and child is established between persons not recognized at common law.

2. **Decline.** The availability of birth control methods, abortion, and a reduced birth rate has severely limited the number of children available for placement in adoption, and this, ironically, has heightened public awareness of and encouragement of adoptions.

B. COMPETING INTERESTS

Involved in the ordinary adoption are the interests of the natural parents, the child, the prospective adoptive parents, and, not infrequently, state agencies attempting to protect state values and children's interests.

1. **Grandparents.**

Matter of Welfare of D.L.

a. **Preference for placement with relatives--Matter of Welfare of D.L.,** 486 N.W.2d 375 (Minn. 1992).

   1) **Facts.** Two-year-old D.L. had been living with Caucasian foster parents since she was four days old. The foster parents and D.L.'s black maternal grandparents both filed petitions to adopt D.L. upon termination of the natural parents' parental rights. The trial court granted the grandparents' petition based on statutory family preference for adoption of minority children. The appeals court found the statute unconstitutional, but affirmed the trial court's result on common law grounds. The foster parents appeal.

   2) **Issues.** Is adoptive placement with family members presumptively in the best interest of the child?

   3) **Held.** Yes. The judgment is affirmed.

      a) All three branches of state government have expressed a preference for placement with family members, regardless of race, when parental rights have been terminated. This consensus reflects the idea that blood relatives are most likely to look out for one another's interests.

      b) Absent a showing of good cause to the contrary or detriment to the child, adoptive placement with a family member is presumptively in the best interest of a child.

c) The fact that initial separation from foster parents would be initially painful to the child is not the "good cause" needed to defeat the preference.

d) In exercising its broad discretion in determining the best interests of potential adoptees, the trial court must make detailed findings of fact showing that the child's best interests are being served. Here, the trial court made findings on the grandparents' health, their emotional and financial stability, the nurturing environment of their home, the presence in their home of D.L.'s two sisters, and the grandparents' willingness to supply the love and comfort D.L. will need in this transitional period of her life.

b. Adoption by same-sex cohabitants--Adoption of Tammy, 619 N.E.2d 315 (Mass. 1993).

Adoption
of Tammy

1) **Facts.** Two unmarried cohabitating women, Susan and Helen, filed a joint petition to adopt Tammy, who is Susan's biological daughter. The women have lived together for 10 years and planned to have a child biologically related to both of them. Susan conceived through artificial insemination by Helen's biological cousin, Francis. Francis is named as the father on Tammy's birth certificate, but Tammy was given a hyphenated surname using Susan's and Helen's last names. Both women have raised and supported Tammy in a secure and comfortable environment. Francis does not participate in parenting Tammy; he signed an adoption surrender and supports a joint adoption by both women. Helen and her living issue are beneficiaries of three substantial irrevocable family trusts, and without the benefit of adoption, Helen's share of the trusts may pass to others. Both women's families unreservedly endorsed the adoption petition. The petition was granted as being in the best interest of the child, and at the same time, the judge reported to the appeals court the evidence and all questions of law in an effort to secure the decree from attack in the future. The appeals court transferred the case.

2) **Issues.**

a) Did the probate judge have jurisdiction to enter a judgment on a joint petition for adoption brought by two unmarried female cohabitants when the judge found that the joint adoption was in the child's best interest?

b) Must Susan's legal relationship to Tammy be terminated if Tammy is adopted?

3) **Held.** a) Yes. b) No. The decree is affirmed in part and vacated in part.

a) There is nothing on the face of the statute which precludes the joint adoption of a child by two unmarried cohabitants such as the petitioners.

b) The statute states "a person of full age may petition . . . for leave to adopt . . . ." In the context of adoption, where the legislative intent of promoting the best interests of the child is evidenced throughout the statute, and the adoption by two unmarried individuals accom-

Domestic Relations - 113

plishes that goal, construing the term "person" as "persons" clearly enhances, rather than defeats, the purpose of the statute.

c) It is in the best interests of Tammy to be adopted jointly; the women have a stable and committed relationship, both participate in parenting, both are viewed as parents by Tammy, the child will benefit practically, and adoption would allow her to maintain her unique filial ties to her mother's partner if her mother predeceases her partner or is separated from her.

d) The statute's provision that all parental rights terminate between the child adopted and his natural parents as a result of the adoption was not intended by the legislature to apply to a natural parent's legal relationship when the natural parent is a party to the adoption petition.

e) The purpose of this provision is to protect the child's newly-created family unit.

4) Dissent. I subscribe to the dissent which follows although I do not agree with the first few sentences (which discuss lifestyle choices).

5) Dissent. I do not disapprove of the petitioners or their lifestyle, nor is my disagreement related to petitioners' sexual orientation. There is nothing in the statute indicating a legislative intent to allow two or more unmarried persons to jointly petition for adoption. The plain meaning of the statute cannot be expanded or altered where the legislature establishes specific criteria or classifications to be satisfied. The Massachusetts statute only allows joint petitions for adoption by married persons.

2. Terminating Parental Rights. Every adoption involves two steps: termination of parental rights and creation of a new legal parent-child relationship. The first step is often difficult.

a. Father of illegitimate children--Stanley v. Illinois, *supra* at p. 4.

Lehr v. Robertson

b. Putative father's right to be heard--Lehr v. Robertson, 463 U.S. 248 (1983).

1) Facts. Lehr (P) brought this action to set aside an adoption order entered for Robertson (D). Jessica was born out of wedlock. D (Jessica's mother) married another man eight months after Jessica's birth. When Jessica was over two years old, D and her husband filed an adoption petition in the Ulster Family Court. At about the same time, P (the child's natural father) filed a visitation and paternity petition in the Westchester Family Court. Before the outcome of the paternity petition, the Ulster Court entered the order for adoption, even though the judge knew of the pending paternity suit. The Westchester Court thereby granted D's motion to dismiss the paternity suit because an adoption order had already been entered. P argues that he, as the father, had a constitutional right to prior notice and an opportunity to be heard before he was deprived of that interest. P also argues that the statute requiring notice to only certain putative fathers, while the mother of an illegitimate child is always in the favored class, is gender-based and violates the Equal Protection Clause.

2) **Issues.**

    a)   Did the State's failure to notify P of the adoption petition constitute a violation of due process?

    b)   Does the statute requiring notice to be given to only certain putative fathers violate the Equal Protection Clause?

3) **Held.** a) No. b) No. The judgment is affirmed.

    a)   Parental rights do not spring full blown from the biological connection between parent and child. They require relationships that are more enduring. Where an unwed father demonstrates a full commitment to the rearing of his child, his interest in personal contact with the child acquires substantial protection under the Due Process Clause, but the mere existence of a biological link does not merit equivalent constitutional protection. P did not seek to establish a legal tie until after Jessica was two years old. The right to receive notice was completely in P's control. By mailing a postcard to the putative father registry, he could have guaranteed that he would have received notice of any proceedings to adopt Jessica. Ignorance of the law is not a sufficient reason for criticizing the law.

    b)   Because P had never established a substantial relationship with his daughter, the statute did not operate to deny him equal protection. If one parent has an established custodial relationship with the child and the other parent has either abandoned or never established a relationship, the Equal Protection Clause does not prevent a state from according the two parents different legal rights.

4) **Dissent** (White, Marshall, Blackmun, JJ.). P's version of the facts paints a far different picture than that portrayed by the majority. P visited D in the hospital every day during her confinement from having the child. From the time D was discharged, however, she kept her whereabouts concealed from P. He had to hire a private detective before he finally located D and his child. He then requested that D permit him to visit Jessica and, perhaps in response, D commenced the adoption action at issue here. The biological connection is itself a relationship that creates a protected interest. The fact that the relationship exists is enough that it is entitled to constitutional protection. States cannot be expected to give every father notice or to use exhaustive methods before a final adoption order is entered. However, in this case the court knew precisely who the father was and where he could be reached to give him notice that his parental rights were about to be terminated. Because they failed to do so, the court violated his right to due process.

5) **Comment.** While *Lehr* is the latest word on the subject of parental rights of unwed fathers, it undoubtedly will not be the last. The actual contact or relationship between father and child is clearly a critical factor.

c. **Unwed father seeks to vacate adoption--Robert O. v. Russell K.,** 604 N.E.2d 99 (N.Y. 1992).

1) **Facts.** Petitioner, Robert O. (P), was engaged to Carol when she became pregnant. The relationship ended, but Carol did not reveal the pregnancy. The respondents, Russell and Joanne K. (D), who were friends of Carol, adopted the child after Carol executed a judicial consent. Carol was never asked to identify the father. She signed a statement indicating, accurately, that under the relevant statute there was no one entitled to notice of the adoption. P had not attempted to contact Carol although she did nothing to conceal her whereabouts or her pregnancy. The couple reconciled and married, and 10 months after the adoption, Carol told P that a child had been born. P, in a belated effort to meet statutory requirements for notice and consent, reimbursed Carol for medical expenses, registered with the Putative Father Registry, and commenced this proceeding to vacate the adoption. The family court rejected P's claim of fraud or concealment of a material fact in the adoption and concluded P had no constitutional right to notice of the adoption proceedings or to veto or consent to the adoption. The appellate court affirmed. P appeals.

2) **Issue.** Because New York laws fail to require notice and consent to one in P's position (an "unknowing" unwed father), has P been denied a constitutional liberty interest?

3) **Held.** No. The order is affirmed.

   a) The Supreme Court has recognized that some unwed fathers, by their conduct in relation to their children, enjoy constitutionally protected parental rights. The biological connection alone is not sufficient; the unwed father must "grasp the opportunity" to form a relationship with his child.

   b) We have recognized that an unwed father has a right to veto an adoption if he manifests a willingness to assume full custody of the child. Factors that indicate that willingness include whether the father paid the mother's medical bills, whether he held himself out to be the father, and, most significantly, whether his manifestation of willingness took place promptly. The standards presuppose the father knows he has a child.

   c) Promptness is measured not by the onset of the father's awareness, but in terms of the baby's life. The demand for promptness is a logical and necessary outgrowth of the state's legitimate interest in the child's need for early permanence and stability.

   d) The constitutionally-protected opportunity, and the one pertinent to this case, was the opportunity to develop a qualifying relationship with the infant.

   e) P seeks to protect not this opportunity, but the opportunity to manifest his willingness, even though no one prevented him from finding out about Carol's pregnancy.

4) Concurrence. Due process does not require the unraveling of a 10-month-old adoption at the request of the biological father whose identity was unknown and unknowable at the time. The law, however, should not hold P accountable for failing to discover his former fiancee's pregnancy. This is out of step with modern mores and the reality of contemporary heterosexual liaisons. In this case, the state's interest in finality of adoptions outweighs P's interest, even though the rule may omit potentially responsible fathers in P's position.

d. Courts are reluctant to terminate parental rights to facilitate stepparent adoption-D.A. v. D.R.L., 727 P.2d 768 (Alaska 1986).

D.A. v. D.R.L.

1) Facts. D.R.L (D) and L.A. were divorced in 1982, and L.A. was given custody of their daughter, L.R.A. D visited the child about once a month for 10 months until L.A. married D.A. (P). D then telephoned about once a month to inquire about the infant (then about two years old), except during a three-month period when L.A. and her new husband were in Arizona. For the next four or five months D did not visit the child. P then filed a petition to adopt the child. P presented evidence that D had sent no Christmas or birthday cards to the child, and that D had requested a few visits but had been denied them. D did not present any evidence but moved for a directed verdict. The Superior Court granted the motion.

2) Issue. Did the Superior Court err in denying P's petition for adoption without the consent of D?

3) Held. No. The judgment is affirmed.

a) Alaska's forfeiture of consent statute has been strictly construed. It provides that if a parent has for at least one year failed significantly and without justification to communicate meaningfully with the child, the parental rights of that parent may be terminated in an adoption proceeding. However, where the child is too young to read or talk over the telephone, the courts have been lenient to the parent.

b) Here the young age of the child, the mother's denial of requested visitation, and the three-month absence from the state excuse the lack of communication by D. There is adequate evidence to support the court's decision. P failed to carry his burden of proof.

4) Dissent. A child's absence from the state does not automatically toll the one-year statutory period. P made a prima facie case of failure to communicate; then the burden shifted to D to produce evidence to excuse that failure. Emotional antagonism by the custodial parent does not excuse failure to communicate.

5) Dissent. There is no evidence that D even tried to communicate with his daughter while she was out of state. Absence from the state does not excuse failure to communicate.

6) Comment. Does Alaska's geographic location have something to do with the emphasis on the effect absence from the state has on the duty to communicate?

e. **Adoption considerations.** It has only been since the 1960s that much attention has been shown to the rights of noncustodial parents when a stepparent wants to adopt. During the past three decades, courts have given priority to the rights of the *de jure* parent (the noncustodial parent) over the rights of the *de facto* parent (the stepparent).

1) **Revocation of consent.** Today withdrawal of consent to adoption is disfavored.

2) **Race and religion.** Consideration of race or religion of competing parents or would-be parents is not prohibited, but may not be solely dispositive and is relevant only as it relates to determining what is in the best interests of the child.

3) **Marital status and sexual practices.** Marital status and sexual behavior are likewise relevant considerations, but may not be totally dispositive factors. The underlying assumption is that it might be in the best interest of the child for a person with one such unusual factor to still be the best choice for custodian of a child. Certainly the facts in some cases seem to vindicate that assumption.

Mississippi Band of Choctaw Indians v. Holyfield

f. **Indian Child Welfare Act gives tribal courts custody jurisdiction despite wishes of Indian parents--Mississippi Band of Choctaw Indians v. Holyfield, 490 U.S. 30 (1989).**

1) **Facts.** The Indian Child Welfare Act ("ICWA") resulted from concern about the separation of Indian children from their Indian heritage and families. Congress heard testimony that 25-35% of all Indian children were placed for adoption, foster care, or in institutions, and that one-eighth of all minor Indian children were placed out for adoption; 90% of Indian placements were in non-Indian homes. The Indian culture was considered at risk. The ICWA section 1911(a) gives tribal courts exclusive jurisdiction of custody-related proceedings of any Indian child residing or domiciled on the reservation. Section 1911(b) gives state and tribal courts concurrent jurisdiction over such proceedings regarding children not domiciled on the reservation. Adoptive placement must favor members of the child's extended family, other members of the child's tribe, and other Indian families over any non-Indian families. The children at issue here, BB and GB, are twins. They were born out of wedlock and off the reservation to Indian parents who were domiciled on the reservation. Their parents signed consent to adoption forms, and they were adopted by the Holyfields (Ds). Two months later, the Mississippi Band of Choctaw Indians (P) moved to vacate the adoption decree on the ground that state court lacked jurisdiction. The court denied the motion, and the Supreme Court of Mississippi affirmed. Both courts found that under state law, the children were not domiciled on the reservation. P appeals.

2) **Issue.** Under the ICWA, is a child born off a reservation to an unmarried Indian woman who immediately relinquishes the child for adoption domiciled on the reservation because the mother's domicile is on the reservation?

3) **Held.** Yes. The judgment is reversed and the case is remanded.

a) The adoption proceeding was a custody proceeding for purposes of the ICWA.

b) The meaning of "domicile" is not specified in the text or history of the ICWA.

c) There is no evidence that Congress intended to incorporate state domicile law into the ICWA. It would result in a lack of uniformity, thus partially defeating the purpose of the ICWA.

d) As a matter of general common law, the domicile of a child is that of the parents; if the child is born out of wedlock, it is the domicile of the mother.

e) The statement of the Mississippi Supreme Court that the children here were never domiciled on the reservation is not the prevailing rule.

f) Tribal court jurisdiction may not be defeated by the acts of the Indian parents. The ICWA was designed to protect Indian tribes and culture, not Indian parents.

g) Three years have passed since the children were adopted by Ds. We hope the tribal court will recognize the ties that have developed, but the decision is the tribal court's.

4) **Dissent** (Stevens, J., Rehnquist, C.J., Kennedy, J.). I agree hat a uniform federal definition of "domicile" must be given to achieve the purposes of the ICWA. But the Court's definition is too narrow. If a child is abandoned by its father, it takes the domicile of its mother; if abandoned by its mother, it takes the domicile of its father; if abandoned by both (as here), it takes the domicile of the person standing in loco parentis—in this case, Ds. The purpose of the ICWA is to prevent unjustified or involuntary removal of Indian children. That did not occur here; the Indian parents have expressed their clear preference for the Mississippi state courts over the tribal court.

C. PLACEMENT

In all states, licensed adoption agencies may assist in arranging adoptions. In some states, "private" (non-agency) adoptions are prohibited. Significant, but not absolute, discretion is vested in such agencies, whether state or private, as the placement decisions are influenced by so many human variables.

1. **Action against adoption agency--M.H. and J.L.H. v. Caritas Family Services,** 488 N.W.2d 282 (Minn. 1992).

   a. **Facts.** During the process of adoption, M.H. and J.L.H. (Ps) indicated they would be open to any child except one with a very serious mental deficiency. They were told the baby they eventually adopted had "incest in the family's background," and that the mother was 13 years old. Before the adoption was final in 1982, Ps were

M.H. and J.L.H. v. Caritas Family Services

informed that the mother was 17 years old and the "possibility of incest" was mentioned in a report. The child was 45 days old when he was adopted. During his childhood, he had serious behavioral problems, attention deficit hyperactivity disorder, exhibited violent behavior, and set fires indoors. When a psychologist requested more information regarding the child's background in 1987, it was revealed that the child's parents were a 17-year-old boy and his 13-year-old sister. The father was considered "borderline hyperactive," had a low range of intelligence, and had been seen at a mental health clinic when he was 11, but was discharged because he did not cooperate with his therapist. D admitted it knew of the child's genetic background at the time of the adoption. Ps sued D for misrepresentation and later moved to amend their complaint to include a claim for emotional distress. The trial court granted D's motions for summary judgment except as to negligent misrepresentation. The court of appeals affirmed in part and reversed in part. D appeals.

b. **Issues.**

   1) Does public policy preclude a negligent misrepresentation action against an adoption agency where the agency, having undertaken to disclose information about the child's genetic parents and medical background to the adoptive parents, negligently withholds information in such a way that the adoptive parents were misled as to the truth?

   2) Were there sufficient allegations to support a claim of intentional misrepresentation?

   3) Were there sufficient allegations to support a claim of intentional infliction of emotional distress?

c. **Held.** a) No. b) No. c) No. The court of appeals decision is affirmed, the certified question answered in the negative, and the case is remanded.

   1) For purposes of negligent misrepresentation, conduct actionable against one class of defendants is not automatically actionable against another class of defendants. Tort liability depends on whether the party accused of the tort owes a duty to the accusing party and the plaintiff's interests are entitled to legal protection against the defendant's conduct.

      a) If a duty is owed, then one who undertakes to act must act with reasonable care.

      b) Even if one has no duty to disclose, if one chooses to speak, one must say enough to prevent the words from misleading the other party.

   2) Adoption agencies have a duty to use due care to ensure that when they disclose information about a child's genetic parents and medical history, they disclose information fully and adequately so as not to mislead.

   3) An intentional misrepresentation claim requires Ps to allege D made a false representation having to do with a past or present material fact susceptible of knowledge that the representor knows to be false or is asserted without knowing whether the fact is true or false, with the intent to induce the other person to act, the person is, in fact, induced to act in reliance on the

representation, and suffers damages. A misrepresentation may be made by a false affirmative statement or by concealing certain facts that render the disclosed facts disclosed misleading.

   a)   Ps failed to allege any facts or produce any evidence implying D intended to mislead by deliberately withholding full facts regarding incest in the child's background, and D's statement regarding the genetic father's "good health" was not shown to be either false on its face or deliberately misleading. Therefore, Ps' allegations were insufficient to support intentional misrepresentation.

4) Infliction of emotional distress generally requires plaintiffs to suffer a physical injury. There was no evidence that D directly invaded Ps' rights by willful, wanton, or malicious conduct, or that Ps suffered physical injury. Therefore, Ps' allegations were insufficient to support a claim of intentional infliction of emotional distress.

D. LEGAL CONSEQUENCES OF ADOPTION

1. **Purpose.** It is generally said that the purpose of adoption is to create in law the same relationship that exists between biological parents and children. However, sometimes the lack of biological relation between adopted family members is legally recognized.

   a. **Marriage of siblings-by-adoption--Israel v. Allen,** *supra* at p. 24.

   b. **Inheritance.** Adopted children are treated the same as biological offspring for most inheritance purposes, but careless choice of words may still create ambiguities.

   c. **Grandparents' visitation usually not allowed after adoption--Bush v. Squellati,** 522 N.E.2d 1225 (Ill. 1988).

      Bush v. Squellati

      1) **Facts.** Gene and Louise Bush (Ps) are the biological maternal grandparents of Anthony. In August 1984, Anthony was adopted by his great aunt Sally Squellati and her husband (Ds). Anthony's biological parents consented to the adoption, then got divorced. Louise and Sally are sisters. Ds refused to let Ps visit Anthony. Ps filed a petition with the circuit court seeking grandparent visitation. Section 607 of the Illinois Marriage and Dissolution of Marriage Act provides that in custody proceedings incident to divorce a court may grant reasonable visitation privileges to grandparents. The court granted the petition. The appellate court reversed. Ps appeal.

      2) **Issue.** May statutory visitation rights be granted under section 607 when the biological parents consent to adoption?

      3) **Held.** No. The judgment is affirmed.

         a)   Grandparent visitation rights did not exist at common law. A prior decision indicated that under exceptional circumstances courts could award grandparents visitation rights, such as when a father is inducted into the military and petitions a court to award his parents visitation with his child, or where a deceased parent named his parents trustees of a special fund for the benefit of the child.

    b)   By statute, grandparents may be awarded visitation in the case of the death of both natural or adoptive parents, but that statute does not apply here because both parents are still alive.

    c)   Section 607 applies only in the case of dissolution of marriage or where one parent has died. The legislative history reveals that section 607 was amended by the legislature to provide for grandparent visitation when one parent has died and the child is adopted by the new spouse of the surviving parent. That is not the case here. The statutory term "related adoption" in those provisions means stepparent adoption. Because Anthony's blood parents voluntarily gave him up, the grandparent visitation provisions do not apply.

    d)   Ps do not have standing under the grandparent visitation statutes, but that does not mean that morally they do not have a just claim to visit their grandson. It does mean that they must get permission of Ds to do so. The court hopes the sisters will stop their quarreling and let Ps visit Anthony.

4)   **Comment.** Some cases have awarded grandparent visitation in circumstances similar to those described in *Bush*, but the majority of courts have agreed with the *Bush* approach.

d.   **Open adoption is not necessarily prohibited--Michaud v. Wawruck, 551 A.2d 738 (Conn. 1988).**

Michaud v. Wawruck

    1)   **Facts.** A Connecticut probate court terminated the parental rights of Jacqueline Michaud (P) with her consent, and the parental rights of the father of her child. The child was placed with James and Cynthia Wawruck (Ds), foster parents. Ds sought to adopt the child. P filed a motion to set aside the decree terminating her parental rights on the ground that her consent had been fraudulently obtained. Ds intervened. P agreed to dismiss her motion and not oppose the adoption after Ds and P signed an "Open Adoption and Visitation Agreement" which granted P visitation twice a month for three hours. The agreement was noted in the record but not incorporated into the adoption decree. When Ds denied P visitation, P filed a complaint to enforce the agreement. The trial court granted Ds' motion to strike the complaint. P appeals.

    2)   **Issue.** Are open adoption agreements contrary to public policy, and thus unenforceable in Connecticut?

    3)   **Held.** No. The judgment is vacated and the case is remanded.

        a)   Connecticut's visitation statute permits the court, on proper application, to grant visitation rights in the best interests of the child. This gives the court great latitude and discretion.

b) We are unpersuaded that the open adoption agreement violates public policy. Cases from other courts agree that adoption does not automatically require complete severance of the child from further contact with former relatives.

c) Traditional models of the nuclear family have been modified and replaced in recent years. The best interests of children do not require adherence exclusively to such a narrow concept of the family.

4) **Comment.** Open adoption is increasingly being favored as a best-alternative-in-difficult-cases model. Such factors as the age of the child involved and the reasonable expectations of all the parties are critical.

E. EQUITABLE ADOPTION

1. **Equitable Relief for Property Claims.** Adoption was not known at common law—it is a strictly statutory proceeding. Full and exacting compliance with all the statutory requirements is necessary to perfect a legal adoption. However, in some cases involving posthumous claims to property by children raised by persons who were not their biological parents, many courts have granted a remedy of treating the child as if he or she were the legal (biological or adoptive) child and heir of the deceased. While this does not create a bona fide parent-child relationship for any other purpose, it is a useful device to accomplish equitable results in probate. The doctrine is variously known by the somewhat misleading labels of "equitable adoption" or "adoption by estoppel."

F. SEALED RECORDS

1. **The Search for Biological "Roots."** For many years it has been the general practice (and law) for courts to seal adoption records in order to protect the reputation and prevent harassment of the biological parents giving up their child, and to protect and prevent interference with the new family unit. Recently, the quest of adopted children to learn about their biological parentage (for medical, genealogical, and personal reasons) has necessitated reconsideration of the established policy.

2. **Right to Know One's Biological Identity--*In re* Roger B.**, 418 N.E.2d 751 (Ill. 1981), *appeal dismissed*, 454 U.S. 806 (1981).

   In re
   Roger B.

   a. **Facts.** Roger B. (P) sought a judgment to declare unconstitutional the state statute that places adoption records and original birth records under seal. P was an adult and testified that he did not need the records for any psychiatric or medical reason. He only sought to know information about his biological background. State statute prevented him from obtaining information about his original birth records unless the court ordered it. The trial court upheld the validity of the statute and denied P's request. P appeals.

   b. **Issue.** Is a statute which prevents an adopted person from gaining access to his original birth records and adoption records unconstitutional?

c. **Held.** No. The judgment is affirmed.

1) We have found no case holding that the right of an adoptee to determine his genealogical origin is explicitly or implicitly guaranteed by the Constitution. It is not a fundamental right, and the statute will be upheld if it is not arbitrary and bears a rational relationship to a legitimate state objective.

2) The state's interest, as shown from the legislative intent, is that confidentiality promotes the integrity of the adoption process. The natural parents, the adoptive parents, and the adopted child all have an important interest in privacy and confidentiality. It is essential to preserve the adoption process so as not to increase the risk of neglect to any child or to force parents to resort to the black market in order to surrender children they cannot care for.

3) The statute allows the court to evaluate the needs of the adoptee and to release the adoption records if needed. The statute therefore is rationally related to a legitimate legislative purpose of protecting the adoption process.

d. **Comment.** At the time of this opinion only three states—Alabama, Florida, and Kansas—grant an adoptee access to original birth records.

G. ADOPTION OF ADULTS

1. **Parens Patriae.** In Roman law (and to some extent in continental civil law), adoption was designed and employed to serve the interests of adults (*e.g.*, inheritance, etc.). In American law, adoption was designed to serve a very different purpose—to provide for the welfare of parentless or neglected children by giving their adoptive parents all the rights and duties of biological parents. Thus, most adoption statutes require findings that the prospective adoptive parents will be "fit parents" and that the adoption will be in the "best interests" of the adopted child. Nevertheless, adoption statutes are generally worded broadly enough that legal adoptions of adults may be accomplished (frequently to formalize a parent-child relationship that has long existed in fact but which has not previously been legally recognized). Sometimes, however, the primary or sole purpose of an adoption petition is to achieve some objective other than to provide for the proper rearing of children or to provide de jure recognition for de facto parent-child relationship.

Adoption of Swanson

2. **No Parent-Child Relationship Required--Adoption of Swanson,** 623 A.2d 1095 (Del. 1993).

a. **Facts.** Richard Sorrels, age 66, sought to adopt James Swanson, age 51, who had been his companion for 17 years, in order to formalize their close relationship and to facilitate estate planning. The family court denied the petition. Sorrels appeals.

b. **Issue.** Is a pre-existing parent-child relationship required under the Delaware adult adoption statutes in order for one adult to adopt another?

c. **Held.** No. The decision is reversed.

1) The relevant statutory language provides: "If the petition complies with the requirements of [other sections of] this title, and if the person or persons to be adopted appear in court and consent to the adoption, the Family Court may render a decree ordering the issuance of a certificate of adoption to the petitioner."

2) If a statute is clear, unambiguous, and consistent with other provisions of the same legislation, the court's role is limited to the application of its literal meaning. Regardless of a judge's views on the wisdom of a statute, his or her role limited to applying the statute objectively. A court may not engraft upon a statute language which has been clearly excluded.

3) Most jurisdictions recognize that adult adoption for the purpose of creating inheritance rights is valid.

4) A pre-existing parent-child relationship is not required under the statute in order for one adult to adopt another, nor was an investigation required as to whether the adoption was in the best interests of the adoptee.

IX. GROUNDS AND PROCEDURES FOR DISSOLUTION OF MARRIAGES

A. HISTORY

Until the middle of the 19th century, termination of marital status was largely dealt with in England in the ecclesiastical courts, applying canon law (Catholic initially, then Anglican). But over time the political law absorbed the ecclesiastical law. In America, divorce regulation took as many different courses as there were states. By the middle of this century, divorce in almost all states was available on demand for all practical purposes in the law as applied, but was somewhat or severely restricted in the law as written. The blatant discrepancy between the law as written and the law as applied, coupled with the individualistic tendencies of the past few decades, produced a virtual revolution in divorce statutes (the "no-fault" revolution of the 1970s). Not surprisingly, divorce rates have risen dramatically. Today, "dissolution" is used by some jurisdictions as the preferred term for no-fault termination of marital relations.

B. ACCESS TO COURTS

Divorce is exclusively a judicial remedy. No American jurisdiction recognizes "common law divorce" or permits subsequent marriage without proper termination of the former marriage. Thus, access to the courts is critical for those seeking to undo or reenter nuptial obligations.

Boddie v.
Connecticut

1. **Filing Fees in Divorce Actions--Boddie v. Connecticut,** 401 U.S. 371 (1971).

   a. **Facts.** Boddie and other welfare recipients (Ps) brought this action in federal court challenging state filing fee requirements in order to initiate a divorce action. An average cost for bringing a divorce action was $60. A three-judge district court held that a state may impose filing fees which effectively bar persons from commencing divorce actions. Ps appeal.

   b. **Issue.** Does a state filing fee requirement which effectively bars indigents from commencing divorce actions violate the Due Process Clause of the Fourteenth Amendment?

   c. **Held.** Yes. The decision is reversed.

      1) The marriage relationship is of basic importance in our society. That is why the state has seen fit to oversee many aspects of this relationship.

      2) Since resort to the state courts is the only means of dissolving the marriage relationship, due process prohibits a state from denying, solely on the basis of inability to pay, access to its courts to individuals who seek a divorce.

      3) Due process requires that everyone have an opportunity to be heard. Persons barred from the courtroom because of inability

to pay filing fees are denied this important right. The state's claims that filing fees prevent frivolous litigation and rationally allocate the state's limited judicial resources do not overcome the individual's interest in access to the only avenue of terminating his or her marriage.

    d.   **Dissent** (Black, J.). Marriage is almost completely under state control, and so is divorce. The states have the deepest interest in the kinds of law regulating marriage. The Court should refrain from expanding federal power over marriage. The Fourteenth Amendment does not justify judges in invalidating state laws on the non-constitutional standard of their view of fairness.

    e.   **Comment.** The Court carefully limited its holding to the facts of the case before it, emphasizing the complete monopolization of means of dissolution of marriage and the absolute bar created by this rule. Nevertheless, some attempts to use this rationale to invalidate other impediments to litigation have followed.

C.   FAULT GROUNDS AND DEFENSES

1.   **The Risk of Strict Construction.** Under the traditional "fault"-based divorce system, there was always the risk that the court would apply the statutory grounds for divorce strictly and deny a divorce where the parties both desired it, or where just one party vigorously objected. Usually courts would only deny divorce if the judge believed that the marriage was not irretrievably broken. This judicial paternalism itself was distasteful to many.

    a.   **More cruelty is required to dissolve a long marriage than a short one--Brady v. Brady,** 64 N.Y.2d 339 (1985).
          Brady v. Brady

        1)   **Facts.** Edward (P) and Dorothy (D) Brady were married in 1956 and had four children. Since 1979, P has not lived at the marital residence at all. P filed this action for divorce in 1981 alleging cruel and inhuman conduct by D, including striking him with various objects, threatening to kill him, berating him, and refusing to have sex with him. D denied these allegations. The trial court found the marriage to be "dead," and granted P a divorce. The appellate division affirmed in relevant part. D appeals.

        2)   **Issue.** Can a divorce for cruelty be granted upon a finding that the marriage is dead?

        3)   **Held.** No. But more cruelty is required for a long marriage than a short one.

            a)   "Cruel and inhuman treatment" is a ground for a divorce. It requires more than mere incompatibility. A prior case indicated that what was required would depend in part on the length of the marriage—the longer the duration of the marriage the more serious the cruelty necessary for divorce.

b)   This rule does not violate gender equality. The financial plight of middle-aged divorced women is sufficient to justify a higher standard of cruelty for divorce after a longer marriage.

c)   However, a finding of a "dead marriage" is not sufficient to constitute grounds for divorce for cruel and inhuman treatment.

4)   Comment. Adultery, like cruelty, was a ubiquitous ground for fault divorce. When it was the sole or nearly the only ground for divorce, it was often collusively manufactured.

b.   Intemperance--Husband D v. Wife D, 383 A.2d 302 (Del. Fam. Ct. 1977).

1)   Facts. Husband (P) brought an action for divorce on the ground that Wife (D) "has been habitually drunk for a period in excess of two years" and that her habitual intemperance has been "so destructive of the marriage relation that petitioner cannot reasonably be expected to continue in that relation" with D. D opposes the divorce action, claiming that the parties drank together frequently and heavily before marriage, so that P was aware of the situation, and that D's problem is not so serious as to make it impossible for P to endure, and claims recrimination, condonation, and connivance. P is 62 and D is 46; they have been married for seven years. She testified that P drinks as much as she does, but complains about her alcohol problem to divert attention from his alcoholism. P admitted that he often drank with D before and after marriage and that D took good care of him and the house. In July 1976, D met P at the door drunk and in her underwear when he returned from a convention, and verbally abused him. They separated but reunited for appearance's sake around Christmas. On December 27, 1976, D had to be hospitalized for the third time because of alcohol and malnourishment. Apparently D has maintained complete sobriety since then, but reconciliation is deemed impossible.

2)   Issue. Is P entitled to a fault divorce because of the habitual, unendurable intemperance of D?

3)   Held. No. The petition for divorce is denied.

a)   According to *Muir v. Muir*, 86 A.2d 857 (Del. Super. Ct. 1952), connivance is unavailable as a defense because, as a matter of Delaware law, no married man should have to forgo his own recreational drinking just because it may lead his wife to alcoholism. Likewise, condonation is unavailable as a defense to habitual drunkenness because it is a continuing cause of divorce. *Muir* is distinguishable because there the petitioner was not guilty of essentially the same fault upon which he sought a divorce. The court concludes that both parties were alcoholics.

b)   Prior to 1974 recrimination was only available as a defense when adultery was alleged. In that year the "fault" defenses were abolished. In 1976 they were restored as they had previously existed. Thus, recrimination is still not available as a defense when habitual drunkenness is the alleged ground for divorce.

c)   Clean hands is not an available defense because it is an equitable defense and in Delaware divorce is a legal, not an equitable, cause of action.

d)   However, fault divorce may only be granted to an "injured and innocent" spouse. If the parties are equally at fault or if the petitioner by his conduct caused the situation on which his action for divorce is based, divorce may not be granted. P's drinking habits are essentially the same as D's, so P cannot obtain a fault divorce on the basis of D's intemperate drinking. It cannot be said that D's excessive drinking was the sole cause of the marital breakup.

f)   Moreover, D's conduct was not "so destructive of the marriage relation that the petitioner cannot reasonably be expected to continue in that relation" as the statute requires.

g)   It was the intent of the legislature which enacted Delaware's no-fault divorce statute to discourage fault divorces except in the most egregious cases; this is not such a case. P admits that D performed her wifely duties very well.

4)   Comment. Apparently the parties would still be able to obtain a no-fault divorce.

D.   NO-FAULT DIVORCE

1.   **Old No-Fault Divorce Grounds.** Long before the modern "no-fault" divorce statutes were enacted, two "no-fault" grounds for divorce were available in many states. One was "separation," where the parties had lived separate and apart (often a decree of legal separation was required) for a specified period of years. The other "no-fault" basis for divorce was insanity, a well-conceived ground for divorce which may have been as socially stigmatizing as some fault grounds for divorce.

2.   **Modern No-Fault Divorce Grounds.** Since about 1970, almost every state has either replaced or supplemented its previous fault grounds for divorce with a no-fault ground, usually termed either "irretrievable breakdown" or "irreconcilable differences."

a.   **Incompatibility--Husband W. v. Wife W.,** 297 A.2d 39 (Del. 1972).

> Husband W. v. Wife W.

1)   **Facts.** Husband (P) brought an action for divorce on the ground of incompatibility. Wife (D) opposed. The undisputed evidence showed that the parties had lived apart for a year and a half. They had often quarreled violently, necessitating police involvement on numerous occasions; a family court judge had remarked on one such occasion that "it is obvious that the marriage is finished and they are incompatible." D put lye on P's food, tried to stab him, and threw a brick through a window. P thrice hit D over the head with chairs, threatened to burn down the house, and locked D out in the cold in winter. P

testified that there was no hope of reconciliation; D said she could not say if reconciliation was possible. The trial court denied the divorce, holding that P had failed to sustain his burden of showing no reasonable possibility of reconciliation.

2) **Issue.** Did the trial court err in denying the divorce on ground of insufficient proof or irreconciliation?

3) **Held.** Yes. The decision is reversed and remanded with direction to grant the divorce decree. The undisputed evidence amply satisfies the legal requirement that the parties be irreconcilable.

Sinha v.
Sinha

b. **Unilateral divorce may require tougher no-fault standards than mutually agreed divorce--Sinha v. Sinha, 526 A.2d 765 (Pa. 1987).**

1) **Facts.** Shrikant (P) and Chandra (D) Sinha were married in India in 1974. Two years later, P came to the United States to study. D was unable to join P because of visa problems. In 1979, P filed for divorce. D came to the United States and P dismissed his divorce action. A year later P filed for no-fault divorce alleging that the parties had lived apart for three years and the marriage was irretrievably broken. The court granted the divorce. D appeals.

2) **Issue.** Must the party seeking unilateral no-fault divorce on the ground of living separate and apart for three years have an intent to divorce before the three years begins to run?

3) **Held.** Yes. The divorce judgment is reversed.

a) P first revealed his intention to divorce D when he filed his divorce complaint in August 1979, 14 months before filing this divorce action. The unilateral no-fault divorce provisions require living apart and separate for three years.

b) The three years the parties lived apart while P was in school does not count because the intent to divorce must precede the running of the separation period. P expressed his love for D as late as 1978.

c) Families often are required to separate for employment, education, or war. Such separations, without intent to end a marriage, do not suffice for the no-fault divorce provision.

E. **DIVORCE JURISDICTION**

1. **Introduction.** Traditionally, divorce jurisdiction has been predicated on the domicile of the petitioner. Even in the absence of personal jurisdiction of the responding spouse, courts have been said to have had jurisdiction to grant divorce if the petitioner was domiciled in the jurisdiction. The

of the rveracity of jurisdictional findings (*e.g.,* domicile) is subject to reexamination under principles of collateral estoppel.

a. Full faith and credit--Sherrer v. Sherrer, 334 U.S. 343 (1948).

1) Facts. Margaret Sherrer (P) and Edward Sherrer (D) lived together for 12 years in Massachusetts. P moved to Florida and instituted divorce proceedings there. D made a general appearance and contested many of P's allegations, including the allegation as to P's Florida residence. The Florida court granted P a divorce. D did not appeal. P immediately married a Massachusetts man. A month later, P and her new husband returned to Massachusetts. Several months later, D instituted an action in Massachusetts to allow him to convey his property as if he were sole owner, alleging that the Florida judgment was invalid because P was not a domiciliary. The Massachusetts courts held for D. P appeals.

2) Issue. Does the Full Faith and Credit Clause require the recognition by one state court of the jurisdictional determination of a sister state that the plaintiff is a domiciliary of that state, where the defendant appeared at the trial, was accorded all his due process rights, and failed to appeal to the highest state court?

3) Held. Yes. The judgment of the Massachusetts court is reversed.

   a) The Massachusetts court erred in permitting the Florida divorce decree to be subject to collateral attack on the ground that P was not a Florida domiciliary. This was an issue for judicial determination, and D had his day in court and was afforded all his due process rights. He failed to appeal the decision to the Florida Supreme Court. Full faith and credit does not require giving a litigant a second opportunity to litigate the issue.

   b) Full faith and credit requires recognizing decrees of divorce entered by courts of sister states. Of course, judicial reexamination of findings of jurisdictional fact made in ex parte proceedings may be permissible, but not where the defendant made a general appearance, contested the issue, and lost. In such cases, the determination of jurisdiction should be final and not subject to collateral attack in the courts of sister states.

   c) That this case concerns "vital interests of domestic relations" only underscores the need for finality of the judgment.

4) Comment. This opinion mixes notions of full faith and credit with concepts of collateral estoppel and res judicata.

b. Residency duration requirements--Sosna v. Iowa, 419 U.S. 393 (1975).

1) Facts. Carol Sosna (P) and Michael Sosna (D) were married in Michigan, but lived in New York between 1967 and 1972. P moved to Iowa and a month later petitioned the district court for a dissolution of her marriage. A durational residency requirement of one year was imposed before such an action could be brought. The court dismissed P's petition. P appeals.

2) **Issue.** Is a one-year residency requirement imposed upon persons desiring to petition for divorce unconstitutional because it discriminates against those who have recently exercised their right to travel?

3) **Held.** No. The judgment is affirmed.

a) Forty-eight states impose a residency requirement similar to Iowa's. The most common is the one-year period selected by Iowa. State statutes that impose durational residency requirements for welfare payments, medical care, and voting have been struck down, but these cases did not intimate that such requirements were never appropriate.

b) Iowa's residency requirement may be justified on other than budgetary and administrative convenience grounds. Iowa may insist that a proceeding as important as one for divorce be granted only to one who has a modicum of attachment to the state. A state can decide that it does not want to become a divorce mill.

c) The one-year requirement provides a safeguard against successful collateral attack in other states.

d) The Iowa statute does not result in the total deprivation of P's ability to obtain a divorce, but only delays her access to the courts.

4) **Dissent** (Marshall, Brennan, JJ.). The Court fails to discuss the main issue, which is whether the right to obtain a divorce is important enough that its denial to new residents constitutes a penalty on interstate travel. The Court also applies the lenient "rational basis" standard of analysis rather than the "compelling state interest" test in this case. The Iowa residency requirement unduly interferes with the right to travel.

5) **Comment.** The durational residency requirement in this case was a type of subject matter jurisdiction limitation concerning divorce. Since the entire subject matter of domestic relations is of particularly local (not federal) concern, the Court's decision is as much a reaffirmation of federalism as it is a statement on due process or equal protection principles.

Perrin v.
Perrin

c. **Recognition of foreign divorces--Perrin v. Perrin,** 408 F.2d 107 (3d Cir. 1969).

1) **Facts.** Mrs. Perrin (P) and Mr. Perrin (D) obtained a bilateral Mexican divorce. She was plaintiff in the action, having met the one- or two-day residency requirement; he was defendant and appeared by counsel and consented to the divorce. The Mexican decree awarded child custody to D. Later P, seeking to gain custody of the parties' child, sued for divorce in the District Court of the Virgin Islands, claiming that the Mexican divorce was invalid because neither party was a domiciliary of Mexico. The district court granted P's petition. D appeals.

2) **Issue.** Should a United States court, under principles of comity, recognize as valid a bilateral foreign divorce decree, where neither party was a domiciliary of the foreign country?

3) **Held.** Yes, at least where, as in this case, the party attacking the foreign decree was the plaintiff in the foreign action. The judgment is reversed.

    a) Ordinarily, a court will not recognize a foreign divorce where neither party was a domiciliary of the foreign country. This is true with respect to "mail order" divorces where neither party appears, and with respect to ex parte proceedings in foreign countries. But this case involved a bilateral divorce, and the party attacking its validity was the plaintiff who procured the divorce upon her representation to the Mexican court that she was a resident of Juarez, Mexico.

    b) In *Coe v. Coe*, 334 U.S. 378 (1948), the United States Supreme Court upheld a divorce procured by a plaintiff who had satisfied Nevada's six-week residency requirement. Mr. Coe's six weeks in Nevada did not give Nevada any more concern with his marriage than did P's one- or two-day residency in Mexico.

    c) Domicile is not always an indispensable prerequisite to divorce jurisdiction.

4) **Comment.** The issue in this case might as well have been approached under an estoppel theory; indeed, that concept seems to underlie the court's jurisdictional analysis.

d. **Estoppel--Kazin v. Kazin,** 405 A.2d 360 (N.J. 1979).

    Kazin v.
Kazin

1) **Facts.** Clara Kazin (P) married Jesse Liss in 1953 and had four children by him. Liss left P to live with another woman. In 1969, Michael Kazin (D) proposed to P. D helped arrange for P and Liss to get a Mexican divorce. D's attorney assured P and Liss that the Mexican divorce would be legal. In reliance on D's agreement to support her and her children, P did not request alimony from Liss, and agreed to minimal child support. D made all the arrangements for P to go to Mexico, paid her expenses, and accompanied her at least to El Paso. Three weeks after the Mexican divorce, D married P in New Jersey and they lived together there for seven years. D then left P, who brought an action for divorce on grounds of desertion, extreme cruelty, and adultery, seeking alimony and equitable distribution. D denied the validity of the marriage, arguing that his marriage to P was null and void because the Mexican divorce was jurisdictionally invalid. The trial court held that D was estopped from affirmatively asserting the invalidity of P's Mexican divorce, but also held that, because the divorce was void, P could not prove a valid marriage, and the court dismissed P's complaint. The appellate division affirmed.

2) **Issue.** Did the trial court err in dismissing P's complaint for divorce because P's prior Mexican divorce decree was void for want of jurisdiction, even though D had knowledge of and encouraged P to obtain the Mexican divorce?

3) **Held.** Yes. The judgment is reversed and the case is remanded.

    a) In 1949, the New Jersey Supreme Court, in *Tonti v. Chadwick*, held that a party in P's position was not entitled to a divorce despite D's lack of clean hands. That decision was consistent with the "powerful legislative mandate against the facile termination of lawful marriages."

b) There have been drastic changes in public policy and law concerning divorce since 1949. Grounds and jurisdiction for divorce have been expanded, and many traditional defenses have been abolished. Social acceptance of divorce, as well as the divorce rate, have increased.

c) Today, equitable principles are of foremost concern in actions for dissolution of marriage. Equitable estoppel depends upon the facts and circumstances of each case. Courts will prevent a party from attacking the validity of a prior divorce decree under "quasi-estoppel" if the party is "blowing both hot and cold" by taking a position inconsistent with his prior conduct.

d) Most cases have applied estoppel to prevent a party from attacking his or her own prior divorce decree, and many cases have likewise precluded a husband from attacking his wife's prior divorce where he took an active role in helping her to procure that divorce. One who has received the benefits of a second marriage should not be able to escape its obligations.

e) The law presumes that the last marriage is valid, and that any prior marriage was lawfully terminated by death or divorce.

f) D's knowledge, participation, acceptance of benefits, and subsequent marriage establish sufficient nexus with P's Mexican divorce to estop him from attacking the validity of that divorce.

4) Comment. This represents the apparent majority rule. Not only is the doctrine of estoppel invoked to justify this result, but some courts hold that a new spouse lacks standing to challenge the validity of his spouse's prior divorce.

Newport v. **Divisible divorce--Newport v. Newport,** 245 S.E.2d 134 (Va. 1978).
Newport

1) Facts. Elswick (D) and Flora (P) were married in 1947 and moved to Virginia in 1966, where P has resided since. In 1973, following military duty in Vietnam, D established residence in Nevada and obtained an ex parte divorce "dissolving the bonds of matrimony." In 1974, P filed a complaint in Virginia state court seeking separate maintenance and support. D answered, arguing that P's right to claim alimony or support was extinguished by the Nevada divorce decree and suggesting that, by statute, Virginia courts could only grant alimony upon decreeing the dissolution of a marriage. The trial court held that the Nevada decree validly terminated marital status but did not terminate P's right to support. D appeals.

2) Issue. Did the trial court err in holding that an ex parte foreign divorce decree did not terminate P's right to support because the Nevada court lacked personal jurisdiction over her?

3) Held. No. The judgment is affirmed.

a) In *Estin v. Estin*, 334 U.S. 541 (1948), the Supreme Court held that full faith and credit did not require New York to recognize an ex parte Nevada divorce decree as terminating a wife's claim for alimony where she had earlier obtained a New York order for support.

b) In *Armstrong v. Armstrong* 350 U.S. 568 (1956), four justices expressed the opinion that an ex parte foreign divorce decree denying alimony to a nonresident wife was invalid as a denial of due process.

c) In *Vanderbilt v. Vanderbilt*, 354 U.S. 416 (1957), the Supreme Court held that an ex parte Nevada divorce decree did not cut off the rights of a New York wife to alimony even though no prior support order had been obtained by her. The Court emphasized that, since the wife was not subject to the personal jurisdiction of the Nevada court, it could not extinguish her personal right to support.

d) D argues that these cases only show that whether the right to alimony survives an ex parte foreign divorce decree depends on the law of the claimant's domicile.

e) Under Virginia law, only the decree of a court having personal jurisdiction over the wife will be recognized as terminating her right to support.

f) As a general rule, full faith and credit will only be accorded a foreign divorce decree as to property and support rights if the court rendering the decree had personal jurisdiction over all the parties. But some jurisdictions have gone further and given preclusive effect to ex parte decrees regardless of personal jurisdiction.

g) Virginia has a profound interest in the economic well-being of its citizens and in vindicating their moral and marital rights to appropriate support after marital dissolution.

f. Jurisdiction for child support--Kulko v. Superior Court of California, 436 U.S. 84 (1978).

Kulko v. Superior Court of California

1) Facts. Ezra (P) and Sharon (D) were New York residents when they got married in California during a three-day stop-over there while P was en route to Korea in military service. They lived together in New York continually after P returned from the service, and their two children were born there. In 1972, D left P and moved to California, but returned to New York to sign a separation agreement and went to Haiti to get a divorce. Under the agreement, D was to keep the children during summers and holidays, and P was to have them the rest of the year. When the daughter wanted to reverse the arrangement, P acceded and bought her a one-way ticket to California. Later, the son also wanted to live with D and she sent him a ticket secretly so he could join her in California. D then filed an action in a California court to modify the custody arrangement and to increase child support. P's motion to quash service on the ground of no minimum contacts was denied. The appellate court affirmed, as did the California Supreme Court. P filed a petition for a writ of certiorari.

2) **Issue.** Does economic burden in a state caused by the husband's acquiescence to a child's request to live in that state with the mother year-round constitute sufficient contact with the state for it to exercise of personal jurisdiction over the husband in a child support action?

3) **Held.** No. The judgment is reversed.

    a) A valid judgment imposing personal obligations on a foreign defendant may be rendered only if he has had minimum contacts with the forum state such that the maintenance of the suit does not offend "traditional notions of fair play and substantial justice."

    b) Neither P's brief presence in California at the time he was married, nor his agreement initially to let the children spend some time there with their mother, is such a minimum contact. To hold otherwise would discourage parents from entering into reasonable visitation agreements, and would arbitrarily subject the parent to jurisdiction wherever the visited parent chose to spend time while having custody.

    c) The unilateral activity of one claiming some relationship with a nonresident defendant cannot satisfy the requirement of contact with the state.

    d) Nor does a father's agreement to a child's request to spend more time than originally allowed with the mother constitute availing himself of the benefits and protections of the laws of the mother's state.

    e) The in-state "effects" of an out-of-state act by a nonresident will generally only suffice as a minimum contact in the context of commercial activity.

    f) D could have brought this action in New York. She might even have been able to institute a two-state URESA action. It was D who left the state of marital domicile.

    g) California's substantial interests in the welfare of resident children is a valid choice-of-law consideration, but it is not a jurisdictional minimum contact reaching P.

4) **Dissent** (Brennan, White, Powell, JJ.). The question is a close one, and the standard of review is such that the decision of the Supreme Court of California ought to be upheld.

g. **Summary dissolution.** In cases in which the marriage is of short duration, no children are born, and no real property and no substantial personal property are acquired, some states provide procedures for summary dissolution by which a marriage is automatically ended by quasi-administrative or clerical entry after the expiration of a cooling-off period.

X. ECONOMIC EFFECTS OF DISSOLUTION

A. SEPARATE MAINTENANCE

While the effect of a decree of divorce or dissolution is final regarding the spousal relationship, it is often impossible to sever all economic ties between the parties. Changing philosophies about the roles, rights, and responsibilities of men and women, married persons and singles, and mothers and fathers further confuse the matter.

1. **Reform Movement.** Since the early 1970s, state legislatures have directed attention first to the grounds for divorce and then to the distribution of marital property. While some states adopted a system of community property, many adopted systems which distributed property to the person in whose name the property was titled during the marriage. This often meant that the primary wage earner would end up with the property; the non-wage earner had to rely on alimony to compensate for such contributions as maintaining the home or raising children. Community property statutes have given way to "equitable distribution" statutes which give courts the authority to distribute marital property on the basis of the parties' individual contributions other than wage earning. Although the strict title approach has disappeared, there is still a great disparity among the states. The New York Domestic Relations Law, section 236, is broad and detailed, and may serve as a basis for study of the factors that are common to much of the new legislation enacted by other states.

B. ALIMONY AND CHILD SUPPORT

Both spousal support (often termed alimony after divorce) and child support involve continuing economic obligations to insure an adequate income stream for persons whose economic dependency has resulted, at least in part, from a family relationship.

1. **Alimony.** Traditionally alimony was only available to women who divorced. Now it is available to economically dependent former spouses regardless of gender. Too often, inadequate or no alimony is awarded the dependent spouse.

   a. **Sex discrimination in alimony--Orr v. Orr,** 440 U.S. 268 (1979).   Orr v. Orr

   1) **Facts.** In 1974, the marriage of Lillian (P) and William (D) Orr was dissolved by a divorce decree. The parties stipulated that D would pay P $1,240 per month alimony, and that agreement was incorporated in the divorce decree. In 1976, P filed contempt proceedings against D for nonpayment. D resisted, arguing that the alimony law of Alabama is unconstitutional in that it only authorizes courts to award alimony to wives. The trial court rejected the argument and entered judgment against D for $5,524 back alimony and attorney's fees. The Alabama Court of Civil Appeals affirmed, and the state supreme court quashed a writ of certiorari. D appeals.

2) **Issue.** Does an alimony law which provides only that wives, but not husbands, may receive alimony upon divorce violate the Equal Protection Clause?

3) **Held.** Yes. The judgment is reversed and the case is remanded.

   a) D has standing to raise the constitutional issue even though he made no claim that he was entitled to an award of alimony and even though his success may not bring him relief from the judgment, because the sex discrimination could be remedied by making the alimony law gender-neutral, as well as by invalidating the law.

   b) It is possible that the constitutional issue might have been avoided had objection been raised to D's tardiness in raising the constitutional question for the first time in the contempt proceeding (and not in the divorce action), or by basing P's claim or judgment upon the stipulated agreement (contract) instead of the divorce judgment. However, neither avoiding action was taken, so the court can proceed to hear the constitutional issue.

   c) In authorizing the imposition of alimony obligations on husbands only, the Alabama law discriminates on the basis of gender. To withstand equal protection scrutiny, gender classifications must serve important governmental objectives and be substantially related to achieving them.

   d) State preference for allocating family responsibilities is not an adequate state interest.

   e) State interests in providing financial assistance for needy spouses and in compensating women for past economic discrimination in marriage are both adequate state interests. But neither is sufficiently related to this sex-based means of achieving them.

   f) Gender is not a sufficiently accurate proxy for "need"; the Alabama law would ironically give the advantage to a financially secure wife whose husband is in need. Moreover, since individualized hearings at which the parties' relative financial circumstances are reviewed are already required, there is no need for the use of a gender-based generalization about economic disparity between married men and married women.

Olsen v.
Olsen

b. **Need for alimony--Olsen v. Olsen,** 557 P.2d 604 (Idaho 1976).

   1) **Facts.** Wilfred Olsen petitioned the court to modify a 1946 divorce decree under which he was required to pay his former wife, Frances, $200 per month alimony. Wilfred showed that, as a result of his retirement from the practice of medicine, his taxable income had decreased from about $45,000 a year to about $22,000 a year, including a pension and social security. Frances also showed a change in her taxable income from about $14,000 a year to about $10,000 a year due to her mandatory retirement. Frances needed the $200 from Wilfred in order to avoid having to withdraw from her $30,000 savings account, from which she drew $125 interest a month. The court denied Wilfred's petition. Wilfred appeals.

2) **Issue.** Must a party show a material, permanent, and substantial change in circumstances in order to justify a modification of a divorce decree and elimination of alimony?

3) **Held.** Yes. The judgment is affirmed.

    a) It is true that Wilfred's income has decreased significantly since his retirement. But he admits that he will return to the active practice of medicine if he finds it necessary. Frances had to retire and her income decreased significantly. She needs Wilfred's alimony payments in order to maintain her standard of living without having to dip into her savings. The trial court held that Wilfred had failed to meet his burden. No abuse of discretion was shown.

4) **Dissent.** Under prior cases, alimony can be awarded (and continued) only if the wife is unable to support herself. Frances has a bank account of $30,000. She can support herself without Wilfred's alimony. Considering the fact that the legislature has accepted the no-fault divorce concept and that women are increasingly able to support themselves, there is no longer a reasonable basis or justification for alimony awards. The alimony concept should be abandoned.

c. **Lump sum and rehabilitative alimony--Pfohl v. Pfohl,** 345 So. 2d 371 (Fla.   Pfohl v. Pfohl
    Dist. Ct. App. 1977).

    1) **Facts.** Mr. Pfohl (P) was granted a divorce from Mrs. Pfohl (D) and was awarded a lump sum alimony of $30,000, rehabilitative alimony of $5,000 a month for 18 months, and $30,000 for attorney's fees. During the marriage, the parties enjoyed an extremely high standard of living supported by D's substantial wealth (D has a net worth over four million dollars). At the time of the divorce, P was in good physical condition but impaired mental health. Both parties appealed. P believed that he should have received permanent alimony and D believed that P should have received none at all.

    2) **Issues.**

        a) Is it an abuse of discretion on the part of a court to award lump sum and rehabilitative alimony to a husband who has been supported at a high standard of living for nine years by his wife?

        b) Is the award of $30,000 against a millionaire wife for her husband's divorce attorney improper?

    3) **Held.** a) No. b) No. The judgment is affirmed.

        a) A wife may be required to pay alimony to her husband. This is in keeping with the current social trend toward establishing equality between the sexes and with the explicit language of recent Florida legislation.

        b) To be entitled to alimony, the husband must show the wife's ability to pay and his own needs, taking into account the standard of living shared by the parties to the marriage. D has a net worth of

$4,250,000; she is very well able to pay. The trial judge found that P had been totally supported by D in an extravagant manner; that whatever small earning skills P ever had were now impaired; and that as a result of the marital difficulties, P was suffering a temporary mental illness.

c) It does not matter that part of the time D supported P on money given to her by her father. What matters is that she supported the family unit, not P. The $120,000 lump sum and rehabilitative alimony is reasonable. P's needs are not so great that the trial court abused its discretion in refusing to award him more. In addition to the award, P has $200,000 in property given him by D during the marriage.

d) Essentially the same considerations support the award of attorney's fees. Need for legal counsel and relative ability to pay legal fees are the touchstones. One hundred twenty hours of attorney/clerk effort, leading to recovery of $120,000 alimony, justifies the $30,000 fee.

Herndon v.
Herndon

d. **Changed circumstances--Herndon v. Herndon,** 305 N.W.2d 917 (S.D. 1981).

1) **Facts.** Mr. Herndon (P) brought an action to reduce his child support payments and terminate his alimony payments to Mrs. Herndon (D). The original divorce decree awarded approximately $100,000 of accumulated property to D and allowed for both child support and alimony payments. However, both kinds of payments have been modified on two different occasions because of changed circumstances. P had been a chiropractor, but developed a severe arthritic condition in his hands which limited his ability to work. Surgery would help P's condition, but his ability would still be limited. Since the last modification of the divorce decree, P sold his practice, and now alleges as changed circumstances: appreciation of D's property awarded in the divorce decree; reduction of P's income; sale of P's practice due to the condition of his hands; and employment income of D. The trial court held that the changed circumstances were not sufficient to justify a reduction in the payments.

2) **Issue.** Have the circumstances of this case sufficiently changed to justify a reduction in support payments?

3) **Held.** No. The judgment is affirmed.

a) We are unable to say that the trial court abused its discretion. The condition of P's hands has remained unchanged since the first modification of the payments. Although D's property has appreciated, it was mostly due to inflation, which has also caused the cost of raising the child to increase.

b) Although P has sold his practice, there is evidence that he is still licensed to work. A person cannot voluntarily reduce his income in order to avoid alimony payments.

4) **Dissent.** Reviewing the economic status of the parties clearly indicates that D is not in need of alimony, and her monetary status greatly exceeds that of P. P's decision not to have surgery at the age of 60 does not mean he voluntarily reduced his income. The economic necessity of an alimony

recipient must be considered when reviewing the equity of such an award as well as the ability to meet the award. The circumstances have sufficiently changed since the last modification to justify termination of alimony payments.

e. **Explicit conditions to receiving alimony--Bell v. Bell,** 468 N.E.2d 859 (Mass. 1984).

1) **Facts.** Mrs. Bell (P) obtained support payments from her former husband Mr. Bell (D), by an incorporated separation agreement. The agreement provided that P was entitled to alimony for 15 years following a final entry of divorce, or until (i) her death, (ii) her remarriage, and/or (iii) her cohabitation with another man so as to give the outward appearance of marriage at any time prior to May 1, 1981. The agreement also provided that the parties would not interfere in each other's personal liberty. P brought a contempt complaint against D for his failure to continue support payments. The probate court dismissed P's complaint because she had cohabited with another man for three years. Although P had never represented that she was married to this individual, and had never commingled assets or kept joint bank accounts, the court found that she had given the outward appearance of marriage within the scope of the original separation agreement. The appeals court reversed and D appeals.

2) **Issue.** Does the cohabitation clause of the separation agreement apply where P is living with another man but does not appear to be receiving financial support from him?

3) **Held.** Yes. The judgment of appeals court is reversed.

   a) The plain language of the agreement does not mention support or P's continuing need in the absence of a new source. The parties could have expressly provided for the termination of alimony in the event of P's substantial support by another man, or if she became contractually entitled to such support.

   b) Furthermore, the termination of alimony payments under such circumstances does not interfere with P's personal liberty as set forth in the separation agreement. Clearly, the parties did not intend that the non-interference provision apply to a possible influence on P's decision to remarry or live with another man.

   c) The court cannot address P's equal protection argument because P did not raise it before the trial court.

4) **Dissent.** The significant factual point in this case is that P's conduct and relationship with her new friend are as consistent with not being married as they are with being married. However, the most troubling policy implication from this decision is that alimony payers, who are usually former husbands, can control the now independent lives of their ex-spouses through the court's interpretation and enforcement of a separation agreement clause.

2. **Child Support.** The amount of unpaid child support in America has reached mammoth proportions (not to mention the number of children living with a single parent whose other parent is under no judicial order to provide child support). The public burden of providing (with public funds) adequate support for the children of parents who have chosen to abandon their support responsibilities is a matter of growing concern.

Rand v. Rand

a. **Equality of support obligations--Rand v. Rand,** 374 A.2d 900 (Md. 1977).

    1) **Facts.** Florence (P) and Robert (D) Rand were divorced in 1971. P was awarded $250 monthly child support. In 1975, P sought an increase in support to finance the child's college education. The trial court found the child's expenses to be $520 per month and ordered D to pay $480 per month (92% of the child's expenses). The court of special appeals found this amount to be excessive and, relying on a statute giving both parents equal liability for child support, held that each spouse should pay a proportionate amount of his/her net income after expenses. In this case, D would pay $325 per month and P would pay the remaining $195 per month. P appeals.

    2) **Issue.** In a state which has made the Equal Rights Amendment part of its laws, is the father still primarily liable for the support of his minor children?

    3) **Held.** No. The case is remanded.

        a) At common law, the father was primarily liable for the support of his minor children. However, Maryland has a statute which places the duty of support on both parents and has also adopted the Equal Rights Amendment. Thus, gender cannot be a factor in determining the support obligation.

        b) The broad, sweeping language of the ERA is evidence that the people of Maryland are fully committed to equal rights for men and women. The parental obligation for child support is one that is shared by both parents. Child support awards must be made without regard to gender.

        c) The court does not mandate any specific formula for determining the share of support to be paid by each parent. But the "net income after personal expenses" test applied by the court of special appeals appears to be a fair one. The case must be remanded to the trial court so that the chancellor may, in the first instance, make the appropriate decision.

Nash v. Mulle

b. **Trial judge not limited to ordinary guidelines--Nash v. Mulle,** 846 S.W.2d 803 (Tenn. 1993).

    1) **Facts.** Mulle (D) fathered a child with Nash (P) in 1981 as the result of an extramarital affair, but has had nothing to do with P or the child since then. In 1984, paternity was established and D was ordered to pay $200 a month for child support, in addition to other expenses. In 1990, P sought an increase in child support because of

D's increased income. The court ordered D to pay $3,092.62 per month, with $1,780.17 reserved for a trust fund for the child's college education. The appeals court reversed, limited the award to $1,312 per month, or 21% of $6,250, the top monthly income to which the support guidelines apply, and disallowed the trust fund. P appeals.

2) Issues.

a) May a court exercise discretion in determining the proper measure of child support to be awarded in this case in view of the fact that D's monthly income exceeds $6,250?

b) Is the educational trust fund award an award of postminority support?

3) Held. a) Yes. b) No. The judgment is reversed and the case is remanded.

a) A court may consider all of the obligor's income in setting a child support award, as opposed to only the income up to the highest amount provided in the guidelines, and may set an award in excess of or lower than the guidelines.

b) A showing of need by the custodial parent is not required for an upward departure from the guidelines.

c) The guidelines require an award to reflect both parents' financial circumstances.

d) The trust fund is not an impermissible award of post-minority support; although child support payments may not extend beyond the child's minority, except in extraordinary circumstances involving physical or mental disability, benefits paid during a child's minority can extend beyond the child's minority.

e) Even though D has had nothing to do with the child, the court had discretion to establish the trust fund and part of the child support award since the purpose of the award was to prevent D from shirking his responsibility for the child he willingly fathered. The trust fund is explicitly provided for in the guidelines and assures that money earmarked for the child actually inures to the child's benefit.

c. Support of stepchildren--Washington Statewide Organization of Stepparents v. Smith, 536 P.2d 1202 (Wash. 1975).

1) Facts. Washington Statewide Organization of Stepparents (P) brought a class action asking the court to hold that laws enacted in 1969 by the Washington state legislature, imposing on stepparents the legal duty to support their stepchildren during the duration of their marriage to the natural parents of the children, did not apply to stepparents who were married to the parents of biologically unrelated children before 1969, or to hold the laws unconstitutional. The trial court dismissed the action on the merits. P appeals.

2) **Issue.** Did the trial court err in holding that legislation imposing the legal obligation on stepparents to support their stepchildren constitutionally applies to stepparents who were married to parents of biologically unrelated children before the support law was enacted?

3) **Held.** No. The judgment is affirmed.

   a) P's claim that the application of the support obligation to persons who were stepparents before 1969 unconstitutionally impairs contracts is groundless. Most jurisdictions have rejected that argument, and the New York cases endorsing it are out of harmony with the general rule. While marriage is a "civil contract," the legal rights and duties flowing from marriage are determined by statute and may be altered like other statutes. If P's position were adopted, it would mean that previously married persons could not enjoy the benefits of modern revised divorce laws, etc.

   b) Application of the 1969 support obligation to persons who were previously stepparents is not retroactive legislation, because the statute applies only to create a present-future obligation, not to create a retroactive duty of past support.

   c) Equal protection is not denied stepparents even though persons who cohabit with single parents without marriage are not put under the same support obligation. The legislature could conclude that marriage betokens a greater commitment to the single parent and her children. Also, it would be difficult and impractical to enforce a support obligation on unmarried cohabitants. Admittedly, children may receive more support from an unmarried cohabitant of their single parent than from stepparents, but the classification scheme need not be perfect in all details.

   d) P's argument that the 1969 legislation will discourage men from marrying women with children should be directed to the legislature.

4) **Concurrence.** While a heightened standard of review is necessary, the 1969 legislation is sustainable because all it does is treat stepparents like natural parents. Now stepchildren have three adults to whom they can look for support. Moreover, the legislation makes it possible for stepchildren to obtain AFDC benefits if a third adult, their stepparent, is unemployed.

5) **Comment.** The concurring opinion seems to have missed the issue. Of course there are "reasons" for making all stepparents support their stepchildren; the question is whether singling out stepparents for special liability not imposed on persons similarly situated is constitutionally permissible. The majority's analysis addressed the proper question.

M.H.B. v.   **d.** **Duty to support an unrelated child may arise by estoppel--M.H.B. v.**
H.T.B.   **H.T.B.,** 498 A.2d 775 (N.J. 1985).

   1) **Facts.** Marilyn (P) and Henry (D) were married in 1966 and had two children. Then P had an affair and became pregnant. D did not know his wife had been adulterous and thought the child, KB, was his. Three months after the child's birth, he learned of P's infidelity and left P. He eventually moved to other states. He continued to have close bonds with all three children. P brought the children to Wisconsin to live with D, but after six months the couple separated again. D said he loved KB and signed a separation agreement providing support for all three children. P dated other men, but none replaced D as KB's father figure. The parties were divorced and D was ordered to support all three children as he had agreed to do. He continued to express his love for and interest in KB. D remarried, and as his second wife did not get along with P, problems between D and P developed. D withheld some support payments. In January 1982, D petitioned for custody of all three children, but the case was dismissed so it could proceed in New Jersey. In March, P sought an increase of child support. D counterclaimed for custody of the children, then amended his counterclaim to deny support liability for KB. Human Levcocyte Analysis blood testing confirmed that D is not KB's father. The trial court nonetheless held that D was equitably estopped from denying support for KB. The appellate division affirmed that point. D appeals.

2) **Issue.** Can an unrelated adult be equitably estopped from denying child support under the terms of a previous support agreement voluntarily made by him?

3) **Held.** Yes. The judgment is affirmed by an equally divided court.

   a) In a previous case, the New Jersey Supreme Court recognized the doctrine of equitable estoppel in a child support context where it was shown that the course of conduct of a stepparent affirmatively encouraged reliance by the child on continuing support.

   b) D's actions here invited reliance and were tantamount to a knowing and affirmative representation of continuing support commitment. D's efforts to obtain custody of KB underscore this. KB's filial dependence on D is undeniable.

   c) The New Jersey Parentage Act does not shield D from support liability. N.J. Stat. Ann. section 9:17-44 provides that a court may order any appropriate party to pay support in the best interests of a child. While imposing support on a stepparent is exceptional, this is an exceptional case.

4) **Concurring in part, dissenting in part.** Expansion of the equitable estoppel doctrine is unwise. In the prior case, the stepparent tore up the support checks sent by the natural father. D did not do anything like that. The development of a close relationship to the child is not sufficient basis to impose a duty of support. D should be held liable for KB's support only until a support order may be entered against the biological father.

e. **Child support may be counted in assessing family income for AFDC purposes--Bowen v. Gilliard,** 483 U.S. 587 (1987).

Bowen v.
Gilliard

1) **Facts.** Beaty Mae Gilliard (P) receives Aid to Families with Dependent Children ("AFDC") benefits. She has eight children. She also received child support from the father of the eighth child pursuant to a child support order. The State of North Carolina included the child support in the family income computation, resulting in a reduction of AFDC benefits. P

brought a class action in 1970, arguing that she had a statutory right to exclude child support in computing family income for AFDC purposes. In 1971, the federal district court agreed and the Supreme Court affirmed the judgment on statutory grounds. In 1984, Congress amended the AFDC program to establish a uniform rule governing what family members must be included in income computations for AFDC, and it includes children receiving child support (except the first $50 of child support per month per child). After North Carolina adopted conforming regulations, P and others moved to reopen the 1971 decree. The district court held that the North Carolina and federal regulations violated the Due Process and Takings Clauses of the Fifth Amendment.

2) **Issue.** Does a welfare rule requiring the inclusion of child support in computing family income to determine eligibility for any amount of AFDC violate the Fifth Amendment?

3) **Held.** No. The judgment is reversed.

   a) It is for Congress, not the courts, to decide the policy questions of balancing and weighing welfare benefits.

   b) While the 1984 amendments severely impacted some families, they clearly furthered Congress's goal of decreasing federal expenditures.

   c) It was rational for Congress to modify the AFDC program to account for the reality that child support money generally provides significant benefits for the whole family.

   d) No standard of heightened scrutiny is appropriate because no fundamental right is infringed. The government is not seeking to impose orthodoxy on the unwilling, although a consequence of the new rule may be that many families change their living arrangements.

   e) No unconstitutional taking has occurred here since family members other than the child who is receiving support have no claim regarding treatment of that child support. Requiring assignment of the child support claim to the state is not a "taking" because the law does not require any custodial parent to apply for AFDC benefits.

C. **PROPERTY DIVISION**

As distinguished from support, property division represents (at least conceptually) a one-time division of economic resources rather than a continuing economic obligation.

1. **Types of Property.**

Mahoney v.
Mahoney

   a. **Professional degrees--Mahoney v. Mahoney, 453 A.2d 527 (N.J. 1982).**

1) **Facts.** Mr. Mahoney (P) filed a complaint of divorce, and Mrs. Mahoney (D) filed a counterclaim also seeking a divorce. The parties had been married for eight years, and both contributed to the household expenses except for a 16-month period when P attended school and received an MBA. During that time P contributed no money to the marriage and D contributed $24,000 to the household. Two years after obtaining his MBA, P filed the divorce complaint. The trial court held that the MBA degree constituted a property right and ordered the award of a reasonable sum as a credit for the maintenance of the household and the support of P during his educational period. The court of appeals reversed, and D appeals.

2) **Issues.**

   a) Is P's degree considered "property" which requires equitable distribution?

   b) If the degree is not property, is D entitled to recover the money she contributed to her husband's support while he pursued his professional education?

3) **Held.** a) No. b) Yes. The judgment is reversed and the case is remanded.

   a) Property has been given an expansive interpretation in regard to equitable distribution. A professional degree is a personal achievement of the holder. It cannot be sold and its value cannot readily be determined. It has none of the characteristics of property in the usual sense of the word. Equitable distribution of a professional degree would require the distribution of "earning capacity"—income that the degree holder might never obtain. The equitable distribution statute is restricted to property acquired during the marriage, not the speculation of what the income might be in the future. Estimating the future income that a professional degree may bring about is futile and will probably be inaccurate. A property division, unlike alimony, may not be adjusted. A professional degree therefore is not property that can be equitably distributed.

   b) Equitable distribution derives from the proposition that the supporting spouse should be reimbursed for contributions to the marital unit that, because of the divorce, did not bear its expected fruit for the supporting spouse. D has voluntarily subjected herself to a lower standard of living during the time that P was getting the degree. As a general principle, this court does not support reimbursement between former spouses in alimony proceedings. However, marriage is not a free ticket to a professional degree, and general fairness and equity would justify a remedial award or reimbursement alimony in the case at hand. Only monetary contributions made with the mutual expectation that both parties will derive increased income should be a basis for such an award.

b. Medical license may be treated as marital property--O'Brien v. O'Brien, 66 N.Y.2d 576 (1985).

O'Brien v. O'Brien

1) **Facts.** Mr. O'Brien (P) and Mrs. O'Brien (D) were married in 1971 while both were teachers. D pursued graduate studies to obtain a permanent teaching certificate, but relinquished the opportunity to further her education while P completed his bachelor's degree and premedical preparations. In 1973, P and D moved to Mexico, where P entered a medical school. D held several jobs to help support the family. In 1976, P and D returned to New York for P to complete his medical education. D resumed her former teaching position. P was licensed to practice medicine in 1980. He filed suit for divorce two months later and at the time of trial was a resident in general surgery, though he disliked that work and wished to specialize in internal medicine. The trial court found that D had contributed 76% of the parties' income. An expert for P testified that the present value of P's medical license was $472,000, based on the lifetime earnings of a general surgeon, and the present value of D's contribution to P's education was $103,390. The court held that the license was marital property and awarded D $188,800 (40% of its value) payable in 11 installments. P was also ordered to pay D's attorney and expert. The appellate division held that a professional license is not marital property. D appeals.

2) **Issue.** Is a medical license acquired during marriage marital property divisible on divorce in New York?

3) **Held.** Yes. The appellate division judgment is modified.

   a) New York's equitable distribution law provides that all property is either marital property or separate property, and that all property acquired by either or both spouses during marriage is marital property regardless of the form in which the title is held. Thus, everything of value acquired by a spouse during marriage is marital property. The legislature did not define the term further, but left that task to the courts.

   b) Like pension benefits, which have been held to be marital property, a medical license acquired during marriage is subject to equitable distribution.

   c) Section 236 of the Domestic Relations Law provides that where equitable distribution of an interest in a business, corporation, or profession would be contrary to the law, the court shall make a distributive award in lieu of actual distribution of the property. This suggests that a professional license may be marital property.

   d) The legislative history of this provision indicates that the legislature intended to replace the common law title system with equitable distribution of marital property, based on the premise that marriage is an economic partnership.

   e) In this case, nearly all of the parties' nine-year marriage was devoted to acquiring P's medical license. D's contributions were truly an investment in an economic partnership.

   f) While a professional license may or may not fit within the traditional concept of property, marital property for equitable distribution is not a traditional notion either.

   g) Limiting a working spouse to a maintenance award would be inconsistent with the economic partnership concept, and would perpetuate a dependency contrary to legislative intent. Equitable distribution is based on partition of economic partnership, not need.

h) Giving D mere reimbursement for her expenditure would ignore the noneconomic contributions of a spouse to acquiring an asset. Valuation of licenses is no more difficult than valuation of damages for wrongful death.

i) Marital fault may be considered in equitable distribution only in egregious cases which shock the conscience of the court, but no such conduct of D is evident here.

4) **Concurrence.** A distributive award may lock P into a kind of practice he dislikes because the amount he must pay is based on the amount he can earn in that practice. The degree of speculation here is disturbing. The equitable distribution provisions were intended to provide flexibility so that equity could be done.

5) **Comment.** Apart from the legal analysis, as a matter of equity should a court ignore the harsh economic consequences inflicted upon a long-supportive spouse by such an exploitive, "dump-her-when-the-work-is-done" spouse?

c. **Retirement or pension rights as "property"**--*In re* **Marriage of Brown,** 126 Cal. Rptr. 633 (Cal. 1976).

In re Marriage of Brown

1) **Facts.** Robert Brown (D) and Gloria Brown (P) sought a divorce after 23 years of marriage. At the time of the divorce decree, D had accumulated 72 of the required 78 points needed to be eligible for his pension from his employer. If D continued to work for two more years, he would have the required 78 points. P sought to have the pension rights divided as community property. The trial court, in following the previous decision of *French v. French*, 17 Cal. 2d 775 (1941), held that because the pension right had not yet vested and was contingent on D's continued employment for two more years, it was not a property right but only an expectancy and therefore could not be divided. P appeals.

2) **Issue.** Is a nonvested pension right an "expectancy" and therefore not subject to division?

3) **Held.** No. The judgment is reversed and the case is remanded.

a) The defining characteristic of an expectancy is that the holder has no enforceable right to its beneficence. California has concluded that a pension right does not derive from the beneficence of the employer, but is properly part of the consideration earned by the employee. It is a contractual right and therefore not an expectancy, but a chose in action. The employing body cannot deny or impair the contingent liability any more than it can refuse to make the salary payments. The pension right is therefore a contingent interest in property.

b) As the date of vesting and retirement approaches, the value of the pension right grows until it often represents the most important asset of the marital community. Under the *French* rule, a valuable pension right would escape division solely because dissolution occurred a few weeks before the maturing date. The *French* rule is therefore overruled.

c) In dividing nonvested pension rights, the court must take account of the possibility that death or termination of employment might destroy those rights before they mature. In some instances, because of the uncertainties of maturation of pension rights, the court may award each spouse an appropriate portion of each pension payment. Although this would require the court to continue jurisdiction to supervise the payments, the mere administrative burden cannot serve as support for an inequitable substantive rule.

d) This decision does not infringe upon the employee's freedom to contract because the employee still retains the right to decide, and by his own decision define, the nature of the retirement benefits owned by the community.

e) This decision cannot be given retroactive effect to cases in which a property decree has been entered, but can be applied in all cases where the property rights have not yet been adjudicated.

Mansell v. Mansell

d. Military benefits are governed by federal law--Mansell v. Mansell, 490 U.S. 581 (1989).

1) **Facts.** Gerald (P) and Gaye Mansell (D) were married for 23 years, during which time P served in the Air Force. At the time of their divorce, P was receiving both retirement pay and disability benefits in lieu of the balance of retirement pay. By agreement P agreed to pay D 50% of the total. Four years after the divorce, P asked the court to modify the decree to relieve him of the obligation of paying D any of the disability pay he was receiving. The California Superior Court denied the motion. The court of appeals affirmed and the California Supreme Court declined review.

2) **Issue.** Is military disability pay distributable as community property upon divorce?

3) **Held.** No. The judgment is reversed.

a) Domestic relations are preeminently matters of state law and Congress rarely intends to displace state authority. This is one of those rare cases.

b) Military personnel who serve for at least 20 years may retire with a pension. Those who become disabled may receive disability benefits, but to prevent double dipping must waive retirement benefits equal to the disability benefits. Since disability benefits are exempt from taxes, many veterans elect disability benefits and waive retirement. California treats military retirement payments earned during marriage as community property. In 1982, Congress passed the Former Spouses Protection Act ("FSPA") to permit state courts to treat military retirement pay as community property, overturning a contrary interpretation of the prior statute. The FSPA modified federal law regarding retirement, not disability pay. The language of the Act mentions only retirement pay, not disability pay.

c) The savings clause merely defeats any inference that the federal direct payments mechanism displaced state court authority to divide and garnish other property, not to *sub silentio* extend the FSPA to disability pay.

4) Dissent (O'Connor, Blackmun, JJ.). Family law is an area of state concern. Congress intended by the FSPA to restore to states their traditional control of domestic relations. The savings clause provides that nothing relieves a veteran of liability for payment of alimony, child support, or any other payments required by a court, and that means that disability pay can be divided as community property. The FSPA is designed to recognize the contributions of military spouses and protect their economic security.

D. ANTENUPTIAL PROPERTY SETTLEMENTS

1. Public Policy. Until recently, antenuptial contracts were disfavored in law as conducive to divorce. Now they are favored as making divorce easier to process (less litigious and more certain).

a. Burden of proof in antenuptial contracts--Matter of Estate of Benker, 331 N.W.2d 193 (Mich. 1982).

Matter of Estate of Benker

1) Facts. Mr. Benker died intestate, leaving as his sole heirs Mrs. Benker and his daughter from a previous marriage, Ruth Counts (P). Mr. Benker was 71 and Mrs. Benker was 60 years of age when the marriage took place, and both signed an antenuptial agreement three days before the marriage. In the agreement, both parties waived all rights of inheritance of the other's estate. Upon Mr. Benker's death, P brought this action to determine the validity of the agreement. Mrs. Benker was adjudicated legally incompetent and her son (D) was appointed legal guardian of the estate. The probate court found as facts that the decedent had a substantial estate of over $640,000, but had been secretive about it and lived a very modest lifestyle. Mrs. Benker's estate totaled about $110,000. The agreement contained no reference to the assets of either party, nor did it make any statement regarding disclosure of assets by the parties to the agreement. One attorney represented both clients in drafting the agreement and testified that he did not press the parties for full disclosure of the assets and could not remember to what extent the assets had been discussed. The attorney also testified that he was not concerned with what Mrs. Benker would receive upon Mr. Benker's death because he felt that the agreement was an "arm's length agreement" between the couple. The probate court held that there was a presumption of nondisclosure and that the evidence presented was not sufficient to rebut the presumption, and held the agreement invalid. The court of appeals reversed, holding that the burden of proof is on the party seeking to invalidate the antenuptial contract. D appeals.

2) **Issue.** Was the trial court correct to invoke a presumption of nondisclosure and in doing so invalidate the antenuptial agreement?

3) **Held.** Yes. The decision of the court of appeals is reversed.

  a) Public policy favors antenuptial agreements; however, in order for them to be valid, they must be fair, equitable, and reasonable in view of the surrounding facts and circumstances. Antenuptial agreements give rise to a special duty of disclosure not required in ordinary contract relationships so that the parties will be fully informed before entering into such agreements.

  b) The court of appeals properly interpreted the general rule of this state as placing the burden of proof on the party seeking to invalidate the agreement on the basis of fraud.

  c) A presumption of nondisclosure is properly invoked when the facts are, in general, as follows: (i) the agreement provides for a complete waiver of all rights and does not make any provision for the widow upon her husband's death; (ii) the husband's estate is very ample in comparison to the wife's; (iii) the decedent was shown to be rather secretive about his financial affairs; (iv) the agreement makes no reference as to whether the parties had been fully informed of the property interests of the other; (v) the widow was not represented by counsel; (vi) the attorney who drafted the agreement testified that he did not normally discuss the assets of the parties or press the full disclosure matter; and (vii) the scrivener testified that he was not concerned with what the widow would receive.

  d) All of the above factors are present in the case at hand and support the trial court's decision to invoke the presumption of nondisclosure.

4) **Comment.** If public policy truly did favor antenuptial contracts, would courts be so willing to indulge a presumption of nondisclosure? Perhaps this case is really about findings of fact based on evidence and not about presumptions.

Osborne v. Osborne

b. **Antenuptial contracts contemplating divorce--Osborne v. Osborne, 428 N.E.2d 810 (Mass. 1981).**

1) **Facts.** Mrs. Osborne (P) and Mr. Osborne (D) met and married while both were attending medical school. P is an heiress to a large family fortune amounting to nearly $17 million. At the time of their marriage, D had no assets of significant value. A few hours before the marriage took place, the parties entered into an agreement to discharge all statutory marital property rights. Also, the agreement provided that if the marriage is legally terminated, neither party shall be entitled to any alimony, support money, or any other money by virtue thereof. Also attached was a schedule accurately showing P's wealth and expectation of inheritance. During the marriage the parties maintained a high standard of living which was completely financed by the income of P's trust accounts. They

acquired over $1 million in personal assets and real estate. D now claims an ownership interest in the assets. The court of appeals upheld the validity of the antenuptial agreement and D was not awarded any of the assets.

2) **Issue.** Is an antenuptial agreement which contemplates divorce valid?

3) **Held.** Yes. The judgment is affirmed.

    a)   Although public policy favors antenuptial agreements entered into in contemplation of the death of a spouse, the majority of Massachusetts cases and current authority are against the validity of antenuptial agreements entered into in contemplation of future separation. This notion was based on the idea that such agreements would support divorce.

    b)   The Florida Supreme Court took the lead in departing from the above notion when the court held that antenuptial agreements settling alimony and property rights upon divorce are not void in all instances. Such agreements are no more likely to encourage divorce than antenuptial contracts in contemplation of death. There is no reason not to allow persons about to enter their marriage the freedom to settle their rights in the event that the marriage proves unsuccessful.

    c)   Such agreements should be judged by the fair disclosure rules. Also, agreements that settle the alimony and property rights of the parties in the event of a divorce should be binding on the courts to the same extent as postnuptial separation agreements. The agreement must be fair and reasonable at the time of entry of the judgment, and it may be modified by the courts in certain circumstances.

    d)   D was not under duress in entering into the agreement because he had learned of P's plan for such an agreement on several occasions before the marriage.

c. **Fraudulent nondisclosure does not invalidate premarital agreement in Florida--Stregack v. Moldofsky,** 474 So. 2d 206 (Fla. 1985).

Stregack v. Moldofsky

    1) **Facts.** Sally (P) and Manuel Moldofsky signed a prenuptial agreement before they married in which they waived all rights in each other's estates. Manuel died and P filed a notice of elective share. Susan Stregack (D), who was Manuel's daughter and his personal representative, moved to strike the notice. P filed an action in Florida Circuit Court to cancel the antenuptial agreement for fraud, claiming that Manuel told her he had no assets, when he was worth $250,000. The trial court dismissed the action. The district court reversed. D appeals.

    2) **Issue.** May a surviving spouse challenge an antenuptial agreement based upon fraudulent nondisclosure in Florida?

    3) **Held.** No. The judgment of the district court is quashed.

        a)   In 1962, this court held that a valid antenuptial agreement must contain fair and reasonable provisions for the spouse waiving his or her rights, or else the spouse obtaining the waiver must make a full and fair disclosure of assets.

    b)   The legislature modified that rule by enacting Fla. Stat. section 732.702, which provides that no disclosure shall be required for an agreement, contract, or waiver executed before marriage.

    c)   Interpreting that provision, this court held that nondisclosure, however pled, could not constitute a basis for invalidating an antenuptial agreement. Since no disclosure is required at all, it would not be fair to punish the dead spouse who attempted some disclosure.

4)   Dissent. Here, Manuel grossly misrepresented his financial worth to P, if her allegations are accepted as true. Section 732.702 relieves one of making any disclosure, but if one steps outside the protection of that provision and makes some disclosure, it must be truthful. This is not a case of nondisclosure but fraudulent disclosure.

Avitzur v.
Avitzur

d.   Enforceability of religious agreements concerning marriage--Avitzur v. Avitzur, 58 N.Y.2d 108 (1983).

1)   Facts. Mr. Avitzur (D) and Mrs. Avitzur (P) were married in accordance with Jewish tradition. Prior to the marriage, both parties signed the "Ketubah," which in essence stated that both parties would live in faithfulness and affection to each other in accordance to Jewish law and tradition. It also provides that the parties agree to recognize the "Beth Din" of the Jewish Theological Seminary as having authority to summon and counsel them. Jewish law also required the counsel and permission of the Beth Din to obtain a religious divorce. After 12 years of marriage, D sought and was granted a civil divorce. P sought to summon D before the Beth Din pursuant to the Ketubah in order for her to obtain a religious divorce, thereby allowing her to remarry. The trial court denied D's motion to dismiss for lack of jurisdiction. The appellate court reversed.

2)   Issue. Does the religious agreement of the Ketubah constitute a marital contract enforceable by a state court?

3)   Held. Yes. The judgment is reversed.

    a)   P and D, in signing the Ketubah, entered into a contract which formed the basis of their marriage. P is not attempting to compel D to obtain a religious divorce, but merely seeks to enforce an agreement made by D to appear before and accept the decision of a designated tribunal.

    b)   The contractual obligation P seeks to enforce is closely analogous to an antenuptial agreement to arbitrate a dispute in accordance with the law and tradition chosen by the parties. The agreement is enforceable so long as its enforcement violates neither the law nor the public policy of the state.

    c)   Enforcement of the Ketubah does not violate the state constitution because the court, in ordering D to appear before the Beth Din, is not intruding upon matters of religious doctrine and practice. The case

can be decided solely upon the application of neutral principles of contract law. D's motion to dismiss the complaint is therefore denied.

4) Dissent. What is sought to be enforced is an aspect of the relationship peculiar to the religion within which the ceremony
creating it took place. The evident objective of the present
action is to obtain a religious divorce, a matter well beyond the
authority of any civil court.

5) Comment. Under the modern Establishment Clause doctrine,
would this be a religious "entanglement" making the decision of
the New York court unconstitutional? Has the New York court
effectively denied D his right to change his religious beliefs?

E. POSTNUPTIAL ECONOMIC (SEPARATION) AGREEMENTS

Agreements negotiated by the parties after marriage are of enormous significance to the modern lawyer; without such agreements, courts and lawyers would
have much more burdensome tasks at the time of divorce, and the parties might
perpetuate to an even greater degree the hostility and bitterness of marital
failure.

1. Modern Issue. Careful consideration of many complex issues is necessary
to make a workable and enforceable separation agreement.

a. Merger and incorporation--Johnston v. Johnston, 465 A.2d 436
(Md. 1983).

Johnston v.
Johnston

1) Facts. Mr. Johnson (P) and Mrs. Johnston (D) were married in
1948, lived together for 23 years, and had four children.
Nearly two years after separating, the parties each retained
separate counsel and negotiated a separation agreement which
provided, *inter alia*, that it would be incorporated in but would
not be merged with their divorce decree. Four months later, a
Maryland court granted P's divorce complaint in a decree that
specifically incorporated the separation agreement. Eight years
later, P filed a petition to have the agreement declared void,
arguing that he was mentally incompetent at the time he signed
the agreement. D opposed and filed a motion to strike the
petition, which the chancellor granted. The court of special
appeals affirmed. Both lower courts concluded that the agreement was merged in the divorce decree. P appeals.

2) Issues.

a) Did the lower courts err in holding that the separation
agreement merged in the divorce decree?

b) Did the courts below err in striking P's petition to nullify
the separation agreement?

3) Held. a) Yes. b) No. The judgment is affirmed.

a) "Merger is the substitution of rights and duties under the judgment or decree for those under the agreement or cause of action sued upon." Incorporation is specific reference to an agreement in a decree for purposes of identifying the agreement and establishing its validity. If an agreement is merged in a decree, the rights under the agreement may be enforced by such decree-effectuation devices as contempt, direct execution, etc. If an agreement is not merged, it retains a separate character and enforcement is under the normal processes for contract enforcement.

b) Whether an agreement is merged in a decree is a question of intent. As a general rule, incorporation of an agreement in a decree merges the agreement into the decree unless the agreement contains an explicit nonmerger clause, in which case incorporation does not affect merger. By approving of the agreement, the court adopts the non-merger clause as its intent unless the court specifically states otherwise. Thus, the agreement here was not merged with the decree.

c) Maryland Rule 625a does not apply to preclude attack by P on the agreement here because that rule only protects judgments from attack, and P is attacking the unmerged agreement.

d) But P is precluded from attacking the validity of the agreement by the doctrine of res judicata. Numerous courts have held that incorporation of an agreement into the decree is tantamount to a final and binding adjudication of property rights and of the validity of the agreement, and cannot be collaterally attacked.

e) Here, P was represented by competent counsel at the time of execution of the agreement, P testified at the hearing giving his consent to the agreement, and the chancellor approved of the lengthy and detailed agreement.

4) Comment. It is generally said that res judicata precludes relitigation of any matter fully and fairly litigated and finally decided in a prior adjudication. Where the parties do not contest a point but stipulate or agree to it in the prior adjudication, should the doctrine of issue preclusion apply?

Carter v. Carter

b. Modification of postnuptial agreements--Carter v. Carter, 211 S.E.2d 253 (Va. 1975).

1) Facts. Mr. Carter (P) and Mrs. Carter (D) obtained a divorce decree that incorporated therein a settlement agreement which provided that D would have custody of the minor children and that P would pay her a sum in "lieu of alimony and as further support and maintenance of the children." The agreement also provided that the payments were to cease upon the emancipation of the youngest child and that D was to keep the family home for the benefit of the children. Soon after the divorce, P took over custody of the children because D developed mental health problems. P then petitioned the court for permanent custody and termination of the monthly payments to D. The trial court found the agreement to be ambiguous, and heard evidence as to the intent of the parties concerning whether the amount paid to D was considered alimony or child support. The agree ment also made the payments to D taxable as to her and deductible by P, by deliberately avoiding apportionment of the payments as between alimony and child support. P testified that no part of the payments was to be alimony for D. D testified that she believed that the payments were in part for her benefit rather than entirely for the children. The trial courtf found that the parties intended one-fourth of the monthly payments to benefit D, which would therefore survive a transfer of custody. D appeals the decision that reduces the payments to her.

2) **Issue.** Did the trial court err in ruling that the ambiguous settlement agreement provided for both alimony and child support?

3) **Held.** No. The judgment is modified and the case is remanded.

   a)   The wording of the agreement and the evidence fully supports the construction that the payments included alimony, but the majority of the money was considered child support.

   b)   In some jurisdictions it is held that the court may apportion unitary awards made pursuant to settlement agreements in divorce proceedings. We adopt this rule.

   c)   The trial court erred, however, in fixing D's share at one-fourth. The oldest child had already become emancipated and therefore only three beneficiaries remained. Therefore one-third of the monthly payments is to be considered alimony, and payment of that amount is to be continued.

c. **Promoting divorce--Glickman v. Collins,** 120 Cal. Rptr. 76 (Cal. 1975).

Glickman
v. Collins

1) **Facts.** Claire Glickman (P) brought an action against Hilda Collins (D) to enforce a guaranty agreement when the former husband of both of them defaulted in his support obligations to P. P had refused to sign a property agreement with her estranged husband, Gerald Glickman, or agree to a divorce, until D, Gerald's new lover, agreed to guaranty Gerald's obligation to make alimony and child support payments. D contended that such an agreement tends to promote divorce and is void as against public policy. The trial court held for P. D appeals.

2) **Issue.** Where a marriage is already irretrievably broken down, does an agreement that facilitates the dissolution of that marriage violate public policy?

3) **Held.** No. The judgment is affirmed and modified slightly to eliminate payments for items not covered in the separation agreement.

   a)   Public policy seeks to foster and protect marriage and to avoid separation. Generally, agreements that promote dissolution are against public policy. However, a different rule applies where the marriage is already irretrievably broken before the agreement is entered into.

    b)   If the marriage has deteriorated to where legal grounds for divorce exist and there is little hope of conciliation, dissolution of the marriage is not against public policy and is often the preferred solution. Here, the trial court found substantial evidence that the Glickman marriage was beyond redemption when the guaranty agreement was executed. Gerald had been living with D, the other woman, for several months. P had ample grounds for divorce.

Levine v.
Levine

d.   Validity of a postnuptial agreement--Levine v. Levine, 56 N.Y.2d 42 (1982).

    1)   Facts. Mr. Levine (D) and Mrs. Levine (P) entered into a separation agreement that was prepared by one attorney representing both parties. The separation agreement provided that the wife was to have custody of the children, and the right to occupy the marital residence and retain all the furniture. D also agreed to pay $125 a week in support for the wife and the two children and pay for all the insurance, clothing, medical expenses, and education of the children. D was to pay all charges on the home and provide P with use of a Cadillac. At the meeting to discuss the terms of the agreement, the attorney instructed the wife that she was free to seek independent counsel. Later the wife commenced this action seeking to have the separation agreement set aside as inequitable and unconscionable, alleging that she was not represented by counsel of her own choosing, and the husband exerted undue influence upon her. The trial court dismissed the action and the appellate court reversed. D appeals.

    2)   Issue. Is a separation agreement prepared by one attorney representing both parties invalid for reasons of unfairness and undue influence?

    3)   Held. No. The judgment is reversed.

        a)   To establish her entitlement to relief, P would have to demonstrate both overreaching and unfairness. Separation agreements are more readily set aside in equity under circumstances that would be insufficient to nullify ordinary contracts. The general rule is that if execution of the agreement was fair, no further inquiry will be made.

        b)   The fact that only one attorney represented the parties in the preparation of the agreement does not require an automatic nullification of the agreement. As long as the attorney fairly advised the parties of both the salient issues and the consequences of joint representation, and the separation agreement arrived at was fair, rescission will not be granted.

        c)   The trial court found that the attorney remained neutral throughout his involvement with the parties. The agreement was designed to maintain the wife and the two children in the style to which they were accustomed to living. The agreement was therefore valid.

F. TAX CONSEQUENCES OF DIVORCE

1. **General Considerations.** Divorce lawyers may not carefully consider the tax consequences of divorce settlement terms, and this is probably due to their clients' insistent preoccupation with other aspects of the litigation. But the tax consequences can have substantial economic impact and can be long-lasting; they must be considered.

2. **Provisions of 1984 Tax Reform Act ("TRA") Affecting Divorce.**

   a. **Property settlements.** Gain or loss will no longer be recognized on a transfer of property to a spouse or to a former spouse if the transfer is incident to the divorce, *i.e.,* if the transfer occurs within one year after the marriage ceases or it is related to the cessation of the marriage. The transferee takes over the transferor's adjusted basis.

   b. **Alimony.** Payments between spouses in connection with marital separation and dissolution are treated consistently, *i.e.,* that which is taxable to the payee is deductible by the payor, but that which is not taxable to the payee is not deductible by the payor. The TRA has abolished the requirements that the payments be periodic and that they discharge a state law duty of support. Now, cash payments under any divorce or separation instrument are taxable to the payee and deductible by the payor unless they are disqualified.

      1) **Disqualifying provisions.**

         a) **Child support.**

         b) **Designated payments.** The spouses may designate in the post-separation instrument that payments are not taxable to the payee or deductible by the payor.

         c) **Cessation at death.** The payments must cease at the payee's death.

         d) **Living together.** Legally separated spouses cannot be living together.

         e) **Excess front-loading.** The Code disqualified excessively front-loaded payments, *i.e.,* those in which the stream of payments called for by the instrument does not last for at least six post-separation years.

   c. **Exemption for children of divorced parents.** The non-custodial parent gets the exemption for children of divorced parents if the custodial parent signs a written release of his right to claim the exemption for the current year. The non-custodial parent must attach this declaration to his return. This permission allows the parents to negotiate over who gets the exemption and to compensate the parent who does not claim it. The custodial parent can waive his right to the exemption.

The law prior to TRA, under which the exemption could be allocated to the non-custodial parent by a divorce decree or a written agreement, remains applicable to pre-1985 decrees or agreements (unless the spouses modify these agreements after 1984, explicitly adopting the new provisions).

d. **Deduction for medical expenses.** In the case of divorced parents, a child will be considered a dependent of both parents for purposes of the medical expense deduction. Thus, if a father is entitled to claim the exemption for a child living with her mother, the mother can still deduct any medical expenses she pays for the child.

e. **1986 Tax Reform Act.** In 1986 Congress modified the front-end loading rules to eliminate the penalty for heavy, early rehabilitative alimony.

G. BANKRUPTCY CONSEQUENCES OF DISSOLUTION

1. **Planning for Financial Failure.** It has been stated that, for many middle and lower income level Americans, bankruptcy follows divorce as night follows day. Many schemes for continuing economic relations, deferred property transfers and pay outs which might be attractive at face value may be rendered virtually worthless if the obligated spouse files bankruptcy.

White v.
White

a. **Bankruptcy case need not automatically stay divorce proceeding-- White v. White,** 851 F.2d 170 (6th Cir. 1988).

1) **Facts.** Patricia White (P) instituted divorce proceedings against John White (D), who was ordered to make temporary alimony payments of $800 weekly. D made no payments, and P moved for the appointment of a receiver for D's property. D then filed Chapter 11 bankruptcy proceedings. Under the automatic stay provisions of the Bankruptcy Code, the state divorce proceeding was halted. P moved to lift the stay in order that the marital estate (which also constituted the bankruptcy estate) might be appropriately divided. The bankruptcy court granted her request and lifted the stay, noting that the state court had prior in rem jurisdiction. D appealed, and the U.S. District Court affirmed. D appeals again.

2) **Issue.** Where a bankruptcy proceeding is instituted in response to a divorce action, may the bankruptcy court lift the automatic stay of state court proceedings in order that a marital estate may be divided?

3) **Held.** Yes. The judgment is affirmed.

a) An earlier case, *In re Washington*, 623 F.2d 1169 (6th Cir. 1980), would have allowed the state court to proceed on general principles of comity, which would give exclusive jurisdiction to the first court exercising in rem jurisdiction over the property at issue. That 1980 case does not control, however, because of recent changes in the Bankruptcy Code intended to preclude this type of jurisdictional dispute.

    b)   Under federal bankruptcy law, a debtor's interest in property is determined after reference to state law. The bankruptcy court's lifting of the stay against state court proceedings here will permit the state court to determine property interests in connection with the divorce, an area in which it has expertise; it will also help keep the bankruptcy court out of family law matters, which are traditionally reserved to the state courts.

    c)   The provisions for lifting the automatic stay should be deemed to apply in these circumstances for the limited purpose of allowing the state court to exercise its domestic relations authority, including deciding the fair allocation of the marital estate. This is not a per se rule, however; each case must be decided on its facts. This will ensure both that bankruptcy law is not used as a weapon in marital disputes and that spouses cannot collude in staging a divorce to defeat creditors.

b. **Pre-existing interest in marital property required to avoid lien--Farrey v. Sanderfoot,** 500 U.S. 291 (1991).

    1)   **Facts.** When Farrey and Sanderfoot divorced, the court divided the property equally between the parties, granting Sanderfoot sole title to all the real estate the parties had owned as joint tenants. Sanderfoot was required to make payments to Farrey to insure equal division of their net marital assets; Farrey was granted a lien against Sanderfoot's real property to secure the award. Sanderfoot made no payments, and subsequently filed for bankruptcy, listing the marital home and real estate as exempt homestead property. The bankruptcy court denied Sanderfoot's motion to avoid Farrey's lien. The district court reversed, and a divided court of appeals affirmed. The Supreme Court granted certiorari to resolve the conflict of authority.

    2)   **Issue.** Whether section 522(f) of the Bankruptcy Code allows the debtor to avoid the fixing of a lien on a homestead, where debtor never possessed the interest to which the lien attached before it attached as a result of a divorce decree?

    3)   **Held.** No. The Court of Appeals decision is affirmed.

    a)   11 U.S.C. section 522(f)(1) provides that a debtor may avoid the fixing of a lien on an interest of the debtor on property to the extent that such lien impairs an exemption to which the debtor would be entitled if the lien is a judicial lien. The relevant part of the statute is "fixing of a lien on an interest of the debtor in property . . . ."

    b)   Unless the debtor had the property interest to which the lien attached at some point before the lien attached to that interest, he or she cannot avoid the fixing of the lien under section 522(f)(1). A fixing

Domestic Relations - 161

that takes place before the debtor acquires an interest, by definition, is not on the debtor's interest.

    c)   In this case, Sanderfoot took his new interest (fee simple ownership of the real estate) and the lien together in the divorce decree, as if he had purchased an already encumbered estate from a third party. Sanderfoot never possessed his new fee simple interest before the lien fixed, thus section 522(f)(1) is not available to void the lien. Sanderfoot cannot be permitted to use the statute to deprive Farrey of protection of her pre-existing homestead interest.

    d)   The purpose of the statute is to protect the debtor's exempt property, and Congress intended it as a device to thwart creditors who, sensing impending bankruptcy, rush to court to obtain a judgment to defeat debtor's exemptions. To permit a lien to be avoided where the debtor at no point possessed the interest without the judicial lien would allow judicial lienholders to be defrauded through the conveyance of an encumbered interest to a prospective debtor.

    4)   **Concurrence** (Kennedy, Souter, JJ.). Later cases may yield a different result depending on the relevant state laws defining the estate owned by the spouse who had a pre-existing interest in marital property and the state laws governing awards of property under a divorce decree. It is crucial in this case that Sanderfoot conceded that the divorce decree extinguished his property rights. Absent this concession, there is no indication in the record that the court divested Sanderfoot of his pre-existing interest. It gave sole title to Sanderfoot; he obtained Farrey's one-half interest while retaining his own interest. Depending on the type of tenancy involved and the language in a decree for property division, a judicial lien could attach to a husband's predecree interest in his one-half of the marital property, and section 522(f)(1) could be used to avoid at least part of his wife's lien. Congressional action may be necessary to avoid an unjust result in future cases.

H. ENFORCEMENT

    1.   **Practical Problems.** In addition to the issue of establishing a legal right to support or property from a former spouse, there is the practical problem of enforcement. Since emotional involvement is so great, it is not uncommon for parties to go to extremes to refuse to comply with orders that offend them.

Hicks on Behalf of Feiock v. Feiock

    a.   **Enforcement of contempt for nonpayment of child support does not violate the Constitution--Hicks on Behalf of Feiock v. Feiock,** 485 U.S. 624 (1988).

    1)   **Facts.** In 1976, Phillip Feiock (D) was ordered to begin making child support payments to his ex-wife for the support of their three children. For six years, D made only sporadic payments of child support. His ex-wife (P) moved to enforce the support order, and in June 1984, the California court ordered him to begin paying $150 per month, commencing July 1984. After two months, D ceased paying child support again. Nine months later, he was served with an order to show cause why he should not be held in contempt of court. At a hearing in August 1985, P made a prima facie showing of contempt by showing that D was ordered to pay child support, D knew of the order, and D did not pay. D's defense of financial inability to pay was proved for four months, but D was found to be in contempt for five months and sentenced to five days incarceration for each incident (25 days total). Sentence was suspended and D was put on probation conditioned on payment of the $150 child support, plus $50 back payments. The California Court of Appeals annulled the contempt order, and the California Supreme Court denied review. P appeals.

2) **Issue.** Does it violate the Constitution to hold a person who fails to pay court-ordered child support in civil contempt of court when the burden of proving inability to pay rests with the defendant?

3) **Held.** No. The judgment is vacated and the case is remanded.

   a) In assessing whether the Due Process Clause of the Constitution is violated, the State's characterization of a contempt proceeding as criminal is not dispositive, for the issue is one of federal law, not state law. This is especially so when the labels or distinctions, as between "civil" and "criminal" contempt, are blurred. The fact that the court of appeals found the contempt provisions to be "quasi-criminal" is not dispositive.

   b) The purpose of civil contempt is remedial, for the benefit of the complainant. The purpose of criminal contempt is punitive, to vindicate the authority of the court. If the court conditions release from confinement for contempt upon compliance with the order, it must be viewed as remedial. Of course, there are incidental effects in either case, but they do not transform civil contempt into criminal contempt.

   c) Ability to pay the child support ordered is an essential element of the cause of action for contempt, but Cal. Civ. P. Code section 1209.5 puts the burden of persuasion regarding inability to pay on the defendant. If applied to a criminal proceeding, this would violate due process because it would violate the presumption of innocence, yet the same provision would not violate due process if applied in a civil proceeding.

   d) D's jail sentence was conditioned upon nonpayment of the support ordered. It is unclear whether the ultimate satisfaction of the past arrearages would purge the sentence entirely. Thus, the matter should be remanded to the trial court to clarify the nature of the sentence imposed, whether criminal or civil.

4) **Dissent** (O'Connor, J., Rehnquist, C.J., Scalia, J.). The Due Process Clause does not prevent a state from assuming that a support-obligated parent is capable of paying the amount of child support ordered by a court, and putting the burden of proving otherwise upon the one claiming inability to pay. The purpose of the proceeding below was to enforce payment of child support, and the conditional

incarceration order is consistent with that remedial intent. The contempt order was coercive, not punitive.

5) **Comment.** On remand, the California Court of Appeals held that the contempt proceedings were really criminal, but that inability to pay was an affirmative defense to a nonmandatory presumption of ability to pay.

State on
Behalf of
McDonnell v.
McCutcheon

b. **URESA--State on Behalf of McDonnell v. McCutcheon,** 337 N.W.2d 645 (Minn. 1983).

1) **Facts.** Jean McDonnell (P) and James McCutcheon (D) were divorced in New York in 1970. Pursuant to agreement, P was awarded custody of their six-year-old daughter, and the decree ordered D to pay child support at the rate of $25 to $40 per week, plus 10% of D's increased gross income. As of December 1981, D was in arrears $24,717, and the amount he would owe for support under the original decree would be $426 per month. P filed an action to recover arrearages and to compel ongoing support in Colorado. The file was transmitted to Minnesota, where D now lives. D opposed, arguing that P had wrongfully interfered with his visitation by moving to Colorado (though prior to P's move to Colorado, D had moved to another part of New York and had ceased to regularly visit the child, and D subsequently moved to Minnesota). The trial court found that P had removed the child from New York to Colorado without compelling personal reason (P says it was for the healthful air; D says it was because P developed a relationship with a man there), canceled the arrearages, and ordered D to pay only $160 per month child support. P appeals.

2) **Issue.** Did the trial court err in refusing to enforce the indebtedness for arrearages and in reducing the amount of child support to $160 per month?

3) **Held.** No. The judgment is affirmed.

a) The 1968 revised version of the Uniform Reciprocal Enforcement of Support Act ("URESA") applies instead of the 1958 version. P's action was filed in Colorado before the effective date of the Minnesota law replacing the 1958 version with the 1968 version, but the file was not transmitted to Minnesota and the case was not commenced here until after the effective date of the 1968 version.

b) This case involves a "standard" action to enforce support under the URESA and not an action to enforce a foreign judgment or to register a foreign support order.

c) Under URESA, the duty of support is determined under the law of the responding state (obligor's residence). A foreign support order is proof of a duty to support, but the responding state is not required to award the same level of support.

d) Under Minnesota law, the amount of support is determined without regard to marital misconduct by reference to five statutory factors. Wrongful deprivation of visitation is not to be considered in setting the level of support. A 1978 statutory provision provides so explicitly. Also, URESA itself provides that the determination or enforcement of support "is unaffected by interference . . . with custody or visitation."

e) While the trial court erred in relying on P's interference with D's visitation rights in reducing the level of support to $160, examination of the proper factors, *e.g.*, the parties' relative financial position, the projected costs of college, potential for summer employment, etc., leads to the conclusion that the sum of $160 per month is not unreasonable.

f) P could have registered the New York order in Minnesota to recover the accrued arrearages. In a standard URESA action, however, the responding state is not bound to conform to the foreign order.

g) Once registered, a foreign support order would be subject to the same defenses and motions as a support order of Minnesota. It is not clear that even New York would require D to pay the full amount of arrearages—D could argue laches or waiver, and D's move to Colorado could be considered.

h) In any event, P should have proceeded by registration and not under URESA. While it was error for the trial court to indicate that it was effectively canceling the New York order, it was not error for the trial court to decide not to enforce the arrearages, based on its evaluation of the evidence as to need, history of payment, etc.

4) **Comment.** The wooden analysis of the Minnesota Supreme Court is a classic example not only of judicial misapprehension of the law of conflicts but of why uniform acts are so often disappointing in practice.

2. **Federalism and Increasing Involvement of the National Government.** As noted by the Supreme Court in *Mansell v. Mansell, supra,* the regulation of domestic relations is "preeminently [a] matter of state law." Traditionally, the federal government has seldom attempted to directly regulate matters of family law. With some notable but relatively rare exceptions, that is still true today. However, that is not to say that federal law and policies do not impact upon and significantly influence state family laws. In the American system of interdependent federal-state government, that would be impossible. Moreover, from time to time (and perhaps with increasing frequency), Congress has deliberately attempted to influence state family law and policy indirectly by conditioning eligibility of states to receive various forms of federal subsidies on the enactment by the state of particular legislation, *e.g.*, child abuse reporting laws, child support guidelines, etc. Likewise, there has been some effort by Congress to remove federally created obstacles to implementation of state domestic relations laws and policies, as the *Mansell* case illustrates.

TABLE OF CASES

(Page numbers of briefed cases in bold)

Notes

Notes

Notes

Notes

Notes

Publications Catalog

Features:
Gilbert Law Summaries
Legalines
Gilbert Interactive Software
CaseBriefs Interactive Software
Law School Legends Audio Tapes
Employment Guides
& Much More!

Prices Subject To Change Without Notice

For more information visit our World Wide Web site at http://www.gilbertlaw.com or write for a free 32 page catalog:
. **Harcourt Brace Legal and Professional Publications, 176 West Adams, Ste. 2100, Chicago, Illinois 60603**

Gilbert Law Summaries are the best selling outlines in the country, and have set the standard for excellence since they were first introduced more than twenty-five years ago. It's Gilbert's unique combination of features that makes it the one study aid you'll turn to for all your study needs!

Administrative Law
By Professor Michael R. Asimow, U.C.L.A.
Separation of Powers and Controls Over Agencies; (including Delegation of Power) Constitutional Right to Hearing (including Liberty and Property Interests Protected by Due Process, and Rulemaking-Adjudication Distinction); Adjudication Under Administrative Procedure Act (APA); Formal Adjudication (including Notice, Discovery, Burden of Proof, Finders of Facts and Reasons); Adjudicatory Decision Makers (including Administrative Law Judges (ALJs), Bias, Improper Influences, Ex Parte Communications, Familiarity with Record, Res Judicata); Rulemaking Procedures (including Notice, Public Participation, Publication, Impartiality of Rulemakers, Rulemaking Record); Obtaining Information (including Subpoena Power, Privilege

Against Self-incrimination, Freedom of Information Act, Government in Sunshine Act, Attorneys' Fees); Scope of Judicial Review; Reviewability of Agency Decisions (including Mandamus, Injunction, Sovereign Immunity, Federal Tort Claims Act); Standing to Seek Judicial Review and Timing.
ISBN: 0-15-900000-9 Pages: 300 $19.95

Agency and Partnership
By Professor Richard J. Conviser, Chicago Kent
Agency: Rights and Liabilities Between Principal and Agent (including Agent's Fiduciary Duty, Principal's Right to Indemnification); Contractual Rights Between Principal (or Agent) and Third Persons (including Creation of Agency Relationship, Authority of Agent, Scope of Authority, Termination of Authority, Ratification,

Liability on Agents, Contracts); Tort Liability (including Respondeat Superior, Master-Servant Relationship, Scope of Employment). Partnership: Property Rights of Partner; Formation of Partnership; Relations Between Partners (including Fiduciary Duty); Authority of Partner to Bind Partnership; Dissolution and Winding up of Partnership; Limited Partnerships.
ISBN: 0-15-900001-7 Pages: 142 $16.95

Antitrust
By Professor Thomas M. Jorde, U.C. Berkeley, Mark A. Lemley, University of Texas, and Professor Robert H. Mnookin, Harvard University
Common Law Restraints of Trade; Federal Antitrust Laws (including Sherman Act, Clayton Act, Federal Trade Commission Act, Interstate Commerce Requirement, Antitrust Remedies);

Monopolization (including Relevant Market, Purposeful Act Requirement, Attempts and Conspiracy to Monopolize); Collaboration Among Competitors (including Horizontal Restraints, Rule of Reason vs. Per Se Violations, Price Fixing, Division of Markets, Group Boycotts); Vertical Restraints (including Tying Arrangements); Mergers and Acquisitions (including Horizontal Mergers, Brown Shoe Analysis, Vertical Mergers, Conglomerate Mergers); Price Discrimination — Robinson-Patman Act; Unfair Methods of Competition; Patent Laws and Their Antitrust Implications; Exemptions From Antitrust Laws (including Motor, Rail, and Interstate Water Carriers, Bank Mergers, Labor Unions, Professional Baseball).
ISBN: 0-15-900328-8   Pages: 193 $16.95

All titles available at your law school bookstore
or call to order: 1-800-787-8717

LAW SCHOOL LEGENDS SERIES

America's Greatest Law Professors on Audio Cassette

Wouldn't it be great if all of your law professors were law school legends? You know — the kind of professors whose classes everyone fights to get into. The professors whose classes you'd take, no matter what subject they're teaching. The kind of professors who make a subject sing. You may never get an opportunity to take a class with a truly brilliant professor, but with the Law School Legends Series, you can now get all the benefits of the country's greatest law professors…on audio cassette!

Administrative Law
Professor To Be Announced
Call For Release Date

TOPICS COVERED (Subject to Change): Classification Of Agencies; Adjudicative And Investigative Action; Rule Making Power; Delegation Doctrine; Control By Executive; Appointment And Removal; Freedom Of Information Act; Rule Making Procedure; Adjudicative Procedure; Trial Type Hearings; Administrative Law Judge; Power To Stay Proceedings; Subpoena Power; Physical Inspection; Self Incrimination; Judicial Review Issues; Declaratory Judgment; Sovereign Immunity; Eleventh Amendment; Statutory Limitations; Standing; Exhaustion Of Administrative Remedies; Scope Of Judicial Review.
3 Audio Cassettes
ISBN 0-15-900189-7 $39.95

Agency & Partnership
Professor Richard J. Conviser
Chicago Kent College of Law

TOPICS COVERED: Agency: Creation; Rights And Duties Of Principal And Agent; Sub-Agents; Contract Liability–Actual Authority: Express And Implied; Apparent Authority; Ratification; Liabilities Of Parties; Tort Liability–Respondeat Superior; Frolic And Detour; Intentional Torts. *Partnership:* Nature Of Partnership; Formation; Partnership By Estoppel; In Partnership Property; Relations Between Partners To Third Parties; Authority of Partners; Dissolution And Termination; Limited Partnerships.
3 Audio Cassettes
ISBN: 0-15-900351-2 $39.95

Antitrust Law
Professor To Be Announced
Call For Release Date

TOPICS COVERED (Subject to Change): How U.S. Antitrust Lawyers And Economists Think And Solve Problems: Antitrust Law's First Principle — Consumer Welfare Opposes Market Power; Methods Of Analysis — Rule Of Reason, Per Se, Quick Look; Sherman Act Section 1 — Civil And Criminal Conspiracies In Unreasonable Restraint Of Trade; Sherman Act Section 2 — Illegal Monopolization And Attempts To Monopolize; Robinson Patman Act Price Discrimination And Related Distribution Problems; Clayton Act Section Section 7 — Mergers And Joint

Ventures; Antitrust And Intellectual Property; U.S. Antitrust And International Competitive Relationships — Extraterritoriality, Comity, And Convergence; Exemptions And Regulated Industries; Enforcement By The Department Of Justice, Federal Trade Commission, National Association Of State Attorneys General, And By Private Litigation; Price And Non-Price Restraints.
2 Audio Cassettes
ISBN: 0-15-900341-5 $39.95

Bankruptcy
Professor Elizabeth Warren
Harvard Law School

TOPICS COVERED: The Debtor/Creditor Relationship; The Commencement, Conversion, Dismissal and Reopening Of Bankruptcy Proceedings; Property Included In The Bankruptcy Estate; Secured, Priority And Unsecured Claims; The Automatic Stay; Powers Of Avoidance; The Assumption And Rejection Of Executory Contracts; The Protection Of Exempt Property; The Bankruptcy Discharge; Chapter 13 Proceedings; Chapter 11 Proceedings; Bankruptcy Jurisdiction And Procedure.
4 Audio Cassettes
ISBN: 0-15-900273-7 $45.95

Civil Procedure
By Professor Richard D. Freer
Emory University Law School

TOPICS COVERED: Subject Matter Jurisdiction; Personal Jurisdiction; Long-Arm Statutes; Constitutional Limitations; In Rem And Quasi In Rem Jurisdiction; Service Of Process; Venue; Transfer; Forum Non Conveniens; Removal; Waiver; Governing Law; Pleadings; Joinder Of Claims; Permissive And Compulsory Joinder Of Parties; Counter-Claims And Cross-Claims; Ancillary Jurisdiction; Impleader; Class Actions; Discovery; Pretrial Adjudication; Summary Judgment; Trial; Post Trial Motions; Appeals; Res Judicata; Collateral Estoppel.
5 Audio Cassettes
ISBN: 0-15-900322-9 $59.95

Commercial Paper
By Professor Michael I. Spak
Chicago Kent College Of Law

TOPICS COVERED: Introduction; Types Of Negotiable Instruments; Elements Of Negotiability; Statute Of Limitations; Payment-In-

Full Checks; Negotiations Of The Instrument; Becoming A Holder-In-Due Course; Rights Of A Holder In Due Course; Real And Personal Defenses; Jus Teril; Effect Of Instrument On Underlying Obligations; Contracts Of Maker And Indorser; Suretyship; Liability Of Drawer And Drawee; Check Certification; Warranty Liability; Conversion Of Liability; Banks And Their Customers; Properly Payable Rule; Wrongful Dishonor; Stopping Payment; Death Of Customer; Bank Statement; Check Collection; Expedited Funds Availability; Forgery Of Drawer's Name; Alterations; Imposter Rule; Wire Transfers; Electronic Fund Transfers Act .
3 Audio Cassettes
ISBN: 0-15-900275-3 $39.95

Conflict Of Laws
Professor Richard J. Conviser
Chicago Kent College of Law

TOPICS COVERED: Domicile; Jurisdiction; In Personam, In Rem, Quasi In Rem; Court Competence; Forum Non Conveniens; Choice Of Law; Foreign Causes Of Action; Territorial Approach To Choice/Tort And Contract; "Escape Devices"; Most Significant Relationship; Governmental Interest Analysis; Recognition Of Judgments; Foreign Country Judgments; Domestic Judgments/Full Faith And Credit; Review Of Judgments; Modifiable Judgments; Defenses To Recognition And Enforcement; Federal/State (Erie) Problems; Constitutional Limits On Choice Of Law.
3 Audio Cassettes
ISBN: 0-15-900352-0 $39.95

Constitutional Law
By Professor John C. Jeffries, Jr.
University of Virginia School of Law

TOPICS COVERED: Introduction; Exam Tactics; Legislative Power; Supremacy; Commerce; State Regulation; Privileges And Immunities; Federal Court Jurisdiction; Separation Of Powers; Civil Liberties; Due Process; Equal Protection; Privacy; Race; Alienage; Gender; Speech And Association; Prior Restraints; Religion—Free Exercise; Establishment Clause.
5 Audio Cassettes
ISBN: 0-15-900319-9 $45.95

Contracts
By Professor Michael I. Spak
Chicago Kent College Of Law

TOPICS COVERED: Offer; Revocation; Acceptance; Consideration; Defenses To Formation; Third Party Beneficiaries; Assignment; Delegation; Conditions; Excuses; Anticipatory Repudiation; Discharge Of Duty; Modifications; Rescission; Accord & Satisfaction; Novation; Breach; Damages; Remedies; UCC Remedies; Parol Evidence Rule.
4 Audio Cassettes
ISBN: 0-15-900318-0 $45.95

Copyright Law
Professor Roger E. Schechter
George Washington University Law School

TOPICS COVERED: Constitution; Patents And Property Ownership Distinguished; Subject Matter Copyright; Duration And Renewal; Ownership And Transfer; Formalities; Introduction; Notice, Registration And Deposit; Infringement; Overview; Reproduction And Derivative Works; Public Distribution; Public Performance And Display; Exemptions; Fair Use; Photocopying; Remedies; Preemption Of State Law.
3 Audio Cassettes
ISBN: 0-15-900295-8 $39.95

Corporations
By Professor Therese H. Maynard
Loyola Marymount School of Law

TOPICS COVERED: Ultra Vires Act; Corporate Formation; Piercing The Corporate Veil; Corporate Financial Structure; Stocks; Bonds; Subscription Agreements; Watered Stock; Stock Transactions; Insider Trading; 16(b) & 10b-5 Violations; Promoters; Fiduciary Duties; Shareholder Rights; Meetings; Cumulative Voting; Voting Trusts; Close Corporations; Dividends; Preemptive Rights; Shareholder Derivative Suits; Directors; Duty Of Loyalty; Corporate Opportunity Doctrine; Officers; Amendments; Mergers; Dissolution.
4 Audio Cassettes
ISBN: 0-15-900320-2 $45.95

Criminal Law
By Professor Charles H. Whitebread
USC School of Law

TOPICS COVERED: Exam Tactics; Volitional Acts; Mental States; Specific Intent; Malice; General Intent; Strict Liability; Accomplice Liability; Inchoate Crimes; Impossibility; Defenses;

Insanity; Voluntary And Involuntary Intoxication; Infancy; Self-Defense; Defense Of A Dwelling; Duress; Necessity; Mistake Of Fact Or Law; Entrapment; Battery; Assault; Homicide; Common Law Murder; Voluntary And Involuntary Manslaughter; First Degree Murder; Felony Murder; Rape; Larceny; Embezzlement; False Pretenses; Robbery; Extortion; Burglary; Arson.
4 Audio Cassettes
ISBN: 0-15-900279-6 $39.95

Criminal Procedure
By Professor Charles H. Whitebread
USC School of Law

TOPICS COVERED: Incorporation Of The Bill Of Rights; Exclusionary Rule; Fruit Of The Poisonous Tree; Arrest; Search & Seizure; Exceptions To Warrant Requirement; Wire Tapping & Eavesdropping; Confessions (Miranda); Pretrial Identification; Bail; Preliminary Hearings; Grand Jurics; Spoody Trial; Fair Trial; Jury Trials; Right To Counsel; Guilty Pleas; Sentencing; Death Penalty; Habeas Corpus; Double Jeopardy; Privilege Against Compelled Testimony.
3 Audio Cassettes
ISBN: 0-15-900281-8 $39.95

Evidence
By Professor Faust F. Rossi
Cornell Law School

TOPICS COVERED: Relevance; Insurance; Remedial Measures; Settlement Offers; Causation; State Of Mind; Rebuttal; Habit; Character Evidence; "MIMIC" Rule; Documentary Evidence; Authentication; Best Evidence Rule; Parol Evidence; Competency; Dead Man Statutes; Examination Of Witnesses; Present Recollection Revived; Past Recollection Recorded; Opinion Testimony; Lay And Expert Witness; Learned Treatises; Impeachment; Collateral Matters; Bias, Interest Or Motive; Rehabilitation; Privileges; Hearsay And Exceptions.
5 Audio Cassettes
ISBN: 0-15-900282-6 $45.95

Family Law
Professor To Be Announced

TOPICS COVERED (Subject to change): National Scope Of Family Law; Marital Relationship; Consequences Of Marriage; Formalities And Solemnization; Common Law Marriage; Impediments; Marriage And Conflict Of Laws; Non-Marital Relationship; Law Of Names; Void And Voidable Marriages; Marital Breakdown; Annulment And Defenses; Divorce — Fault And No-Fault; Separation; Jurisdiction For Divorce; Migratory Divorce; Full Faith And Credit; Temporary Orders; Economic Aspects Of Marital Breakdown; Property Division; Community Property Principles; Equitable Distribution; Marital And Separate Property; Types Of Property Interests; Equitable Reimbursement; Alimony; Modification And Termination Of Alimony; Child Support; Health Insurance; Enforcement Of Orders; Antenuptial And Postnuptial Agreements; Separation And Settlement Agreements; Custody Jurisdiction And Awards; Modification Of Custody; Visitation Rights; Termination Of Parental Rights; Adoption; Illegitimacy; Paternity Actions.
3 Audio Cassettes
ISBN: 0-15-900283-4 $39.95

Federal Courts
Professor To Be Announced

TOPICS COVERED (Subject to change): History Of The Federal Court System; "Court Or Controversy" And Justiciability; Congressional

Power Over Federal Court Jurisdiction; Supreme Court Jurisdiction; District Court Subject Matter Jurisdiction—Federal Question Jurisdiction, Diversity Jurisdiction And Admiralty Jurisdiction; Pendent And Ancillary Jurisdiction; Removal Jurisdiction; Venue; Forum Non Conveniens; Law Applied In The Federal Courts; Federal Law In The State Courts; Collateral Relations Between Federal And State Courts; The Eleventh Amendment And State Sovereign Immunity.
3 Audio Cassettes
ISBN: 0-15-900296-6 $39.95

Federal Income Tax
By Professor Cheryl D. Block
George Washington University Law School

TOPICS COVERED: Administrative Reviews; Tax Formula; Gross Income; Exclusions For Gifts; Inheritances; Personal Injuries; Tax Basis Rules; Divorce Tax Rules; Assignment Of Income; Business Deductions; Investment Deductions; Passive Loss And Interest Limitation Rules; Capital Gains & Losses; Section 1031, 1034, and 121 Deferred/Non Taxable Transactions.
4 Audio Cassettes
ISBN: 0-15-900284-2 $45.95

Future Interests
By Dean Catherine L. Carpenter
Southwestern University Law School

TOPICS COVERED: Rule Against Perpetuities; Class Gifts; Estates In Land; Rule In Shelley's Case; Future Interests In Transferor and Transferee; Life Estates; Defeasible Fees; Doctrine Of Worthier Title; Doctrine Of Merger; Fee Simple Estates; Restraints On Alienation; Power Of Appointment; Rules Of Construction.
2 Audio Cassettes
ISBN: 0-15-900285-0 $24.95

Law School ABC's
By Professor Jennifer S. Kamita
Loyola Marymount Law School, and
Professor Rodney O. Fong
Golden Gate University School of Law

TOPICS COVERED: Introduction; Casebooks; Hornbooks; Selecting Commercial Materials; Briefing; Review; ABC's Of A Lecture; Taking Notes; Lectures & Notes Examples; Study Groups; ABC's Of Outlining; Rules; Outlining Hypothetical; Outlining Assignment And Review; Introduction To Essay Writing; "IRAC"; Call Of The Question Exercise; Issue Spotting Exercise; IRAC Defining & Writing Exercise; Form Tips; ABC's Of Exam Writing; Exam Writing Hypothetical; Practice Exam And Review; Preparation Hints; Exam Diagnostics & Writing Problems.
4 Audio Cassettes
ISBN: 0-15-900286-9 $45.95

Law School Exam Writing
By Professor Charles H. Whitebread
USC School of Law

TOPICS COVERED: With "Law School Exam Writing," you'll learn the secrets of law school test taking. In this fascinating lecture, Professor Whitebread leads you step-by-step through his innovative system, so that you know exactly how to tackle your essay exams without making point draining mistakes. You'll learn how to read questions so you don't miss important issues; how to organize your answer; how to use limited exam time to your maximum advantage; and even how to study for exams.
1 Audio Cassette
ISBN: 0-15-900287-7 $19.95

Professional Responsibility
By Professor Erwin Chemerinsky
USC School of Law

TOPICS COVERED: Regulation of Attorneys; Bar Admission; Unauthorized Practice; Competency; Discipline; Judgment; Lawyer-Client Relationship; Representation; Withdrawal; Conflicts; Disqualification; Clients; Client Interests; Successive And Effective Representation; Integrity; Candor; Confidences; Secrets; Past And Future Crimes; Perjury; Communications; Witnesses; Jurors; The Court; The Press; Trial Tactics; Prosecutors; Market; Solicitation; Advertising; Law Firms; Fees; Client Property; Conduct; Political Activity.
3 Audio Cassettes
ISBN: 0-15-900288-5 $39.95

Real Property
By Professor Paula A. Franzese
Seton Hall Law School

TOPICS COVERED: Estates—Fee Simple; Fee Tail; Life Estate; Co-Tenancy—Joint Tenancy; Tenancy In Common; Tenancy By The Entirety; Landlord-Tenant Relationship; Liability For Condition Of Premises; Assignment & Sublease; Easements; Restrictive Covenants; Adverse Possession; Recording Acts; Conveyancing; Personal Property—Finders; Bailments; Gifts; Future Interests.
4 Audio Cassettes
ISBN: 0-15-900289-3 $45.95

Remedies
By Professor William A. Fletcher
University of California at Berkeley, Boalt Hall School of Law

TOPICS COVERED: Damages; Restitution; Equitable Remedies (including Constructive Trust, Equitable Lien, Injunction, and Specific Performance); Tracing; Rescission and Reformation; Specific topics include Injury and Destruction of Personal Property; Conversion; Injury to Real Property; Trespass; Ouster; Nuisance; Defamation; Trade Libel; Inducing Breach of Contract; Contracts to Purchase Personal Property; Contracts to Purchase Real Property (including Equitable Conversion); Construction Contracts; and Personal Service Contracts.
3 Audio Cassettes
ISBN: 0-15-900353-9 $45.95

Sales & Lease of Goods
By Professor Michael I. Spak
Chicago Kent College of Law

TOPICS COVERED: Goods; Contract Formation; Firm Offers; Statute Of Frauds; Modification; Parol Evidence; Code Methodology; Tender; Payment; Identification; Risk Of Loss; Warranties; Merchantability; Fitness; Disclaimers; Consumer Protection; Remedies; Anticipatory Repudiation; Third Party Rights.
3 Audio Cassettes
ISBN: 0-15-900291-5 $39.95

Secured Transactions
By Professor Michael I. Spak
Chicago Kent College of Law

TOPICS COVERED: Collateral; Inventory; Intangibles; Proceeds; Security Agreements; Attachment; After-Acquired Property; Perfection; Filing; Priorities; Purchase Money Security Interests; Fixtures; Rights Upon Default; Self-Help; Sale; Constitutional Issues.
3 Audio Cassettes
ISBN: 0-15-900292-3 $39.95

Torts
By Professor Richard J. Conviser
Chicago Kent College of Law

TOPICS COVERED: Essay Exam Techniques; Intentional Torts—Assault; Battery; False Imprisonment; Intentional Infliction Of Emotional Distress; Trespass To Land; Trespass To Chattels; Conversion; Defenses; Defamation—Libel; Slander; Defenses; First Amendment Concerns; Invasion Of Right Of Privacy; Misrepresentation; Negligence—Duty; Breach; Actual And Proximate Causation; Damages; Defenses; Strict Liability; Products Liability; Nuisance; General Tort Considerations.
4 Audio Cassettes
ISBN: 0-15-900185-4 $45.95

Wills & Trusts
By Professor Stanley M. Johanson
University of Texas School of Law

TOPICS COVERED: Attested Wills; Holographic Wills; Negligence; Revocation; Changes On Face Of Will; Lapsed Gifts; Negative Bequest Rule; Nonprobate Assets; Intestate Succession; Advancements; Elective Share; Will Contests; Capacity; Undue Influence; Creditors' Rights; Creation Of Trust; Revocable Trusts; Pourover Gifts; Charitable Trusts; Resulting Trusts; Constructive Trusts; Spendthrift Trusts; Self-Dealing; Prudent Investments; Trust Accounting; Termination; Powers Of Appointment.
4 Audio Cassettes
ISBN: 0-15-900294-X $45.95

**All titles available at your law school bookstore
or call to order: 1-800-787-8717**

Legalines

Legalines gives you authoritative, detailed case briefs of every major case in your casebook. You get a clear explanation of the facts, the issues, the court's holding and reasoning, and any significant concurrences or dissents. Even more importantly, you get an authoritative explanation of the significance of each case, and how it relates to other cases in your casebook. And with Legalines' detailed table of contents and table of cases, you can quickly find any case or concept you're looking for. But your professor expects you to know more than just the cases. That's why Legalines gives you more than just case briefs. You get summaries of the black letter law, as well. That's crucial, because some of the most important information in your casebooks isn't in the cases at all...it's the black letter principles you're expected to glean from those cases. Legalines is the only series that gives you both case briefs and black letter review. With Legalines, you get everything you need to know—whether it's in a case or not!

Administrative Law
Keyed to the Breyer Casebook
ISBN: 0-15-900169-2   206 pages $17.95

Administrative Law
Keyed to the Gellhorn Casebook
ISBN: 0-15-900170-6   268 pages $19.95

Administrative Law
Keyed to the Schwartz Casebook
ISBN: 0-15-900044-0   155 pages $17.95

Antitrust
Keyed to the Areeda Casebook
ISBN: 0-15-900046-7   209 pages $17.95

Antitrust
Keyed to the Handler Casebook
ISBN: 0-15-900045-9   174 pages $17.95

Civil Procedure
Keyed to the Cound Casebook
ISBN: 0-15-900314-8   316 pages $19.95

Civil Procedure
Keyed to the Field Casebook
ISBN: 0-15-900048-3   388 pages $21.95

Civil Procedure
Keyed to the Hazard Casebook
ISBN: 0-15-900324-5   253 pages $18.95

Civil Procedure
Keyed to the Rosenberg Casebook
ISBN: 0-15-900052-1   312 pages $19.95

Civil Procedure
Keyed to the Yeazell Casebook
ISBN: 0-15-900241-9   240 pages $18.95

Commercial Law
Keyed to the Farnsworth Casebook
ISBN: 0-15-900176-5   170 pages $17.95

Conflict of Laws
Keyed to the Cramton Casebook
ISBN: 0-15-900056-4   144 pages $16.95

Conflict of Laws
Keyed to the Reese (Rosenberg) Casebook
ISBN: 0-15-900057-2   279 pages $19.95

Constitutional Law
Keyed to the Brest Casebook
ISBN: 0-15-900059-9   235 pages $18.95

Constitutional Law
Keyed to the Cohen Casebook
ISBN: 0-15-900261-3   235 pages $18.95

Constitutional Law
Keyed to the Gunther Casebook
ISBN: 0-15-900060-2   395 pages $21.95

Constitutional Law
Keyed to the Lockhart Casebook
ISBN: 0-15-900242-7   348 pages $20.95

Constitutional Law
Keyed to the Rotunda Casebook
ISBN: 0-15-900315-6   281 pages $19.95

Constitutional Law
Keyed to the Stone Casebook
ISBN: 0-15-900236-2   296 pages $19.95

Contracts
Keyed to the Calamari Casebook
ISBN: 0-15-900065-3   256 pages $19.95

Contracts
Keyed to the Dawson Casebook
ISBN: 0-15-900268-0   188 pages $19.95

Contracts
Keyed to the Farnsworth Casebook
ISBN: 0-15-900067-X   219 pages $18.95

Contracts
Keyed to the Fuller Casebook
ISBN: 0-15-900069-6   206 pages $17.95

Contracts
Keyed to the Kessler Casebook
ISBN: 0-15-900070-X   340 pages $20.95

Contracts
Keyed to the Murphy Casebook
ISBN: 0-15-900072-6   272 pages $19.95

Corporations
Keyed to the Cary Casebook
ISBN: 0-15-900172-2   407 pages $21.95

Corporations
Keyed to the Choper Casebook
ISBN: 0-15-900173-0   270 pages $19.95

Corporations
Keyed to the Hamilton Casebook
ISBN: 0-15-900313-X   248 pages $19.95

Corporations
Keyed to the Vagts Casebook
ISBN: 0-15-900078-5   213 pages $17.95

Criminal Law
Keyed to the Boyce Casebook
ISBN: 0-15-900080-7   318 pages $19.95

Criminal Law
Keyed to the Dix Casebook
ISBN: 0-15-900081-5   113 pages $15.95

Criminal Law
Keyed to the Johnson Casebook
ISBN: 0-15-900082-3   169 pages $17.95

Criminal Law
Keyed to the Kadish Casebook
ISBN: 0-15-900083-1   209 pages $17.95

Criminal Law
Keyed to the La Fave Casebook
ISBN: 0-15-900084-X   202 pages $17.95

Criminal Procedure
Keyed to the Kamisar Casebook
ISBN: 0-15-900088-2   310 pages $19.95

Decedents' Estates & Trusts
Keyed to the Ritchie Casebook
ISBN: 0-15-900339-3   277 pages $19.95

Domestic Relations
Keyed to the Clark Casebook
ISBN: 0-15-900090-4   128 pages $16.95

Domestic Relations
Keyed to the Wadlington Casebook
ISBN: 0-15-900091-2   215 pages $18.95

Enterprise Organization
Keyed to the Conard Casebook
ISBN: 0-15-900092-0   316 pages $19.95

Estate & Gift Taxation
Keyed to the Surrey Casebook
ISBN: 0-15-900093-9   100 pages $15.95

Evidence
Keyed to the McCormick Casebook
ISBN: 0-15-900095-5   310 pages $19.95

Evidence
Keyed to the Sutton Casebook
ISBN: 0-15-900096-3   310 pages $19.95

Evidence
Keyed to the Waltz Casebook
ISBN: 0-15-900334-2   224 pages $17.95

Evidence
Keyed to the Weinstein Casebook
ISBN: 0-15-900097-1   241 pages $18.95

Family Law
Keyed to the Areen Casebook
ISBN: 0-15-900263-X   262 pages $19.95

Federal Courts
Keyed to the McCormick Casebook
ISBN: 0-15-900101-3   213 pages $17.95

Income Tax
Keyed to the Freeland Casebook
ISBN: 0-15-900222-2   154 pages $17.95

Income Tax
Keyed to the Klein Casebook
ISBN: 0-15-900302-4   174 pages $17.95

Labor Law
Keyed to the Cox Casebook
ISBN: 0-15-900107-2   211 pages $17.95

Labor Law
Keyed to the Merrifield Casebook
ISBN: 0-15-900108-0   202 pages $17.95

Partnership & Corporate Taxation
Keyed to the Surrey Casebook
ISBN: 0-15-900109-9   118 pages $15.95

Property
Keyed to the Browder Casebook
ISBN: 0-15-900110-2   315 pages $19.95

Property
Keyed to the Casner Casebook
ISBN: 0-15-900111-0   291 pages $19.95

Property
Keyed to the Cribbet Casebook
ISBN: 0-15-900112-9   328 pages $20.95

Property
Keyed to the Dukeminier Casebook
ISBN: 0-15-900264-8   186 pages $17.95

Real Property
Keyed to the Rabin Casebook
ISBN: 0-15-900114-5   208 pages $17.95

Remedies
Keyed to the Re Casebook
ISBN: 0-15-900116-1   333 pages $20.95

Remedies
Keyed to the York Casebook
ISBN: 0-15-900118-8   289 pages $19.95

Sales & Secured Transactions
Keyed to the Speidel Casebook
ISBN: 0-15-900166-8   320 pages $19.95

Securities Regulation
Keyed to the Jennings Casebook
ISBN: 0-15-900253-2   368 pages $20.95

Torts
Keyed to the Epstein Casebook
ISBN: 0-15-900120-X   245 pages $18.95

Torts
Keyed to the Franklin Casebook
ISBN: 0-15-900240-0   166 pages $17.95

Torts
Keyed to the Henderson Casebook
ISBN: 0-15-900123-4   209 pages $17.95

Torts
Keyed to the Keeton Casebook
ISBN: 0-15-900124-2   278 pages $19.95

Torts
Keyed to the Prosser Casebook
ISBN: 0-15-900301-6   365 pages $20.95

Wills, Trusts & Estates
Keyed to the Dukeminier Casebook
ISBN: 0-15-900127-7   192 pages $17.95

For more information visit our World Wide Web site at http://www.gilbertlaw.com or write for a free 32 page catalog:
Harcourt Brace Legal and Professional Publications, 176 West Adams, Ste. 2100, Chicago, Illinois 60603

Current & Upcoming Software Titles

Gilbert Law Summaries
Interactive Software For Windows
Gilbert's Interactive Software features the full text of a Gilbert Law Summaries outline. Each title is easy to customize, print, and take to class. You can access the Lexis and Westlaw systems through an icon on the tool bar (with a valid student I.D.), as well as CaseBriefs Interactive Software, and Gilbert's On-Screen Dictionary Of Legal Terms (sold separately).

Administrative Law 0-15-900205-2	Asimow $27.95
Civil Procedure 0-15-900206-0	Marcus, Rowe $27.95
Constitutional Law 0-15-900207-9	Choper $27.95

Contracts 0-15-900208-7	Eisenberg $27.95
Corporations 0-15-900209-5	Choper, Eisenberg $27.95
Criminal Law 0-15-900210-9	Dix $27.95
Criminal Procedure 0-15-900211-7	Marcus, Whitebread $27.95
Evidence 0-15-900212-5	Kaplan, Waltz $27.95
Income Tax 1 0-15-900213-3	Asimow $27.95
Property 0-15-900214-1	Dukeminier $27.95
Secured Transactions 0-15-900215-X	Whaley $27.95
Torts 0-15-900216-8	Franklin $27.95

Legalines

Summary of Subjects Available

- Administrative Law
- Antitrust
- Civil Procedure
- Commercial Law
- Conflict of Laws
- Constitutional Law
- Contracts
- Corporations
- Criminal Law
- Criminal Procedure
- Decedents' Estates & Trusts
- Domestic Relations
- Enterprise Organization
- Estate & Gift Taxation
- Evidence
- Family Law
- Federal Courts
- Income Tax
- Labor Law
- Partnership & Corporate Taxation
- Property
- Real Property
- Remedies
- Sales & Secured Transactions
- Securities Regulation
- Torts
- Wills, Trusts & Estates

CaseBriefs
Interactive Software For Windows
Each title is adaptable to *all* casebooks in a subject area. For example, the Civil Procedure CaseBriefs title is adaptable to Civil Procedure by Cound, Hazard, Yeazell, etc... Simply select the casebook you're using when installing the software, and the program will do the rest! CaseBriefs is easy to customize, print, and take to class. You can access the Lexis and Westlaw systems through an icon on the tool bar (with a valid student I.D.), as well as Gilbert Law Summaries Interactive Software, and Gilbert's On-Screen Dictionary Of Legal Terms (sold separately).

Administrative Law 0-15-900190-0	Adaptable To All Casebooks $27.95
Civil Procedure 0-15-900191-9	Adaptable To All Casebooks $27.95
Conflict Of Laws 0-15-900192-7	Adaptable To All Casebooks $27.95
Constitutional Law 0-15-900193-5	Adaptable To All Casebooks $27.95

Contracts 0-15-900194-3	Adaptable To All Casebooks $27.95
Corporations 0-15-900195-1	Adaptable To All Casebooks $27.95
Criminal Law 0-15-900196-X	Adaptable To All Casebooks $27.95
Criminal Procedure 0-15-900197-8	Adaptable To All Casebooks $27.95
Evidence 0-15-900198-6	Adaptable To All Casebooks $27.95
Family Law 0-15-900199-4	Adaptable To All Casebooks $27.95
Income Tax 0-15-900200-1	Adaptable To All Casebooks $27.95
Property 0-15-900201-X	Adaptable To All Casebooks $27.95
Remedies 0-15-900202-8	Adaptable To All Casebooks $27.95
Torts 0-15-900203-6	Adaptable To All Casebooks $27.95
Wills, Trusts & Estates 0-15-900204-4	Adaptable To All Casebooks $27.95

Gilbert's On Screen Dictionary Of Legal Terms:
Features over 3,500 legal terms and phrases, law school shorthand, common abbreviations, Latin and French legal terms, periodical abbreviations, and governmental abbreviations.

ISBN: 0-15-900-311-3   Macintosh $24.95
ISBN: 0-15-900-308-3   Windows $24.95

All titles available at your law school bookstore
or call to order: 1-800-787-8717

Current & Upcoming Titles

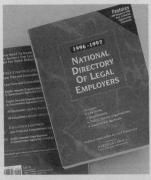
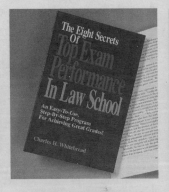

Gilbert's Pocket Size Law Dictionary
Gilbert

A dictionary is useless if you don't have it when you need it. If the only law dictionary you own is a thick, bulky one, you'll probably leave it at home most of the time — and if you need to know a definition while you're at school, you're out of luck!

With Gilbert's Pocket Size Law Dictionary, you'll have any definition you need, when you need it. Just pop Gilbert's dictionary into your pocket or purse, and you'll have over 3,500 legal terms and phrases at your fingertips. Gilbert's dictionary also includes a section on law school shorthand, common abbreviations, Latin and French legal terms, periodical abbreviations, and governmental abbreviations.

With Gilbert's Pocket Size Law Dictionary, you'll never be caught at a loss for words!

Available in your choice of 4 colors, $7.95 each:
- Black ISBN: 0-15-900255-9
- Blue ISBN: 0-15-900257-5
- Burgundy ISBN: 0-15-900256-7
- Green ISBN: 0-15-900258-3

Limited Edition: Simulated Alligator Skin Cover
- Black ISBN: 0-15-900316-4 $7.95

What Lawyers Earn: Getting Paid What You're Worth
NALP

"What Lawyers Earn" provides up-to-date salary information from lawyers in many different positions, all over the country. Whether you're negotiating your own salary — or you're just curious! — "What Lawyers Earn" tells you how much lawyers really make.
ISBN: 0-15-900183-8 $17.95

The 100 Best Law Firms To Work For In America
Kimm Alayne Walton, J.D.

An insider's guide to the 100 best places to practice law, with anecdotes and a wealth of useful hiring information. Also included are special sections on the top law firms for women and the best public interest legal employers.
ISBN: 0-15-900180-3 $19.95

The 1996-1997 National Directory Of Legal Employers
NALP

The National Association for Law Placement has joined forces with Harcourt Brace to bring you everything you need to know about 1,000 of the nation's top legal employers, fully indexed for quick reference.

It includes:
- Over 22,000 job openings.
- The names, addresses and phone numbers of hiring partners.
- Listings of firms by state, size, kind and practice area.
- What starting salaries are for full time, part time, and summer associates, plus a detailed description of firm benefits.
- The number of employees by gender and race, as well as the number of employees with disabilities.
- A detailed narrative of each firm, plus much more!

The National Directory Of Legal Employers has been published for the past twenty years, but until now has only been available to law school career services directors, and hiring partners at large law firms. Through a joint venture between NALP (The National Association For Law Placement) and Harcourt Brace, this highly regarded, exciting title is now available for students.
ISBN: 0-15-900179-X $49.95

Proceed With Caution: A Diary Of The First Year At One Of America's Largest, Most Prestigious Law Firms
William R. Keates

In "Proceed With Caution" the author chronicles the trials and tribulations of being a new associate in a widely coveted dream job. He offers insights that only someone who has lived through the experience can offer. The unique diary format makes Proceed With Caution a highly readable and enjoyable journey.
ISBN: 0-15-900181-1 $17.95

The Eight Secrets Of Top Exam Performance In Law School
Charles Whitebread

Wouldn't it be great to know exactly what your professor's looking for on your exam? To find out everything that's expected of you, so that you don't waste your time doing anything other than maximizing your grades?

In his easy-to-read, refreshing style, nationally-recognized exam expert Professor Charles Whitebread will teach you the eight secrets that will add precious points to every exam answer you write. You'll learn the three keys to handling any essay exam question, and how to add points to your score by making time work for you, not against you. You'll learn flawless issue spotting, and discover how to organize your answer for maximum possible points. You'll find out how the hidden traps in "IRAC" trip up most students… but not you! You'll learn the techniques for digging up the exam questions your professor will ask, before your exam. You'll put your newly-learned skills to the test with sample exam questions, and you can measure your performance against model answers. And there's even a special section that helps you master the skills necessary to crush any exam, not just a typical essay exam — unusual exams like open book, take home, multiple choice, short answer, and policy questions.

"The Eight Secrets of Top Exam Performance in Law School" gives you all the tools you need to maximize your grades — quickly and easily!
ISBN: 0-15-900323-7 $9.95

Guerrilla Tactics for Getting the Legal Job of Your Dreams
Kimm Alayne Walton, J.D.

Whether you're looking for a summer clerkship or your first permanent job after school, this revolutionary new book is the key to getting the job of your dreams!

"Guerrilla Tactics for Getting the Legal Job of Your Dreams" leads you step-by-step through everything you need to do to nail down that perfect job! You'll learn hundreds of simple-to-use strategies that will get you exactly where you want to go.

"Guerrilla Tactics" features the best strategies from the country's most innovative law school career advisors. The strategies in "Guerrilla Tactics" are so powerful that it even comes with a guarantee: Follow the advice in the book, and within one year of graduation you'll have the job of your dreams… or your money back!

Pick up a copy of "Guerrilla Tactics" today…and you'll be on your way to the job of your dreams!
ISBN: 0-15-900317-2 $24.95

Checkerboard Careers: How Surprisingly Successful Attorneys Got To The Top, And How You Can Too!
NALP

Fast paced and easy to read, "Checkerboard Careers" is an inspirational guide, packed with profiles and monologues of how successful attorneys got to the top and how you can, too.
ISBN: 0-15-900182-X $17.95

FREE! Gilbert Law Summaries 1st Year Survival Manual

Available from your BAR/BRI Bar Review Representative or write:

Gilbert Law Summaries
176 West Adams, Ste. 2100
Chicago, Illinois 60603

**Also available on our World Wide Web site at
http://www.gilbertlaw.com**

To Order Any Of The Items In This Publications Catalog, Call Or Write:
Harcourt Brace Legal and Professional Publications, 176 West Adams, Ste. 2100, Chicago, Illinois 60603

1-800-787-8717